Real Vampires, Night Stalkers and Creatures from the Darkside

BRAD STEIGER

VISIBLE
INK
PRESS

Detroit

Real Vampires, Night Stalkers and Creatures from the Darkside

Visible Ink Press®
43311 Joy Rd., #414
Canton, MI 48187-2075

Visible Ink Press is a registered trademark of Visible Ink Press LLC.

Most Visible Ink Press books are available at special quantity discounts when purchased in bulk by corporations, organizations, or groups. Customized printings, special imprints, messages, and excerpts can be produced to meet your needs. For more information, contact Special Market Director, Visible Ink Press, www.visibleink.com or 734-667-3211.

Project Manager: Kevin Hile
Art Director: Mary Claire Krzewinski
Typesetting: Marco Di Vita
Proofreader: Sarah Hermsen and Amy Marcaccio Keyzer
Indexer: Lawrence W. Baker

ISBN 978-1-57859-255-5

Library of Congress Cataloging-in-Publication Data
Steiger, Brad.
   Real vampires, night stalkers, and creatures of the night / by Brad Steiger.
      p. cm.
   Includes index.
   ISBN 978-1-57859-255-5
1. Vampires. I. Title.
   BF1556.S73 2010
   133.4'23--dc22
                                                         2009023106

Printed in the United States of America

10 9 8 7 6 5 4 3 2 1

Contents

CONTRIBUTING ARTISTS

Thanks to the following gifted artists for contributing
original illustrations to this publication

Ricardo Pustanio

Ricardo Pustanio is an enduring icon in the world of New Orleans Mardi Gras float design and local artistry. Today, his phenomenal creative talents are witnessed by thousands upon thousands of locals and tourists who throng the streets of New Orleans each year to catch a glimpse of one of the oldest and most prestigious parades of the season, the Krewe of Mid-City. And, according to Ricardo, "The best is still to come!"

Born in New Orleans, Ricardo is the third son of local golfing legend Eddie "Blackie" Pustanio, a well-known icon of the sport. When Ricardo was baptized, the famous "Diamond Jim" Moran was hailed as his godfather, and all the major golfing pros who visited the elder Pustanio at his City Park Golf Course digs bounced little Ricardo on their knees at one time or another.

Early in life Ricardo demonstrated a profound talent for art, first expressed in kindergarten and grammar school artwork that was well ahead of its grade level. From an early age, Ricardo's work was distinguished with prizes and praise.

Like nearly every child brought up in the city of New Orleans, Ricardo was brought out by his parents to enjoy the pageantry and revelry of the great old-line Mardi Gras parades. These halcyon Mardi Gras days of his youth were Ricardo's first taste of the passion that would become the artistic pinnacle of his later career.

During the 1960s Ricardo's entries won first place awards, and he rode with the King of Mid-City three years in a row: a true precursor of things to come. The winner of many art competitions throughout his life, his earliest prize-winning work was created while Ricardo was still in kindergarten; the piece hung in the children's area of the New Orleans Museum of Art for many years. Other early works could be found on display in the New Orleans Cabildo: most are now in private art collections in New Orleans and across the United States.

Ricardo Pusi-tanio

In the early 1970s Ricardo began a long association with local New Orleans radio station WRNO-FM, where he distinguished himself as art director for many years. Ricardo has also worked for several decorating companies in the New Orleans area, including Freeman, Spangenberg; Schmidt Brothers; Andrews Bartlett and Associates, Exhibition Contractors; and International Productions to name only a few.

Ricardo served Le Petit Theatre du Vieux Carré as technical director for its 1992–1993 season, during which he contributed his considerable artistic talents to the creation of scenery and backdrops for the season's major productions. He worked on scenery for *West Side Story* and *The Baby Dance,* for which he created a giant 60 foot by 30 foot papier maché pyramid, one of the highlights of the season. Ricardo's set designs for the production of *King Midas and the Golden Touch* and *The Snow Queen* each won him numerous awards.

In 1992 Ricardo also began his long association with William Crumb and the Children's Educational Theatre. His work on scenery and backdrops has toured with the company in 13 major productions across the United States, and he continues to contribute his talents to the organization to this day. Ricardo has also donated his time and talent to a number of nonprofit organizations, including the Save Our Lake Foundation and the March of Dimes.

Ricardo's special style was also very visible in his work on numerous backdrops and displays for the 1984 New Orleans World's Fair. Several of his original pieces from that Fair have garnered high prices at auctions throughout the United States and Europe.

Ricardo also displayed his talent with scenic design in some of the best-known, locally produced films, including *Angel Heart,* starring Mickey Rourke; *The Big Easy,* starring Dennis Quaid and Ellen Barkin; Anne Rice's *Interview with the Vampire,* starring Tom Cruise and Brad Pitt; and, more recently, in the much anticipated *A Love Song for Billy Long,* which stars John Travolta and was filmed on location in historic New Orleans.

Ricardo has conceptualized and designed numerous book covers and illustrations for major works of science fiction and fantasy. He was voted Best New Artist of the Year at World Cons held in New Orleans and Amsterdam, Netherlands. Ricardo has also illustrated children's books, created portraits and artwork for private clients across the United States and in Europe, and has to his credit three original action comic books. In addition, he has illustrated and designed the long-running *International Middle Eastern Dancer* magazine and several decks of personalized Tarot cards. It is no wonder Ricardo has been named one of the Hardest Working Artists in the City of New Orleans.

Reflecting on his artistic achievements, Ricardo has said: "I have paid my dues many times over the years and I am always in a constant state of expectation: I can't wait for the next challenge, the next thing to approach me. I am probably most proud of my work with the Krewe of Mid-City in recent years, because they have allowed me an unlimited palette to create with: the only limit is my imagination, and as you see, that has never had any limits!"

Ricardo Pustanio's hands have been busy creating artworks that have brought joy and pleasure to literally thousands of people over the years. He is truly The Hardest Working Mardi Gras Artist in the City of New Orleans and in the history of Mardi Gras design.

Dan "Wolfman" Allen

Dan "Wolfman" Allen is the owner of Ronin Studio, where he has been perfecting his unique style of comic book art for many years. Wolfman also does incredible renderings of vampires, werewolves, and other assorted monsters in a very compelling and graphic manner. He is not really into the "super-hero" genre that permeates the American comic book industry. Rather, most of his characters are more a part of the fantasy and sci-fi genre; his protagonists, while thought by some of their peers to be antisocial or disreputable, continue to be themselves and try to rise above their superficial visages or reputations to solve a key problem, rather than trying to save the entire world.

Dan "Wolfman" Allen

Dan is also fascinated by Native American lore and shares both tribal and Viking blood in his genes. As much as possible, he attempts to follow shamanic teachings in combination with Christian philosophy. He has studied the paranormal and the mystical since he was a boy, and he has experienced many aspects of the so-called supernatural on a personal basis. Contact him at plan9 motorsports @charter.net.

Bill Oliver

Artist Bill Oliver is also a musician, composer, and award-winning song writer. His music is sometimes reflective and moody, and his compositions, like his art, often act as "sound photographs." They are aimed at capturing a moment of life and freezing it in time for further contemplation—even if that moment of contemplation involves a vampire, zombie, UFO visitor, or a werewolf.

Oliver resides in Vancouver, British Columbia, where he has nourished a lifelong interest in the paranormal, UFOs, the metaphysical, and all things esoteric, stemming from many personal experiences. His enthusiasm for pursuing the unknown brought him into personal contact and

Bill Oliver

interview opportunities with experiencers in all aspects of the paranormal. These encounters have had significant influences on much of Bill's work.

Brad Steiger first became familiar with Oliver's exciting artwork when the Canadian won the Christmas Art contest on the Jeff Rense Program in 2005. In the Art contest for Halloween 2006, Bill won honorable mention.

As the two men became better acquainted, Steiger was honored to learn that he had been one of Oliver's boyhood heroes with his work on the paranormal, the esoteric, and things that go bump in the night.

"To be reading one of Brad's classic books one day and being asked to do some art for one of his new books another is truly paranormal," Oliver said. You can visit Bill Oliver's website at www.boysoblue.com.

OTHER CONTRIBUTORS

Thanks go to the following people who contributed their personal tales of vampires, night stalkers, and creatures of the night for this publication.

Chris Holly

Chris Holly

Chris Holly lives on Long Island, where she presently writes and publishes the site Endless Journey (endlessjrny.blogspot.com) with Chris Holly's Paranormal World (www.fttoufo.com/chrishollysparanormalworld.htm) and the Knightzone (www.blog talkradio.com/Knightzone).

Although Chris has spent her life building different entrepreneurial ventures, her one true passion has always been writing. She feels it is her destiny to tell these true events to the world. Chris is working on a series of books based on her paranormal writing, which she hopes will be finished by late winter 2009.

Chris is grateful to all her readers and extremely happy to receive and read the emails sent to her concerning the world of the paranormal. "I always read every email sent to me and try hard to respond to each and every one who takes the time to write to me."

Sharon McCabe

Shannon "Ms. Macabre" McCabe is president of HPI (Haunted and Paranormal Investigations International), which seeks hard evidence to support alleged hauntings. She has been studying the paranormal for about 14 years and has been the president of HPI International since 2004. Her complete bio can be found at www.ShannonMcCabe.com .

Nick Redfern

Nick Redfern runs the U.S. Office of the British-based Center for Fortean Zoology. He has written dozens of articles on the paranormal, and his books on cryptozoology

Nick Redfern

Paul Roberts with
a real vampire

Tim R. Swartz

Robin Swope

and strange creatures include *There's Something in the Woods, Memoirs of a Monster Hunter, Man-Monkey,* and *Three Men Seeking Monsters.* He can be contacted at www.nick redfern.com.

Paul Roberts

Paul Dale Roberts is the general manager/ghostwriter of Haunted and Paranormal Investigations International (www.hpiparanormal.net). He is a prolific writer who has investigated ghosts, werewolves, witches, vampires, and demons. Roberts is pictured here with one of San Francisco's real vampires.

Tim R. Swartz

Tim Swartz is an Indiana native and Emmy Award-winning television producer/videographer. He is the author of a number of popular books, including *The Lost Journals of Nikola Tesla, Time Travel: A How-To-Guide,* and *Admiral Byrd's Secret Journey Beyond the Poles.* As a photojournalist, Tim has traveled extensively and investigated paranormal phenomena and other unusual mysteries from such diverse locations as the Great Pyramid in Egypt to the Great Wall of China. As well, he is the writer and editor of the Internet newsletter *Conspiracy Journal,* a free, weekly email newsletter considered essential reading by paranormal researchers worldwide. Visit his website at www.conspiracyjournal.com.

Robin Swope

Pastor Robin Swope is known as the "Paranormal Pastor." He has been a Christian minister for more than 15 years in both mainline and Evangelical denominations. He has served as a missionary to Burkina Faso in West Africa, and he has ministered to the homeless in New York City's Hell's Kitchen. He is the founder and chief officiant of Open Gate Ministerial Services and a member of St. Paul's United Church of Christ in Erie, Pennsylvania. His blog is at theparanormalpastor.blogspot.com.

ACKNOWLEDGEMENTS

In addition to the artists and writers mentioned in the Contributors section, I must give my sincere appreciation to the other dozens of men and women, the experiencers, who suffered attacks from vampiric spirit parasites and who chose to remain anonymous, but who told me their stories. Others, who were willing to present their stories with a first name only or a pseudonym, also receive my hearty thanks for their time and their courage in sharing their accounts with me.

Among the investigators into the strange and unknown who were kind enough to share their accounts and their research with is Angela Thomas, the executive coproducer and co-host of the P.O.R.T.A.L. Paranormal Talk Radio Show. Her website is http://www.oct13baby.com/. Other useful web sites included the Vampire Community Resource Directory (www.veritasvosliberabit.com/resourcelinks.html), and TWILIGHT at www.meetup.com/twilight.

Although they have their own special page of recognition in the Contributors section, I wish to give another robust round of applause to the magnificent artists Ricardo Pustanio, Bill Oliver, and Dan Allen, who made us feel the very breath of vampires upon our necks.

I also found the following books useful in researching the history of vampirism as it evolved from prehistoric times to the modern day.

Constable, T.J. *The Cosmic Pulse of Life*. London: Merlin Press, 1976.

London, Sondra. *True Vampires*. Los Angeles: Feral House, 2004.

Maccoby, Hyam. *The Sacred Executioner*. London: Thames & Hudson, 1982.

Masters, R.E.L. *Eros and Evil*. New York: The Julian Press, 1962.

Masters, R.E.L., and Eduard Lea. *Perverse Crimes in History*. New York: The Julian Press, 1963.

Melton, J. Gordon. *The Vampire Book*. Detroit: Visible Ink Press, 1994.

Noll, Richard. *Bizarre Diseases of the Mind*. New York: Berkley Books, 1990.

Seligmann, Kurt. *The History of Magic*. New York: Pantheon Books, 1948.

Trevor-Roper, H.R. *The European Witch-Craze*. New York: Harper & Row, 1967.

INTRODUCTION

We've always known that they really exist, lurking in the shadows, stalking their victims, seeking whom they may devour.

However, they are not the undead, returning from crypt or cemetery plot to steal blood, the vital fluid of existence from the living. Although they may look like us—and when it serves their purpose they may skillfully impersonate us in order to deceive and to prey upon us—they have never been human. Real vampires are parasitic, shape-shifting entities that feed upon the energy, the life force, and the souls of humans.

From whatever dimension of time and space they may have originated, real vampires may be compared to an ancient, insidious virus that first infects, then controls its host body, causing it, in turn, to possess other victims, feeding upon its life essence and its very soul. Some who have sought to appease or to control this parasitic blight from the far reaches of the multidimensional universe have only found themselves being exploited and cruelly inspired to form secret societies, blood cults, and hideous rituals of human sacrifice.

Regardless of the seductive aura of the vampire depicted in contemporary novels, films, and television series, none of these romantic transformations of an ancient menace to humankind portray *real* vampires. While the vampiric virus may infest handsome men and beautiful women, none of those infected have superhuman powers. Real vampires and those whom they possess are loathsome slashers, rippers, and murderers who do not promise immortality with their sensual "bite," only a painful death.

Real vampires and their human hosts can walk freely in the light of day. The rays of the rising sun do not send them scurrying back to their coffins. Crucifixes do not cause real vampires to shrink back in fear of the symbol of Christ's triumph over sin.

Real vampires are the spawn of ancient entities such as Lilith, the seductive fallen angel, or of other paraphysical beings—such as the Jinn, the Cacodaemons, the Raskshasas, and the Nephilim—who have traversed the boundaries of time and space to prey upon humankind.

Real vampires are immortal, and when the spirit parasite that has invaded a human body has tired of that fleshly residence, it dispassionately discards its temporary dwelling and possesses another, abandoning its former host to death and decay, rather than to an existence of attractive eternal youth and everlasting sexual prowess.

Although these entities cannot be killed, they can be driven away from their potential victims. We can resist them. We can become immune to their power. We can fight them and defeat them.

Real Vampires, Night Stalkers and Creatures from the Darkside follows a shadowy path that ventures into the uncertain dimensions of time and space that many choose to call the supernatural. Denizens from this invisible world have intruded into our own domain since prehistory and have used our blood to perpetuate their own existence.

Also, we will delve further into the psychological pattern that may present itself by someone who has become an unwilling host of an uninvited spirit parasite. We shall enumerate many of the character weaknesses that may invite a vampiric entity to possess an individual's body, mind, and spirit.

While the very essence of the real vampire originates in other dimensions of reality, down through the centuries psychopathic murderers have envisioned themselves as vampires who must feed upon human blood in order to gain power over their fellow humans. And, in one of those bizarre twists of the human psyche, in the Middle Ages self-righteous individuals who were in power condemned men and women as monsters who must be slaughtered in order to establish a triumph of God, faith, and conformity.

Real Vampires, Night Stalkers and Creatures from the Darkside also expands its vistas to include a number of non-vampires who present eerie manifestations of mystery and wonder. Could careless dabbling in the occult bring forth parasitic entities who subsist on the psychic energy of their victims? Could entities from UFOs who claim to come from other worlds, and strange teenagers with haunting black eyes who beg your permission to enter your home, really be vampires in less familiar guises?

While this book focuses on the supernatural, the multidimensional, and the paraphysical beings who have interacted with our species since prehistoric times, I shall also visit the vampire community living among us today. I do not suggest for one moment that these men and women are murderers, sociopaths, or supernatural beings. They present a subgroup within our society of individuals who are perhaps unusual and unique, but are not after the blood of those who choose to leave their interaction with vampires to motion pictures, television, and books.

Far more than a book that contains a number of frightening true accounts and a collection of truly magnificent original art, what I hope to accomplish with *Real Vampires, Night Stalkers and Creatures from the Darkside* is expand the definition of the vampire—the most popular monster in the world—to include the more complete definition of "parasitic entities that enter our reality from the far reaches of the multidimensional universe to possess their victims and to feed upon their life essence and their very soul."

—Brad Steiger

The Sons and Daughters of Lilith

The plural form of "Lilith" in Hebrew is "lilim," which is found in Talmudic and Kabbalistic literature as a term for spirits of the night. Lilith is most often depicted as a beautiful woman with long, unkempt hair and large, bat-like wings. According to the Midrash, Lilith preys not only on males as they lie sleeping, but also upon mothers who have just given birth, as well as their newborn babes.

Lilith quite likely was first feared in ancient Babylon as Lilitu, who, together with Ekimmu, wandered the night world in search of victims for their insatiable blood lust. In Hebrew folklore, Lilith was Adam's wife before the creation of Eve, the true chosen mother of humankind. The terrible night creatures known as the incubi and the succubi were the children of Adam and Lilith. The incubi materialize before human women as handsome men, hypnotically seducing them and withdrawing from them their life force. Succubi appear to human men as lovely, sensual women, tempting and promising, disguising their thirst for human blood.

While those human males who consort with a succubus often meet an untimely end, drained of their life forces, on occasion their interactions with these entities brings about a horde of demonic children, who will one day gather at the deathbeds of their human fathers, hail them as their sires, then scatter to capture as many human souls as possible.

The Sacred Magic of Abramelin the Mage, translated by MacGregor Mathers from a manuscript written in French in the eighteenth century, is dated 1458 and claims to be translated originally from Hebrew. The text states that the universe is teeming with hordes of angels and demons that interact with human beings on many levels. Humans are somewhere between the angelic and the demonic intelligences on the spiritual scale, and each human entity has both a guardian angel and a malevolent demon hovering near him or her from birth until death.

Venerable traditions state that such entities as Lilith and her spawn first manifested on Earth at a time when the gods were said to walk freely among humankind.

Real vampires are those vulnerable humans who have been possessed by the spawn of ancient entities such as Lilith, the seductive fallen angel (illustration by Ricardo Pustanio).

To these godlike creatures of darkness, the primitive humans who regarded them with such awe and reverence were property, chattel from which to gain energy and sustenance.

The apocryphal Book of Enoch tells of the order of angels called "Watchers," or "The Sleepless Ones." The leader of the Watchers was called Semjaza or Shemhazai (in other places, Azazel, the name of one of the Hebrews' principal demons), who led 200 Watchers down to Earth to take wives from among the daughters of men. It was from such a union that the Nephilim were born. The Nephilim are said in the Old Testament to have been the progeny of the "sons of god," whose union with Earth women produced "giants … men of great renown." Although often translated as "giants," the word Nephilim actually means "the fallen ones."

Since the Watchers manifested on Earth as angels, the Watchers were beings of spirit essence, rather than of flesh and blood. What these fallen ones invading Earth needed from humans was their blood and their flesh so that they might become corporeal beings. The Watchers and the Nephilim were the first real vampires to exploit humankind, and they continue today to feed on the life force of humans—both their blood and their spirit.

Once in physical bodies, the fallen angels taught their human wives to cast various spells and to practice the arts of enchantment. They imparted to the women the lore of plants and the properties of certain roots. Semjaza did not neglect human men, teaching them how to manufacture weapons and tools of destruction.

Serpent Masters from Other Worlds

In many ways, Semjaza is synonymous with the Serpent who tempted Eve and Adam with the fruit from the Tree of Knowledge. Nearly every known Earth culture has its legends of wise Serpent People who ruled the planet in prehistoric times and assisted humankind in rising in status from hairless apes to the lords of the planet. Many of these Serpent People were said to come from the sky to promulgate the beneficent and civilizing rule of the Sons of the Sun, or the Sons of Heaven, upon Earth. Quetzacoatl, the "feathered serpent" and culture-bearer of the Aztecs, was said to have descended from Heaven in a silver egg. Ciuacoatl, the Great Mother of the Gods for the ancient people of Mexico, was represented as a serpent woman. Among many African tribes, it is Aido Hwendo, the Rainbow Serpent, that supports the Earth.

The Babylonian priest-historian Berossus chronicled the legend of Oannes, an entity described as a serpent-like half-man, half-fish, who surfaced from the Persian Gulf to instruct the early inhabitants of Mesopotamia in the arts of civilization. Before the advent of the serpent master Oannes, Berossus stated, the Sumerians were savages, living like the beasts with no order or rule.

Like so many accounts of the Serpent People, Oannes appeared to be some kind of amphibious Master Teacher endowed with superior intelligence, but possessing an appearance that was frightening to behold. Oannes had the body of a fishlike serpent with humanlike feet and a head that combined the features of fish and human. Berossus explained that the creature walked about on land during the day, counseling and teaching the Sumerians, but returned to the ocean each evening. The amphibious master gave the once primitive Sumerians insight into letters and sciences and every kind of art. He taught them to construct houses, to found temples, to compile laws, and explained to them the principles of geometrical knowledge. He made them distinguish the seeds of the Earth and showed them how to harvest fruits. In short, Oannes instructed them in everything that could tend to soften the manners of and civilize humankind.

The ancient texts tell of the Watchers, the Nephilim, the fallen ones who were the first real vampires to exploit humankind (illustration by Ricardo Pustanio).

Because of the respect for the great Serpent Masters of prehistoric times, the serpent was regarded as both a symbol of immortality and of death in ancient Egypt, and the pharaoh wore a snake emblem on his headdress as a mark of royalty and divinity. Apollo, the Greek god of healing and medicine, was originally invoked and worshipped as a serpent. Aesculapius, another deity associated with medicine, often materialized as a serpent, and his crest of the double snakes remains today as a symbol of the medical profession: the caduceus.

In the Hebrew account of the Fall from Paradise, the Serpent was the king of beasts, walking on two legs. The Serpent became jealous when he saw how the angels honored Adam. For his part in the seduction of Eve, the Serpent was punished by having his limbs removed and being forced to crawl on his belly. In the Muslim tradition, it is Archangel Michael who chops off the serpent's limbs with the sword of God.

In many Native American legends, the great hero Manabozho must battle many Serpent People to free his people from bondage. According to many tribal traditions, in the beginning of time humans and snakes could converse freely. It was believed that

Snakes appear in the mythology and legends of cultures worldwide, including the familiar biblical tale of the Garden of Eden. Could this commonality among ancient civilizations be a clue about creatures visiting early mankind?

shamans and others who were powerfully attuned to the spirit level could still communicate with serpents and learn secrets about the future and powerful healing medicines.

Serpent People remain popular as shape-shifting entities in the local folklore of many areas around the world. Some cultures still believe that an underground race of reptilian beings secretly control all the major events of life on this planet. Certain UFO investigators have theorized that the Serpent People of prehistoric times are the same beings who today visit Earth in spaceships as Overlords surveying the evolution of humankind.

Beware of Demons in Disguise

The science of alchemy was introduced to the Western world at the beginning of the third century C.E. by Zosimus of Panapolis, a Greek-Egyptian alchemist and Gnostic mystic. Zosimus cited the familiar passage in Genesis as the origin of the arcane art: "The sons of God saw that the daughters of men were fair." To this scriptural reference, Zosimus echoed the Book of Enoch in stating the tradition that in reward for their favors, the "sons of God" endowed these women with the knowledge of how to make jewels, colorful garments, and perfumes with which to enhance their earthly charms.

In the opinion of the clergy, the alchemists were being deceived by demons in disguise. Church Father Tertullian (c. 160–240 C.E.) argued that the "sons of God" referred to in Genesis were evil perverters of humans who bequeathed their wisdom to mortals with the sole intention of seducing them to mundane pleasures.

Ignoring the warnings of the clergy, alchemists believed that they could also acquire control over the Elementals, the unseen intelligences who inhabit the four basic elements of the material plane. The creatures of the air are known as sylphs; of the earth, gnomes; of fire, salamanders; and of water, the nymphs or undines.

According to ancient tradition, before the Fall, Adam had complete control over these entities. After the Fall from Grace in the Garden of Eden, Adam lost his command over the elementals, but he was still able to demand their obedience by means of certain incantations and spells. That same ancient tradition suggests that such communication with the unseen entities can be established by the sincere magician who seeks out the old spells.

The appearance of the elementals when discerned by the human eye is that of attractive males and beautiful females. Because they are created of the pure essences of their element, they may live for centuries; but because they were fashioned of terrestrial elements, their souls are not immortal, as are those of humans. If, however, an elemental should be joined in marriage to a human, their union can transform the creature's soul into a spirit that may enjoy eternal life. Some of the greatest figures of antiquity such as Zoroaster, Alexander, and Merlin were reported to have been the children of elementary spirits.

While most traditions hold the elementals to be friendly to humans some authorities warn that each of the four elements contains a number of mischief makers and entities that tend more toward the demonic than the angelic.

Supernatural Shape-shifters from Parallel Dimensions

It is interesting to note that all of the world's major religions speak of a duality of the gods or demigods that came to Earth—some to exploit; others to teach; some to enslave; others to free.

In Arabian and Muslim traditions, the *Jinns* are evil demons who possess a wide variety of supernatural powers. Some scholars declare the Jinns a bit lower than the angels, because they were created of smoke and fire. Their leader is Iblis, once hailed as Azazel, the Islamic counterpart of the Devil.

The Jinns are mentioned frequently in the Qur'an, but the entities were known before the Prophet Muhammad wrote of their existence. In pre-Islamic Arabia, the Jinns were revered as godlike beings who inhabited a world parallel to that of humans.

The idea of Jinns later evolved in Western culture as the "genie in the lamp," but real Jinns are shape-shifters who are mentioned often in the holy Qur'an.

The Jinns are accomplished shape-shifters, capable of assuming any form in their avowed mission to work evil on humans. On the other hand, Jinns may also, on occasion, influence humans to do good, and they may also perform good deeds for those who have the power to summon them. According to some traditions, King Solomon possessed a ring that gave him the power to summon the Jinns to fight beside his soldiers in battle. In addition, it is said that Solomon's temple was constructed with the help of the Jinns.

Primarily, though, the Jinns are feared as creatures who exist for the purpose of tormenting humans. Some old beliefs affirm that a human dying an unrepentant sinner may become a Jinn for a period of time.

Many scholars of mysticism and the esoteric declare one type of *Rakshasas* as the Hindu equivalent of the Nephilim, the giants of the Bible, who declared war on the greater gods. The evil Rakshasas most often appear as beautiful women who drink the blood and feed off the flesh of men and women. The Rakshasas also possess shape-shifting abilities, and they take great delight in possessing vulnerable human hosts and causing them to commit acts of violence until they are driven insane.

In appearance, the Rakshasas are most often described as being yellow, green, or blue in color with vertical slits for eyes. They are feared as blood-drinkers and detested for their penchant for animating the bodies of the dead and stalking new victims.

The great Hindu goddess Kali is herself a vampire, and it is said that her image manifests over battlefields, her long tongue lapping up the blood of the fallen.

In the Shinto traditions, there are millions of *Kami*, nature spirits that can do either good or evil to humans. Although the Kami are by no means angelic, neither is it their sole purpose to harm humans. They can be brutal or benevolent, depending upon the intent or the purpose of the individual. Even the *Kappa*, a bloodsucking demon that haunts the night and is generally considered the most evil of the Kami, can reverse its nature and single out individual humans to teach both medical and magical practices.

The ancient Persians and Chaldeans named those angels who fell to Earth the *Cacodaemons*. Cast out of Heaven (another world, another universe) for rebelling against the prevailing order, their leader, *Ahrimanes,* was determined to rule Earth and the primitive humans who resided there. However, regardless of where Ahrimanes endeavored to establish his kingdom, the *Agathodaemons*, the representatives of universal law, prevented him from exploiting or interfering with the natural evolution of humans.

After attempting to wage a violent war of defiance on Earth against the Agathodaemons, Ahrimanes and his army were once again defeated. According to the Persians, the Cacodaemons were rejected from Earth and took refuge in the space between Earth and the fixed stars, a domain which is known as Ahriman-abad. It is from this dimension that Ahrimanes, resentful and revengeful, takes his pleasure in directing his demons to afflict and torment human beings. Throughout all of history, these paraphysical beings, mimicking our human forms, have walked among us unnoticed, sowing discord wherever they wander, sapping our soul energy, invading host bodies whenever possible, causing vulnerable humans to seek the blood of their fellow beings.

There are numerous ancient legends that refer to a great war that occurred in "Heaven" before the defeated angels or demigods came to Earth; and, after the Nephilim had transgressed against the laws of God, there was another violent conflict that raged on Earth between the forces of light and darkness in humankind's prehistory. It was the defeat of the armies of darkness that forced them to return to their noncorporeal state and withdraw to other dimensions of time and space. Because of the dark forces' continued efforts to corrupt and to possess humans, some mystics argue that the warfare continues unabated and that the great prize is the spiritual essence of humankind.

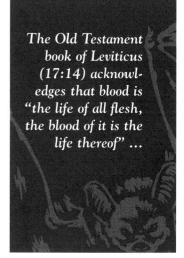

The Old Testament book of Leviticus (17:14) acknowledges that blood is "the life of all flesh, the blood of it is the life thereof" …

Human Blood Becomes Sacred to the Old Gods

At some point in those fierce and frightening prehistoric years, there came the realization that the shedding of a person's blood was connected with the release of the life force itself. And because it was required by the gods, blood became sacred.

After the gods in their various guises retreated to their other dimensional universe, some of their most devoted human servants recalled the power inherent in blood and the life force, and a large number of magical and religious rituals became centered around the shedding of blood. In an effort to call back the gods to Earth and beseech them to grant favors, thousands of members of ancient priesthoods raised chalices filled with the dark, holy elixir of life over thousands of altars stained with both animal and human blood. In an effort to become like the gods, many individuals began to practice the drinking of blood as it pulsed from the veins of their victims.

Biblical scholar Hyam Maccoby in his book *The Sacred Executioner* maintains that Cain was the hero in the original telling of the slaying of Abel in Genesis. Cain built the first city and became the patriarch of metallurgists, musicians, and pastoralists (Genesis 4:16–22). In Maccoby's reconstruction of Genesis, Cain's killing of his brother was not a vicious homicide, but the primeval human sacrifice that secured the civilization of the human race.

As civilization advanced and humankind began to free itself from the demands of the old gods and their priests who demanded blood sacrifice, the life force and the fluid that symbolized it demanded a new kind of respect. Blood became holy.

The Old Testament book of Leviticus (17:14) acknowledges that blood is "the life of all flesh, the blood of it is the life thereof," but the children of Israel are instructed that they "shall not eat of the blood of no manner of flesh; for the life of all flesh is the blood thereof: whosoever eateth it shall be cut off."

Again, in Deuteronomy 12:20–24, the Lord warns, "… thou mayest eat flesh, whatsoever thy soul lusteth after … Only be sure that thou eat not the blood: for the blood is the life; and thou mayest not eat the life with the flesh."

Similar warnings against the ingesting of blood were soon a part of the teachings of all major religious faiths; however, the dictates of culture, magic, and religion could merely issue prohibitions concerning the shedding of blood by humans. Clerical dictates and civic pronouncements hold no threat to those who heed the whispers of the Old Gods to satisfy their bloodlust with the vital fluid of others. Ecclesiastical dogma and the terrors of Inquisitions can do nothing to quell the hunger of the real vampires who possess the bodies of their disciples and command them to crouch in the darkness and wait to drink the blood of men, women, and children and to drain them of their life force.

Mythic Vampires

The vampire legend has always been with us—from the shadows of the ancient Egyptian pyramids to the bright lights of New York City, the vampire's evil remains eternal. From the villages of Uganda and Haiti to the remote regions of the Upper Amazon, indigenous people know the vampire in its many guises. The traditional Native American medicine priest, the Arctic Eskimo shaman, the Polynesian Kahuna, all know the myth of the vampire and take precautions against those whom they believe were once human and who are now among the undead who seek blood by night to sustain their dark energies.

Every culture has its own name for the night stalker. The word with which most of us are familiar rises from the Slavonic Magyar—*vam*, meaning blood; *Tpir*, meaning monster. To cite only a few other names for the vampire from various languages, there is the older English variation, *vampyr*; the Latin, *sanguisuga*; Serbian, *vampir*; Russian, *upyr*; Polish, *Upirs*; and the Greek, *Brucolacas*.

The physical appearance of a vampire in European folklore is grotesque, a nightmarish creature with twisted fangs and grasping talons. The cinematic depiction of the vampire in F.W. Murnau's *Nosferatu* (1922) presented moviegoers with an accurate depiction of the traditional vampire. In this film, which was Murnau's unauthorized version of the Count Dracula saga, we see actor Max Schreck's loathsome bloodsucker, Count Orlock, skittering about in the shadows with dark-ringed, hollowed eyes, pointed devil ears, and hideous fangs. With his long, blood-stained talons, his egg-shaped head and pasty white complexion, Schreck's Nosferatu captures the classic appearance of the undead as seen in the collective nightmares of humankind.

During many demon-haunted centuries in Europe, the dark powers of the vampire grew even stronger in the mind of the average man or woman. According to nervous admonitions, after dusk fell, the vampire's hypnotic powers were irresistible, and his strength was that of a dozen men. He could transform himself into the form of a bat, a rat, an owl, a fox, or a wolf. He was able to see in the dark and to travel on

Vlad III the Impaler, a fifteenth-century Romanian prince, was the historical character upon whom Bram Stoker's Count Dracula was based. The prince had a reputation for torturing his enemies in unspeakable ways.

moonbeams and mist. Sometimes, he had the power to vanish in a puff of smoke.

Desperate, frightened people sought to garland their windows with garlic or wolf bane, to obtain a vial of holy water, hang a crucifix on every wall, and say their prayers at night, but there was no certain protection from the attack of a vampire. Even a recently buried relative could have been cursed to become a vampire, and once night fell, the corpse, animated by blood lust, would claw his way out of the rot of the grave to seek unholy nourishment from his own family members. The vampire was a hideous predator that could only be killed by a stake through the heart and decapitation.

An alternate course of action against the vampire was to pry open its coffin during the daylight hours while it lay slumbering and pound a wooden stake through its heart—or, perhaps a bit safer, destroy the coffin while it was away and allow the rays of the early morning sun to scorch the monster into ashes.

Because we are so conditioned to hearing so many of the classic cinematic vampires speak with the same kind of foreign accent, some of us may be somewhat surprised when we learn that people around the world fear the nocturnal visits of the vampire.

In China, the *Chiang-shih* may appear as a corpselike being covered in green or white hair. Taking the lives of individuals traveling at night is the Chiang-shih's only motivation in its wretched existence. The creature is equipped with long, sharp claws, jagged fangs, and glowing red eyes.

The Chiang-shih may also possess a human body so that it can appear as a seductive woman or a handsome man to its unsuspecting victim. In some instances, the entity reanimates a recently deceased corpse, especially that of someone who committed suicide.

In Chapter One I mentioned the seductive, blood-sucking Rakshasas of the Hindus, but this beautiful night stalker is not alone in Indian tradition. Throughout the centuries Mother India has endured a wide variety of vampiric night stalkers.

The *Bhuta* haunts the wilderness and the wastelands and often signals its presence by an eerie display of glowing lights. Because these hideous beings feed on rotting corpses, the bite of the Bhuta brings illness and sometimes fatal disease.

The rapacious *Brahmaparush* is said to seize its victims by the head and drink their blood through a hole that it punctures in their skulls. Once it has had its fill of blood, the Brahmaparush eats the brains of those who have fallen into its clutches.

According to ancient tradition, the vampire must return to his crypt, coffin, or hiding place before sunrise or the Sun's rays will destroy him (illustration by Bill Oliver).

When the gory feast has been completed, the vampire engages in a bizarre dance of triumph around the corpse.

The *Churel* certainly extinguish the beautiful, seductive image that has been established by so many female vampires around the world. The Churel are nightmarishly ugly with wild strands of hair, sagging breasts, black tongues, and thick, rough lips. Since luring a handsome man to accompany them into the shadows is definitely out of the realm of possibility, the Churel throw seduction aside and viciously attack young men.

The aboriginal people of Australia speak of the *Yara-Ma-Yha-Who*, a nasty shadow dweller who uses the suckers on the ends of his fingers and toes to feast on the blood of its victims.

The Ashanti people of southern Ghana fear the *Asasabonsam*, vampiric entities that favor luring people into the deep forests. The Asasabonsam appear as regular humans—until they suddenly sprout hook-like legs and savage teeth to drink their victim's blood.

Another vampiric being that bothers the tribes of Africa's Gold Coast is the *Obayifo*. This creature might be explained as the spirit form of a male or female practitioner of the Dark Arts that leaves the host body at night and goes in search of human blood. Sometimes the being appears as a glowing ball of light before it rematerializes as a vampire and claims its victim.

The Contemporary Vampire Mythos: Seductive and Sexy

After Bram Stoker's novel *Dracula* (1897) became a popular stage play—and, in 1931, a classic horror film with Bela Lugosi portraying the Count as a sophisticated aristocrat—the image of the vampire as a hideous demon began to transform in the popular consciousness into that of an attractive stranger who possesses a bite that, while fatal, also promises eternal life.

In the decades that followed Lugosi's iconic appearance as a sophisticated, seductive, hypnotic member of the undead, the vampire of legend—a demonic presence, wrapped in a rotting burial shroud, intent only on sating its bloodlust—gradually became replaced by beguilingly romantic figures.

Anne Rice, who has certainly contributed greatly to the literary rebirth of the vampire as a romantic figure in such novels as *Interview with the Vampire*, has said that the vampire is an "enthralling" figure. She perceives the vampire's image to be that of a "person who never dies … [who] takes a blood sacrifice in order to love, and exerts a charm over people." In her view, the vampire is "a handsome, alluring, seductive person who captivates us, then drains the life out of us so that he or she can live. We long to be one of them, and the idea of being sacrificed to them becomes rather romantic."

It seems that in the great majority of the current cinematic and literary portrayals of the undead, attractive, buff male vampires and beautiful, seductive female night stalkers drink human blood only from hospital storage units or get along by feasting on animal blood. In certain contemporary variations of the classic tales, the vampires have developed a synthetic bloodlike formula that enables them to avoid the taking of human vital fluid. A number of popular television series have even portrayed conscientious vampires in the roles of police officers or private detectives who defend human society from vicious fanged mavericks who still seek human victims.

The sexual metaphors to be found in the cinematic and literary portrayals of the vampire's seductive bite are many, and Anne Rice has touched a responsive, atavistic chord in her many enthusiastic readers. In the view of Rice and other authors and screenwriters who have popularized the mythical vampire, the vampire's overall goals may be incomprehensible to a human being's limited point of view, but to the undead, human value judgments do not apply to them.

Closing the Curtain of Myth to View Real Vampires

The moment one begins seriously to discuss the possibility that the ancient multidimensional spirit-parasites may truly be responsible for predatory acts of the real vampires that have stalked humankind since pre-history, one may receive a raised eyebrow and the accusation that one is attempting to push the study of mental illness and antisocial behavior back into the Middle Ages. Nonetheless, there are a growing num-

Christopher Lee's Dracula (left) emphasized even more than Lugosi that the vampire was both sensual and seductive, while Bela Lugosi's iconic interpretation of Count Dracula as a sophisticated aristocrat in the 1931 motion picture version of Bram Stoker's novel changed the image of the vampire in film from hideous demon to an attractive stranger that promises immortality in his bite (illustrations by Ricardo Pustanio).

ber of medical doctors, psychiatrists, clinical psychologists, and members of the clergy who are becoming open-minded enough to suggest that we might reconsider certain areas of mental health and particular categories of abnormal psychic states to be demonic possession by spirit parasites rather than mental illness.

In recent years, a growing number of parapsychologists and other researchers have been investigating the possibility that mental slavery to a spirit parasite may be rather commonplace. Humankind has progressed to a plateau of enlightenment where we condemn the slavery of one human being to another. Soul slavery is more sinister, however, because the phenomenon remains largely unrecognized and undetected.

Many researchers believe that the spirit parasite can seize the controlling mechanism of the host body and direct the enslaved human to perform horrible, atrocious deeds. The spirit parasite might implant murderous thoughts in a host's mind, such as the desire to taste human blood, to slash a victim's throat, even to eat some of the person's flesh. After the crime has been committed, the vampiric spirit parasite withdraws back into another dimension of time and space, thus leaving the confused human being alone, charged with murder, while the true assassin has escaped.

The physical appearance of a vampire in European folklore is a grotesque, nightmarish creature with twisted fangs and grasping talons (illustration by Ricardo Pustanio).

Certain psychical researchers have created a kind of pattern profile of what may occur when someone has become the unwilling host of an uninvited spirit guest.

The host-being may begin to hear voices that direct him to perform acts that he had never before considered. He may begin to use obscene and blasphemous language in situations that make his friends or relatives feel very offended or uncomfortable. Friends and family will remark that he is acting like a "totally different person." He may frequently see grotesque images of the parasite spirit as it exists in its paraphysical dimension.

In the weeks and months that follow, the host-being may fall into states of blacked-out consciousness, times of which he has absolutely no memory.

On occasions, in the midst of conversations, the host-being may find his conscious mind blocked and a trancelike state will come over him.

The host-being will be observed walking differently, speaking in a different tone, and acting in a strange, irrational manner.

In the worst of cases, the parasitic spirit will completely possess the host-being's mind and body. The evil inhabitation may reach a climax with the host-being committing murder, suicide, or some violent antisocial act.

It is hardly comforting to read the reports of some investigators of such phenomena who state that possibly everyone at one time or another may become susceptible to a spirit parasite.

An examination of the case histories of diagnosed schizophrenics reveals that many of them underwent a period of severe stress prior to the onset of the illness. People under stress seek to control the tension in their lives. Unfortunately, far too many use alcohol or drugs in order to put themselves into a relaxed state—which very often deteriorates into a drunken or a drugged stupor. Alcohol and drugs leave the user wide open to spirit parasites.

Traditionally, researchers of the human psychological condition have assumed that the change of personality in one habituated to drugs or alcohol is due to the ingestion of the substance of preference. Certain psychical researchers have found that parasitic spirits frequently move into the mind and body of drug and alcohol users and actually encourage the host-beings to use more drugs or alcohol, for they are more easily controlled while under the influence of mind-altering substances.

Current literary and cinematic portrayals of the vampire have made the ancient blood-sucking creature of darkness the most popular monster in the world. In this present book, however, we deal with Real Vampires who continue to prey mercilessly on their victims and brush aside human values.

A Gallery of Classic Vampires

At the meeting of the American Academy of Forensic Sciences held in Denver, Colorado, in March 2009, Matteo Borrini of the University of Florence in Italy said that he may have forensically examined the first skeletal remains of a vampire.

While excavating the mass graves of victims of the Venetian plague of 1576 on the island of Lazzaretto Nuovo, Borrini found the skull of a woman with a brick in her mouth. According to Borrini, grave-diggers placed small bricks in the mouths of vampires, those men and women who were suspected of spreading the plague, as well as drinking people's blood.

Undoubtedly, during the demon-haunted Middle Ages, there were many corpses buried with bricks in their mouths for there were numerous recently deceased individuals under suspicion of being vampires. In the popular mind, Vlad Tepes, Dracul (1431–1476), might well have been responsible for creating a good number of blood-drinking night stalkers.

Vlad Tepes, King of Wallaschia, present-day Romania, may have been one of the inspirations for Bram Stoker's classic work *Dracula,* and his very name may be synonymous worldwide with vampires, but he will not be included in our Gallery for the very good reason that he was not a vampire. His bloody sobriquet, Vlad the Impaler, did not come from fangs that impaled the throats of his victims, but from the stakes that were driven though the warriors who had yielded to him in battle. History records that Vlad might have tortured, roasted, boiled, and impaled as many as 100,000 enemy soldiers, but he was never seen drinking a single drop of their blood.

In 1410, King Sigismund of Hungary had founded a secret fraternal order called the "Order of the Dragon" to defend Christian Europe from the onslaught of the Ottoman Turks. The emblem of the order was a dragon, wings spread, defending a cross. Vlad Tepes's father was known as "Vlad the Dragon" in honor of his courage in warfare against the Turks. Therefore Vlad Tepes (Vlad III) became at his birth Vlad Dracul or "Son of the Dragon."

In present day Romania, Vlad Dracul is regarded as a national hero for his success in resisting the invading Ottoman Turks and for establishing at least a brief period of peace, independence, and sovereignty. To call Vlad Dracul a shape-shifting creature of darkness while a tourist in Romania would be comparable to visitors to the United States naming our Colonial hero and leader George Washington a vampire.

However, there does exist a historical connection between Dracul and the first true vampire in our Gallery. In 1476, Steven Bathóry of Transylvania, whose family crest also bears the image of a dragon, helped Vlad Tepes regain his throne. In 1560, Erzsebet (Elizabeth) Bathóry was born.

The Countess of Blood

Born into a family of aristocrats, Elizabeth Bathóry inherited a dark reputation from her family. The name of Bathóry had either been that of the wisest rulers or the most depraved despots.

At age 15 Elizabeth, known for her beauty and her flawless complexion, became engaged to Ferenc Nadasdy on New Year's Eve 1575. Nadasdy was another family name with a sinister reputation, and the young Count Ferenc had a streak of barbaric cruelty and intense sadism running through him.

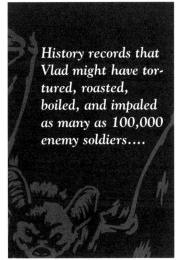

History records that Vlad might have tortured, roasted, boiled, and impaled as many as 100,000 enemy soldiers....

Together they were a perfectly matched pair. Elizabeth was constantly at Ferenc's side as the jaded young aristocrat dabbled in the dark arts. An intelligent, educated woman, Elizabeth could read and write in four languages and was completely capable of managing the affairs of the castle or uttering complex satanic rituals. Elizabeth and Ferenc were married on May 18, 1575, with a wedding that included about 4500 guests. Elizabeth retained the Bathóry name because her family's name was more powerful than that of her husband.

It is likely that Elizabeth would have remained just another depraved aristocrat if her husband had stayed at home to keep her happy. Instead, Ferenc vented his lust for blood by becoming one of Hungary's greatest warriors, earning the title of The Black Hero for his constant battles against the Turks. In 1578, Nadasdy was named the commander-in-chief of the Hungarian army, and he led the troops to fight another war with the Ottomans.

Although Nadasdy was often away for months at a time, in 1585 Elizabeth bore their first child, a daughter, Anna. A few years later, another daughter, Ursula, and a son, Andrew, were born, but they died at a very early age.

With Nadasdy so often engaged in warfare for long periods of battle and blood, the castle guests began taking on a strange appearance, as Elizabeth's personal serving maid Iloona Joo and two lesbian witches named Darvula and Dorka summoned bizarre acquaintances from all over the countryside to amuse their lonely mistress. Some of the visitors claimed to be vampires or werewolves. Others were witches, wizards, and alchemists.

Many hideous and gruesome experiments were performed by these disciples of Satan, which often featured the torturing of servant girls to enliven a dull afternoon. Jonas Ujvary, the castle's chief torturer, would select girls from the staff on whom to practice his skills with branding irons and executions, including beheadings. Johannes, a dwarf, would sometimes flog a young woman to death while the crowd counted aloud the lashes. On other occasions, he sliced off pieces of the women's flesh and passed the bits and pieces around the circle of the guests, eager to sample the gory appetizers before the main course of a lavish feast. Stoked on cruelty and several bottles of wine, the evening would climax with a sexual orgy unmatched in all of Europe for its licentiousness.

By 1598, two more children, Kate and Paul, had been born to Elizabeth and Ferenc; and the Countess, said to be a loving mother, devoted herself to rearing her children—with the help of a number of governesses.

Elizabeth Bathóry, the Countess of Blood (illustration by Ricardo Pustanio).

When Ferenc died in battle in 1604, Elizabeth found herself a single woman in her forties. She began to be concerned that she was no longer young and beautiful and that she may have difficulty finding another consort.

It was when she had begun to fear losing her legendary beauty that we can envision a scenario that was said to have begun with a serving maid who made the mistake of spilling a small portion of the wine that she had been pouring for her mistress. To emphasize her displeasure, the Countess struck the girl in the face and sent a splattering of blood on her hand.

When Countess Bathóry brushed the drops of blood away, it seemed to her that the skin beneath appeared softer and younger.

Quickly the Countess summoned Iloona Joo and asked if the dark arts held the recipes for potions to preserve youth. "Yes, my lady," the woman answered. "There are such potions locked in the secrets of the black rituals."

The Countess considered this, then told the woman that she believed that she had just discovered a vital element to the secret of eternal youth. She summoned the guards and had them bring the serving maid whom she had struck. While the burly men held the terrified girl firmly in their grasp, the Countess drew a pan of blood from her veins.

Ignoring the unconscious maid who had slumped to the floor, Elizabeth Bathóry began bathing her body with the blood she had stolen. "You see," she exclaimed to

Iloona Joo, who had watched the entire proceedings carefully. "My complexion has improved immediately. I have found the secret of remaining eternally youthful. I need never know the ravages of age. All I have to do is bathe in the blood of maidens."

Elizabeth Bathóry believed that she had made the discovery at just the right time, for the mirror had begun to reveal the lines of age encroaching upon her once flawless beauty.

With a desperate passion for retaining her allure, the fiery-eyed Elizabeth Bathóry of Hungary set out to keep a regular supply of maidens in stock to bleed for her bath. For eleven terrible years the peasants in the village below the Bathóry castle cowered behind the locked doors of their houses after dark and listened to the wailing cries of the young women being snatched up by the terrible black carriage that rumbled through the streets.

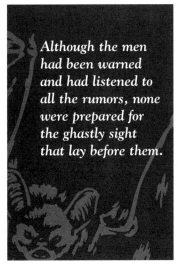

Although the men had been warned and had listened to all the rumors, none were prepared for the ghastly sight that lay before them.

Maidens, kidnapped from the village, were brought directly to the pens in the basement where they were fattened, then bled for the Countess's daily bath.

The horrible acts of torture, murder, and the gruesome blood baths could not go on forever. Beginning in 1602, Istvan Magyari, a Lutheran pastor, began making protests with the court in Vienna regarding the atrocities being committed by the Countess. Although other voices were soon added to that of the Pastor, the accusations against a woman of such a well-respected name were ignored until 1610.

A Bathóry or not, King Matthias at last decided, the rumors about Countess Elizabeth had to be investigated. The raiding party on the castle was led by Juraj Thurzo, the Palantine of Hungary, on New Year's Eve, 1610. Thurzo, a cousin of the infamous countess, had discussed the accusations made against Elizabeth with members of the family, none of whom wished to have her found guilty of such terrible crimes as those being levied against her. None of them wished to surrender the Bathórys' ownership of vast lands and wealth to the Crown. An informal agreement was reached where Elizabeth might be secreted in a nunnery. Those plans for sanctuary were forgotten when the raiding party arrived at the castle.

Although the men had been warned and had listened to all the rumors, none were prepared for the ghastly sight that lay before them as they crashed through the castle door. The dead and dying bodies of young women were strewn about the floor, some of them horribly mutilated. From the sounds upstairs they knew that a huge, drunken revelry was taking place. The raiders quietly sealed off the exits from the castle and arrested everyone inside.

On January 7, 1611, Royal Supreme Court Judge Theodosious de Szulo and 20 associate judges ordered Dorka, Iloona Joo, Janos Ujvary, and number of other witches put to death and their bodies burned. Because of her influential name, Countess Bathóry was imprisoned under house arrest and placed in a walled up set of rooms.

Investigators continued to collect testimonies from more than 300 witnesses to the horrors committed by the Countess of Blood—men and women who had seen their daughters and sisters lured or taken to the castle. Although the exact number of young women who were tortured, bled, and murdered by Elizabeth Bathóry may never be known, the most accepted total of her victims is 650.

The body of Elizabeth Bathóry was found on August 21, 1614, but the exact day of her death is unknown since several plates of food lay untouched in her cell. According to the guards and servants who brought her meals or checked in on her, not once did she ever speak a single word. Nearly 50 when she died, the Countess of Blood was still a remarkably beautiful woman.

Vincent Verzini

Vincent Verzini's crimes in Italy were committed between 1867 and 1871. The sexual nature of the 22-year-old vampire's acts is unmistakable. It is reported that he achieved orgasm by grasping his female victim by the throat and tearing her flesh with his teeth. He then proceeded to suck the blood through the wound.

One day pretty Maria Previtali, a 19-year-old cousin of Verzini, went out into the fields to work. Suddenly she became aware of footsteps other than her own. Frightened, she looked over her shoulder. Vincent was following.

Maria's footsteps picked up speed as she fought back waves of fear and panic. She thought of 14-year-old Johanna Motta, who had been viciously murdered the preceding December as she traveled on foot to a nearby village.

She remembered how she had lain awake that night, too frightened to sleep, and listened to Papa as he told her mother of the incident. "Si, Mama," he had said, his voice filled with emotion, "her throat was black and blue, and her mouth was full of dirt. All of her clothes were ripped off and her thighs were bloody with teeth marks. Her belly was cut wide open, and her insides were pulled out. And the parts that make her a woman had been torn out." With such a memory to goad her, Maria shuddered and began to run.

Maria recalled Mrs. Frigeni, who had gone out to work in the fields one morning, and by nightfall, had still not returned. When her husband had gone out to look for her, he found her naked and mutilated body. She had been strangled with a leather thong and flesh had been torn from her abdomen.

> *Fingers like bands of steel closed around her throat. She started to faint, and the hasty vampire relaxed his grip on her throat.*

Maria was almost breathless now. She could run no more. Her footsteps faltered, and two powerful hands grabbed her. She felt herself thrown to the ground. Fingers like bands of steel closed around her throat. She started to faint, and the hasty vampire relaxed his grip on her throat. Drawing in her breath, the courageous girl brought up her knee and kicked her insane cousin in the stomach. Maria's blow had temporarily drained the vampire of his blood lust. He muttered obscenities, then walked off across the field.

Maria ran home, told her horrified mother of the attack by her cousin, and she was taken at once to the village prefect. Verzini was immediately arrested, and after being questioned at length, made a full and detailed confession. He was tried, convicted, and sentenced to life imprisonment.

Verzini's vampirism was the expression of deep derangement and sexual perversion. In Verzini's own words:

> I had an unspeakable delight in strangling women, experiencing during the act erections and real sexual pleasure. The feeling of pleasure while strangling them was much greater than that which I experienced while masturbating.
>
> I took great delight in drinking Motta's blood. It also gave me great pleasure to pull the hairpins out of the hair of my victims.
>
> It never occurred to me to touch or to look at the genitals.... It satisfied me to seize the women by the neck and suck their blood.

The Woman Who Collected Coffins

Vera Renczi's trouble had begun very early in life. Born in Bucharest, Romania, in 1903 to a wealthy family with ancestral links to Hungarian nobility, she had no trouble obtaining everything she wanted. Her mother died when Vera was only a child, and her father had the chore of turning a temperamental and spoiled young girl into a mature woman. He had no idea what a job that could be. Before her fifteenth birthday young Vera had been chased from a boys' dormitory after midnight.

Vera's father's attempts to curb her radical social life were not very successful at first, but he congratulated himself when Vera presented the man whom she said she wanted to marry. Her father quickly agreed, even though the bridegroom-to-be was much older than Vera.

Vera bore the man a son, Lorenzo, but shortly after the child's birth, she told the neighbors that she feared that her husband had left her for another woman. The neighbors scoffed at Vera's suspicions. Her husband was known as a pillar of the community.

Vera stuck to her story, and after a few months without the presence of the husband to deny his infidelity, everyone believed that the lovely young mother had been deserted. No one suspected that the man lay in coffin number one in the cellar of the house. Before Vera had ended her bizarre collection, there would be 35 coffins neatly arranged in rows for her to admire as evidence of her powerful sex appeal to men.

Without a mate to keep her home, Vera roamed the streets of the city of Berkerekul, loving dozens of men, until she finally settled upon Josef Renczi. It was shortly after she had chosen Renczi as her next husband that she told friends and relatives that she had received word that her first husband had died in an automobile accident, and that she was now free to remarry.

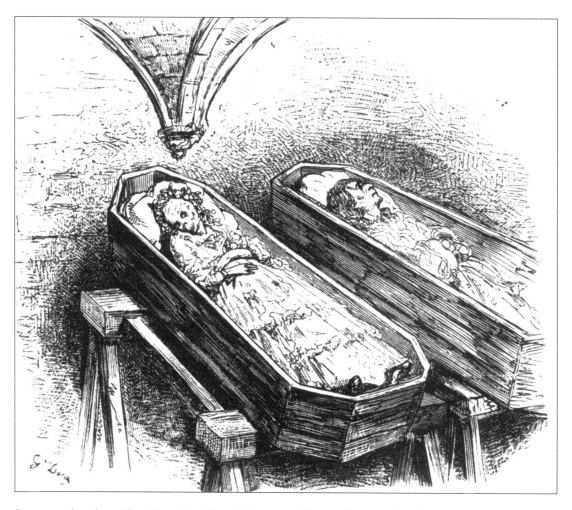

Inspectors found a grisly sight in Vera Renczi's basement (Fortean Picture Library).

Renczi had sought thrills, women, and excitement all over Europe, and it was not long before he tired of the ordinary world in Berkerekul. Sensing his wandering spirit, Vera made sure that Josef would never leave her side—or at least her cellar. She fed him a dose of poison and watched him die an agonizing death.

From then on, throughout the 1920s and 1930s, Vera Renczi did not bother to marry her victims. If she had made her choice of temporary mates from any other strata of society, she most surely would have been discovered sooner. But she was content to have and to hold and to kill only those whose presence would not be missed by the permanent residents of the town. It was, in fact, when she changed her choice of man of a higher caliber that she was discovered.

Invited to a party in town, Vera noticed a young banker, who was obviously very much in love with his new wife. With jealousy flashing through Vera's brain, she knew she had to possess that man. After being introduced to the handsome banker, her sophisticated good looks quickly gained his interest. It was not very long thereafter that he was learning the techniques of love from a very experienced mistress.

To Vera's dismay, the banker had a very strong sense of guilt. When his wife announced to him that she was pregnant, he knew he could no longer see his demanding mistress. He paid her one last visit to tell her that their affair had ended. The visit was fatal. Vera already had a coffin inscribed for him in the basement. But Vera Renczi had never before had to contend with a determined wife. The banker's bride explained to the police that the young man was missing and that he had confessed to having had an affair with Vera Renczi. The police questioned Vera, but she was able to divert them by saying that she did not know that the man was married. Since the police had no other evidence, they had to drop the case.

But the wife of the banker was persistent. She poked around, asking questions and finally turned up enough evidence to link Vera with the disappearance of over a dozen men. The police reopened the case, and a search of the Renczi house revealed the incredible basement crypt with the body of the young banker and over 30 other occupied coffins. In the raid that uncovered this grisly secret, the police found Vera Renczi sitting among her lovers. Inspection of the coffins showed that one of them contained the body of a young boy. "My son," Vera explained coldly. "He threatened to expose me."

When asked why she did it Vera's only explanation was that she could not stand the thought of her lovers in the arms of another woman, so she had successfully kept them "faithful" to her.

Vera Renczi entered prison, feeling no remorse for her crimes; but a few years after her imprisonment she went insane, spending the nights laughing and talking with her dead lovers. Not many years later she joined them.

Fritz Haarmann, The Hanover Vampire

In their *Perverse Crimes in History*, R.E.L. Masters and Eduard Lea identify Fritz Haarmann as one of the vampire breed, but add that it is "somewhat more accurate to regard him as a homosexual sadist and lust murderer—and of course as a cannibal." Haarmann had at least a six-year reign of terror (1918–1924) before he was apprehended by the authorities. During that time, he cannibalized as many as 50 victims. However, some researchers point out the alarming statistics that during that same period of time over 600 boys disappeared from Hanover, Germany, a city of about 450,000.

Some of his posthumous analysts and biographers have characterized him as a dull and stupid youth who served a number of jail sentences for child-molestation, indecent exposure, and homosexuality. Haarmann's antisocial acts graduated from the petty to the perverse when he became enamored with a young male prostitute, Hans Grans.

Haarmann, then in his forties, had made a token effort to work at gainful employment and had opened a small combination butcher shop and restaurant. With the urging of Grans, Haarmann would lure a young man to his shop, overpower him, and begin biting and chewing at his throat. In some instances, he did not cease his bloody attack until he had nearly eaten the head away from the body.

After Haarmann had satisfied his desire for blood and flesh, the body of the victim would be butchered and made into steaks, sausages, and other cuts of meat. Both Haarmann and Grans ate regular meals from their private stock of human flesh. What they didn't eat, Haarmann sold in his butcher shop. His patrons never questioned how it was that his shop always had choice cuts of meat for sale when fresh meat became scarce in other stores throughout the city.

When the sensational news of Haarmann's vampirism and butchery came to light, there may have been a number of citizens of Hanover who were horrified to consider that by patronizing his butcher shop they had become unwitting cannibals.

After his conviction at about the age of 46, Haarmann was beheaded with a sword. His brain was removed from its skull and delivered to Göttingen University for study.

Albert Fish, A Different Kind of Christ

Albert Fish was a cannibal and a vampire who was believed to have killed, eaten, and drunk the blood of between 8 and 15 children. He somehow believed in his demented interpretation of the Old Testament that he was paying homage to Abraham's near-sacrifice of his son, Isaac by actually completing the sacrificial acts. In addition, official estimates tallied that Fish had molested more than one hundred children and castrated a number of boys before his criminal career finally ended.

Born in 1870 in Washington, D.C., Fish came from an extremely dysfunctional family in which nearly every member was mentally deficient in some way. Systematically whipped and abused as a small boy, Fish later grew to become erotically stimulated by the cruel treatment.

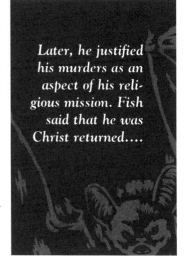

Later, he justified his murders as an aspect of his religious mission. Fish said that he was Christ returned....

Later, he justified his murders as an aspect of his religious mission. Fish said that he was Christ returned, and he proclaimed that it was his divine duty to administer God's vengeance upon a sinful and depraved humanity. His killings of the children, he explained, were actually sacrifices that spared the chosen children from living a life of depravity and sin that would have led to their eternal damnation.

For six years after one of his most heinous crimes—the murder, dismemberment, and eating of 10-year-old Grace Budd—Fish continued to send obscene letters to the girl's parents, describing in perverse detail the sadistic acts that he had performed upon their daughter. It was this series of profane correspondence that led to Fish's eventual capture.

The monster died in the electric chair without showing any signs of fear or an awareness of his own mortality. It was witnessed that he even helped the attendants adjust

The ceremonial drinking of blood inspires a sense of religious ecstasy for some fanatics.

the straps and apparatus as he sat in the chair awaiting the moment when the warden pulled the lever.

Blood Drinking as Religious Ecstasy

John Haigh was another vampire who justified his thirst for human blood by his religious fanaticism and an incredibly distorted interpretation of the Old Testament's admonition to "drink water out of thine own cistern and running waters out of thine own well." By some bizarre process of Haigh's twisted mind, the Bible passages became a commandment that he should start drinking his own urine and blood.

The only child of a pious Plymouth Brethren couple, little Johnny had been a devout boy until he was sexually abused by a member of the Brethren. Later, in his confessions, Haigh said that shortly after the abuse, he began to have dreams of bloody trees and strange men offering cups of blood for him to drink.

Haigh matured to become a fairly resourceful businessman leading a very tranquil and nonviolent life until 1935 when, at the age of 25, he was imprisoned for forgery.

In 1944, the vampire had his first taste of human blood—his own. He was in an automobile crash in which he suffered a scalp wound that bled profusely. The blood flowed down his face and into his mouth, thereby creating a subsequent thirst that would lead him to the gallows.

Perhaps it was the wound's accompanying blow to the head that had somehow deepened Haigh's psychosis. Shortly after the incident, he had a dream that he interpreted to mean that his early religious fervor had so sapped his spiritual strength that he could only restore his rightful energies by the regular consumption of fresh human blood.

Haigh's first taste of another human's blood came with his murder of William Donald McSwan when the young man brought a pinball to his workshop for repair on September 9, 1944. Haigh simply got the idea that he needed blood to drink, so he hit McSwan over the head, slit his throat, caught the flow of blood in a mug, and drank it. He disposed of McSwan's body by placing it in a tub of sulfuric acid.

In keeping with the religious trend of his illness, Haigh evolved a ritual that he generally followed with each of his subsequent murders. He would sever the jugular vein of his victim, then he would carefully draw off the blood, a glassful at a time. The actual drinking of the vital fluid was observed with great ceremony. Haigh later became convinced that his faith could only be sustained by the sacrifice of others and by the drinking of their blood. With a supply of sulfuric acid at hand, their corpses would be transformed into a sludge that could be poured into the sewer drain. When police investigators checked Haigh's workshop for traces of the missing persons, some human gallstones were discovered in the sludge.

Some theorists have wondered if feelings of guilt arising from his homosexual abuse experience drove the impressionable Haigh to offer such terrible propitiation of blood sacrifice. Or, perhaps, Haigh may have mistaken the intoxication he reportedly felt from blood drinking to the "high" that comes from religious ecstasy.

As fascinating as such theories may be as attempts to cast further light on vampirism, they will never be answered in the case of John Haigh, for his further testimonies became increasingly muddled until he was sentenced to death for the murders of nine victims and delivered to the hangman on April 6, 1949.

The Immortal Count de Saint-Germain

Today, many occult groups claim the Count de Saint-Germain as their spirit guide, and he remains popular as a spiritual mentor from other dimensions of reality. Others maintain that the Count de Saint-Germain continues to walk Earth, so that he might on occasion offer his counsel to men and women in high political places.

I have thought that the Count would be a strong candidate for the perfect vampire. He never stayed in any one place for too long; many people went missing in those days and disappeared without a trace; persons of the lower classes were often murdered by their superiors without suffering severe consequences.

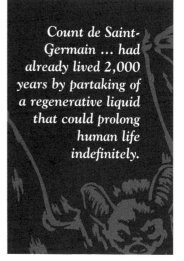

Count de Saint-Germain … had already lived 2,000 years by partaking of a regenerative liquid that could prolong human life indefinitely.

In the 1780s, Frederick the Great of Prussia called the Count de Saint-Germain the man who could not die, for according to the Count, a self-professed master alchemist, he had already lived 2,000 years by partaking of a regenerative liquid that could prolong human life indefinitely. Could an integral element in that elixir of life have been human blood?

Saint-Germain spoke and wrote Greek, Latin, Sanskrit, Arabic, Chinese, French, German, English, Italian, Portuguese, and Spanish. He was also a talented painter. His skill at mixing pigments was extraordinary, and famous painters begged in vain for the count to reveal his formulas. As if his mastery of brush and pigments were not extraordinary enough, Saint-Germain was also an accomplished virtuoso on the harpsichord and violin.

Obviously, since he claimed to have walked the Earth for 2,000 years, Saint-Germain's knowledge of history was unsurpassed. He would refer to a pleasant chat with the Queen of Sheba and relay amusing anecdotes of Babylonian court gossip. He would speak with reverence of the miraculous event that he had witnessed at the marriage feast at Cana when the young rabbi Jesus turned water into wine.

The remarkable count was first and foremost a successful alchemist, and it was widely rumored that he had succeeded in transforming base metals into gold. He could remove flaws from diamonds, and in this way improved one of the gems of King Louis XV. His chemical training far surpassed that of his contemporaries of the eighteenth century.

Members of Europe's royal courts also heard him speak often of an invention which would occur in the next century and which would unite people of all lands. He called it a steamboat, and he implied that it would be he who would be on hand in the future to help create the vessel.

Who was the Count de Saint-Germain and what was his true place of origin? It has been advanced by some scholars that the man was a clever spy on a secret mission who had deliberately shrouded his past with mystery. Why, these scholars ask, would the skeptical Prussian King Frederick promote such fantastic tales of the count unless he had some reason to do so?

Saint-Germain seems to betray himself as a diplomat with his astounding knowledge of the political past. Having gained access to secret court files, he could have studied European history methodically and with earnest purpose. His wide range of claimed artistic talents may have been wildly exaggerated by those who would stand to gain by the Count's missions.

Old records show that Saint-Germain died in the arms of two chambermaids at the court of the Landgrave of Hessen-Cassel, a fervent alchemist. But in spite of his supposed death, there are many recorded instances of the reappearance of the count. Many believe that he only feigned death, just as he had done many times before, so that he could go on sipping of his elixir of life and observing world events from a more quiet perspective.

After the fall of the Bastille in July 1789, Marie Antoinette received a letter of warning that was allegedly signed by the Count de Saint-Germain. Madame Adhemar, Marie Antoinette's confidant, kept a rendezvous with the Count in a chapel. Saint-Germain, then supposedly dead for five years, told her that he had done everything that he could to prevent the Revolution, but that the great magician Cagliostro, a former pupil and a fervent antimonarchist, had taken control of the events. It was further said that Count de Saint-Germain showed himself many times during the French Revolution. He was said to have been observed often near the guillotine, sadly shaking his head.

Could Saint-Germain truly have been a paraphysical being who had been taken over by a spirit parasite in ancient times?

It was claimed by many that Saint-Germain could render himself invisible—a remarkable accomplishment said to often have been witnessed. He was also a proficient hypnotist and could himself fall at will into a state of self-hypnosis.

Since I first wrote of the Count in the 1950s, I have heard from numerous individuals who claim to have encountered the legendary being. I am not referring to members of various secret societies who claim Count de Saint-Germain as their master teacher, but serious minded individuals—many of them experienced paranormal researchers. Only recently some investigators have told me that they have spoken with the Count as he stood in the shadows and that he promised to return to them and make himself more fully known to them. My advice is to practice extreme caution when arranging such a rendezvous.

As an interesting postscript to my theorizing that Count de Saint-Germain would have made the perfect vampire, I learned that Chelsea Quinn Yarbo has written a series of novels in which the eternal Count moves through time as a vampire. I guess I was not the only one who had begun to suspect the "man who lives forever."

Vampires and Werewolves

In 1941, Hollywood reinvented the centuries-old legend of the werewolf in *The Wolf Man* starring Lon Chaney Jr., Evelyn Ankers, and Claude Rains. Just as the motion picture *Dracula* transformed the hideous vampire of folklore into an elegantly attired sex symbol granting eternal life to those once bitten, *The Wolf Man* transformed the savage lupine shape-shifter into a sympathetic individual tortured by the full Moon into becoming half-man/half-wolf. In both fictional reinventions of the monsters, vampires and werewolves increase their kind by biting or scratching humans, thereby initiating a process that will remake their victims in their own image.

In the old records that recounted vicious attacks by creatures described as werewolves, the victims were described as being torn to bloody pieces. In some cases, there was nothing left of the unfortunate victim but gory shreds of flesh and a few bones to be carried away by smaller predators. Surely, such bloody scraps could not begin the process of metamorphosis into a werewolf.

Although sprigs of garlic and crucifixes were deemed by some venerable traditions as a first line of defense against both vampires and werewolves, wolfbane, the silver bullet, and other means of warding off a werewolf were largely imagined by screenwriter Curt Siodmak for the 1941 classic film. Even the ancient "gypsy folklore" repeated by Ms. Ankers, the heroine, was created by Siodmak: "Even a man who's pure in heart and says his prayers at night, may become a wolf when the wolfbane blooms and the autumn moon is bright."

There is no known culture on this planet that has not at one time or another cowered in fear because of a belief in the savage attacks of a nocturnal predator known as a therianthrope, a human-animal hybrid such as a werewolf or a werebear. Such creatures were painted by Stone Age artists more than 10,000 years ago and represent some of the world's oldest cave art.

The truth of the matter is that 10,000 years ago, humans truly wanted to become wolves—or at least be able to absorb some of their skills and their strengths. To the

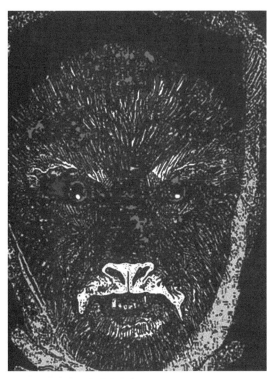

Drawings of the werewolf can be found etched in cave walls by stone age artists more than 10,000 years ago. There is no culture on Earth that has not, at one time or another, feared the attacks of a therianthrope, a human-animal hybrid (illustration by Ricardo Pustanio).

Native American tribes, the wolf was the great teacher. Such respect was also given to the wolf by the early Europeans. From the wolf, humans learned to hunt in packs, to cooperate in group survival, and to practice fidelity to one mate and their offspring.

Native American tribes tell of bear-people, wolf-people, fox-people, and so forth, and state that in the beginning of things, humans were as animals and animals as humans. Stories of women who gave birth to werecreatures are common among the North American tribal myths. Early cultures throughout the Americas, Europe, Asia, and Africa formed totem clans and often worshipped minor deities that were half-human, half-animal.

Warriors went into battle wearing the skins of wild animals, hoping that the ferocity and strength of the beasts would magically rub off on them. In the Northern European tribes, the fierce animal of choice was the wolf or the bear.

In ancient Scandinavia, the Norse words *ulfhedhnar* ("wolf-clothed") and *ber-werker* refer to the wolf or bear skins worn by the fierce Viking warriors when they went "berserk," or war-mad, and fought with the fury of vicious animals against opponents. In the Slavonic languages, the werewolf is called *vlukodlak*, which translates to "wolf-haired" or "wolf-skinned," once again suggesting the magical transference desired from wearing the skin of a brave animal into battle.

The prefix *were* in Old English means "man," so coupled with wolf, it designates a creature that can alter its appearance from human to beast and become a "man wolf." In French, the werewolf is known as *loup garou*; in Spanish, *hombre lobo*; Italian, *lupo manaro*; Portuguese *lobizon* or *lobo home*; Polish, *wilkolak*; Russian, *olkolka* or *volkulaku*; in Greek, *brukolakas*.

Although ritual dances and the wearing of wolf skins remain a part of the heritage of many Native American tribes, in early Europe the shamans began to create a magic and a sorcery that seemed more efficient than the old ways of achieving trance states and seemingly being transformed into wolves. By at least 850 B.C.E., the Greeks were fond of relating accounts of shape-shifters and sorcerers who would turn people into animals. A millennium later, circa 930, those who deliberately sought to become werewolves were generally evil sorcerers who sought the ability to shape-shift into the form of a wolf so that they might more effectively rob or attack their victims. Through incantations, potions, or spells, these wicked men took delight in their savage strength and their ability to strike fear into the hearts of all whom they encountered. Those

Stories of werewolves have horrified people in European communities for centuries (Fortean Picture Library).

who became werewolves against their will were individuals who had somehow run afoul of an evil sorcerer who had placed a curse of lupine transformation upon them.

According to a number of ancient magical texts, one of the methods by which a sorcerer might willingly become a werewolf was to disrobe and to rub completely over one's naked body an ointment made of the fat of a freshly killed animal and a special mixture of herbs. The person who wished to accomplish the lupine transformation should also wear a belt made of human or wolf skin around the waist, then cover his body with the pelt of a wolf. To accelerate the process of shape-shifting, the apprentice werewolf should drink beer mixed with blood and recite an ancient magical incantation.

To the people of the Middle Ages, there was little question that such creatures as werewolves truly existed. Switzerland can lay claim to the first official execution of werewolves, when in 1407, several individuals so accused were tortured and burned in Basel.

The Inquisitors in France have the dubious distinction of recording the most cases of werewolfism in all of Europe—30,000 between 1520 and 1630. The werewolf trials began at Poligny in 1521 when, after enduring the torture chamber, three men admitted to consorting with she-wolves and demons in order to gain the power to transform themselves into wolves—then they confessed to having killed and devoured many small children over a 19-year period. They were summarily burned at the stake.

The famous case of Gilles Garnier, who was executed as a werewolf at Dole, France, in 1573, provides grim details of attacks on numerous children, in which Garnier used his hands and teeth to kill and to cannibalize his young victims. In view of the heinous crimes and Garnier's confession that he was a werewolf, the court was quick to decree that he should be executed and his body burned and reduced to ashes.

The infamous werewolf Peter Stubbe of Cologne revealed that he possessed a magic belt that could instantly transform him into a wolf. To return to human form, he had but to remove the belt. Although the authorities never found his magical werewolf belt, they beheaded him for his crimes in 1589.

In his book *Discours des Sorciers* (1610), Henri Boguet, an eminent judge of Saint-Claude in the Jura Mountains, recounts his official investigation of a family of werewolves and his observation of them while they were in prison in 1584. According to his testimony, the members of the Gandillon family walked on all fours and howled like wolves. Their eyes turned red and gleaming; their hair sprouted; their teeth became long and sharp; and their fingernails turned horny and claw-like.

Real Vampires and Real Werewolves
Are Both Victims of Spirit Parasites

At the time of the Inquisition and the reign of demonic terror in Europe, many judges and learned men believed that an individual who had made a pact with Satan could become both a vampire and a werewolf. In Bram Stoker's novel *Dracula*, the Count is capable of transforming himself into a bat and a wolf. The popular stage version of the novel, which preceded the classic motion picture, dealt with this metamorphosis by having a German Shepherd run across the stage at the proper time when Dracula was in werewolf mode. Francis Ford Coppola's 1992 version of *Dracula* references the vampire's ability to become a werewolf with Gary Oldman as Dracula.

Although in principle I am loathe to agree with the judges of the Inquisition on anything, I will have to state that my opinion that it is the same ancient multidimensional spirit parasites who create Real Vampires that can possess individuals and create Real Werewolves. It is also soon apparent to the serious researcher that victims of these paraphysical invaders exist today as in centuries past and that they seek to enlist innocent men and women into their ranks not necessarily by drinking their blood or devouring their flesh, but by stealing their souls.

An Encounter with a Skin Walker

In many Native American traditions, the werewolf, were coyote, or whatever form the therianthrope or demon may assume is known as a "Skin Walker." My good friend, Priscilla Garduno Wolf, an Apache Medicine woman from New Mexico, told me of her encounter with such an entity which occurred when she was a teenager. Sister Wolf related the following story.

It was a beautiful day, and I was ready for the prom. I caught a ride with a friend, Molly, and the night went very well. However, at the end of the prom, Molly told me to catch a ride home with someone else; she was going to Alamosa with her boyfriend. I asked several people, but no one offered to take me home. I lived three miles from the school, and at that time all the roads were dirt.

I had no choice but to walk home in my formal, holding my heels in my hands. The moon was shining, but it was still very dark. I wasn't scared until I got close to the area where people claimed the Wolf Boy was buried. Grandpa said that the old people buried him there in the 1500s. Nearby, there was this huge tree that my grandfather had named the Skin Walker tree, because of sightings of Skin Walkers in that area.

I wanted to walk back to my grandmother's home, but I was scared that the Wolf Boy would appear to me, so I continued walking east toward my mother's home. When I crossed the old bridge, I heard a noise coming from under it. I looked back, and I saw what appeared to be a calf walking toward me. I started to run, and it began to run, following me.

It was about 300 feet to my mom's home, and I took off running fast. The animal stood up on its hind legs and almost caught me. I could hear its loud breathing. It sounded not human or animal like, but different.

I made it to my mother's farm land, and the thing jumped across the fence. When I got to the door of the house, I banged so hard to wake up Mom. "Open up!" I kept yelling! "Something is chasing me."

Mom made it to the door. I pushed her aside and shut the door, and we locked it. She shut the lights off so no one could look in the house. My baby brother, Adam, was sleeping, and after a while I lay down. I was so worn out from running. I heard someone turning the knob of the door—and open-

In recent years, Hollywood has released a number of motion pictures, such as the "Underworld" series, that have created a pseudo-history of a centuries' old conflict between vampires and werewolves (illustration by Dan Allen).

ing it! I could hear what sounded like the footsteps of a horse moving from room to room toward me.

All of a sudden it was next to my bed. I screamed for Mom to turn the lights on, but she was having a hard time getting up. It was like she was in a daze. I felt the Skin Walker's hand on me, touching my face and throat! His smelly breath and loud breathing were right next to me. The monster was tall and skinny half human and half something that looked like a cow. His hands were rough and hairy, and he had long nails.

I couldn't breathe! I screamed again and asked God to help me. It scratched my neck, and I was bleeding. When Mom managed to turn on the light, it vanished. Mom saw three scratches on my neck and said it was the Devil that had left his claw marks on me. We got up and checked the door. It was still locked, but the door hadn't mattered to the Skin Walker.

By morning the scratches were gone, just vanished. I wrote two stories years later that I called "The Devil's Claws" and "The Skin Walker."

Encountering a Demonic Black Dog of Evil

Paranormal researcher and author Angela Thomas is also executive co-producer and co-host of the P.O.R.T.A.L. Paranormal Talk Radio Show (http://www. oct13baby.com/). In this eerie account, she shares an encounter with a demonic entity which at first assumed the form of a black dog. Historically, as many readers are aware, the Black Dog specter has been commonly linked with haunting phenomenon and often as a precursor to werewolf or vampiric activity. The following is in Angela Thomas's words.

The sun was setting when I arrived at the strange house my grandparents now called home. The house was nothing compared to the two-story, farm house they moved from that sat on two hundred acres nestled near the only lake in the area. It was plain with wide, white planks that resembled every other house on Second Street in Bloomfield, Indiana. There was something eerily different about it. I wanted to leave, and I should have left, but the others with me would not have understood. An uninviting aura surrounded the house, and it appeared to have a life of its own.

I quickly dismissed the thoughts when we were shuffled in the house, and led directly into the bedrooms we were to sleep in that night. Nothing looked unusual in the bedroom that my sister Sandy and I were to share except an antique, cast iron crib that had been passed down through several generations to my grandmother.

The rest of the evening was spent listening to my grandmother chatter about the move into town, and how my grandfather had taken ill shortly thereafter. He was not present in the living room among relatives. Instead he lay ill on his bed. The bedroom door was open, and I could see him lying there almost lifeless. The doctors have no explanation. "He has been like this for awhile," my grandmother said. As she continued to speak, I saw what I thought was a large, black dog passing in front of my grandfather's bed.

"When did you start bringing a large dog into the house?" I asked. I was concerned. After all, it was out of character for her to permit a large animal in the house. "We don't have a dog. We gave all of the animals away before we moved here," she explained.

I knew I had seen something in front of his bed, and I quickly followed the path of where I thought this "dog" had gone. I searched every room—nothing. Making my way back into the living room, I noticed the lights had dimmed, and the room seemed filled with a foggy haze. The lights blinked bright again.

"It's an old house," Grandmother said, looking directly at me. She must have sensed how uncomfortable the entire house made me. Her explanation, I assumed, was to reassure me that nothing was wrong with the lights, but I had a feeling her words meant a little more than the mere wiring functions of an old place. Old places typically did not bother me. In fact, I had an affinity to all things old. Perhaps it was due to my own intuitive sensitivity that made such things inviting.

For several years, I had experienced unusual things, and a special knowing which I automatically thought others shared. Holding items, touching

In the true werewolf folklore, those cursed to become werewolves actually shape shift into the creature and do not become a wolfman—half human, half wolf (illustration by Dan Allen).

walls and expecting things to happen before they happened were part of my abilities, but there was no control then, or any way for me to alter my experiences. If I had touched the walls within the old house, I may have known what would soon change my life, and influence my perceptions of the world.

The feeling in the pit of my stomach was sensing fear, and yet nothing in the bedroom alerted me to anything abnormal. Two double beds with a nightstand in between them, a small desk, and the antique crib were all that filled the room. A small Gerber doll rested on the inside of the crib. I had not noticed it earlier. My sister who had traveled with me was already sleeping in the bed next to mine. By this time, I was eager for sleep to come. Sleep would be welcomed if nothing more than to relieve the feelings of the place.

Sleep would not come. I tossed and turned until I finally settled to the right side of the bed. The moonlight fell into the room providing the only source of light. Suddenly, a loud noise echoed from the other side of the room. Sitting up, I glanced in the direction of the crib, and saw a shadow of a large dog with its back hunched over. It appeared to be vomiting, and the noise coming from it was nothing like I had ever heard.

"Sandy, get up!" I called to my sister. No response. The dog was between the bed she was sleeping in and the wall that the crib was butted up against.

"Sandy," I said loudly, but she did not hear me. I tried screaming, but nothing would come out. In a split second, the animal was beside my bed. I saw its shadow and heard the same noise coming from it as I had heard before. A rank odor filled the air. By this time, I felt light-headed, and paralyzed with fear. The moonlight crossed its face, and then I knew it was not a dog. It was a demon!

Its face was twisted and resembled half-man, half-beast. Instantly, I began to pray to God. Recalling the scriptures, I began to telepathically command the demon to leave:

In the name of Jesus, I command you to leave this place! The demon was still there. Hours seemed to pass, but I was relentless in prayer. The demon was inches from me and seemed to torture me with its presence. At one point, laughter filled the room, its sound bouncing from one corner to the next above me. With all of my conviction, I drowned out the sound with prayer in my head, and I closed my eyes so I would not see the demon any longer. Prayer was my only concern, my deepest conviction.

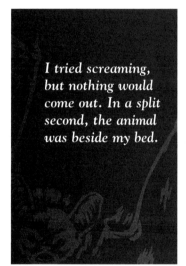

I tried screaming, but nothing would come out. In a split second, the animal was beside my bed.

All at once, I heard my voice speak out loud, commanding the demon to leave. Opening my eyes, I saw that the demon was gone, and I could see the light from the sun coming up outside. With the light of day, I felt rescued. I jumped up, headed for the door, and looked back into the room to make sure it was no longer there. I was startled. There on the bed was the Gerber doll that had been in the crib the night before.

With my sister still sleeping, I tip-toed into the kitchen, and put on a pot of coffee. From the corner of my eye, I saw something moving. It was my grandfather making his way to the kitchen table. He was weak, but there was color and life in his face.

"I had a dream about you," he said. "You were fighting with a dog that was trying to eat me alive."

Although I wanted to tell him desperately about the demon, I did not. He was too ill. It was not long before the others began to make their way into the kitchen, and the subject turned to breakfast.

Over the next couple of days, my grandfather gained strength, and sat with the family. We talked about God, hope, prayer and the ways of the world. Little did he know how my world had changed dramatically right there in his home. I no longer looked at the world the same way. There was definitely evil among us, and by the grace of God, I was spared from it. My prayers that night spared him, too.

As I was packing, my grandmother came into the bedroom carrying a small, wooden trunk. She unlocked it, and pulled out the Gerber doll and the clothes that she had made for it. She was proud of it, and said she thought it looked identical to the Gerber baby on the cereal box.

"Where's the other one?" I asked looking around to see if it was back in the crib.

She matter-of-factly stated, "I have just one, and I keep it under lock and key so nothing happens to it. It's a collectible!"

I told her that I had seen it in the crib the first night there, but she just shook her head, and told me it was impossible. It didn't take long for me to gather up the rest of the family, and drive away. Looking into the rear view mirror, I saw my grandfather standing there waving one last, long good-bye. A part of me wanted to go back, and ask him what he had experienced while he was so ill, but I kept driving. A sense of relief came over me knowing he had been released from the bonds of evil that had brought him to the brink of death. As I rounded the corner, I waved back. We never saw each other again.

A Conversation with a "Werewolf Girl"

Paul Dale Roberts, General Manager/Ghostwriter of Haunted and Paranormal Investigations International, sent me an account of his recent conversation with a young woman who claimed to be a modern-day werewolf.

The young woman claimed to be possessed by the spirit of a wolf.

Paul, who lives in Sacramento, agreed to meet the "werewolf girl" in Vallejo at a coffee shop. According to Paul, he was able to spot her easily: She wore a cat ears head band, a pentagram ring and a black T-shirt that read "Live Animal." Not hard to find at all.

This is her story. About four years ago, she was bitten by a mountain lion while doing voluntary work at the San Diego Zoo. The male mountain lion was playing with her at first and had her arm in his mouth, then he got rough and actually bit her. She (let's call her Diana, in honor of the Huntress) told me that everyone has an animal spirit within their being, and when she got bit, it brought out the wolf-like attributes that she was born with. When she got bitten that day, the essence of the wolf took over her persona. It possessed her.

Diana said that it's rare for werewolves to really transform into wolves and that she can't transform at all, but she added that she does have heightened senses, such as hearing, smell, eyesight, and even the sense of touch. She can feel the fluctuations around a person's body.

When she became a werewolf, the hairs on her arms became dark. She pulled up her pants leg and displayed a whole lot of hair on her leg. Diana displayed no canine teeth, but she craves meat. She has eaten raw meat, but mostly orders medium rare steaks. During a full moon, her senses sky rocket in intensity. This happens the day before a full moon, during the full moon, and after a full moon—three nights of sensationally heightened senses.

She told me that silver cannot harm her, but she has heard that silver can cause an allergic reaction to some werewolves. She lives a normal working life as a hostess at the Olive Garden. She has a boyfriend and her boyfriend is not "awakened," but he is also a werewolf. None of her relatives are werewolves.

She knows a few energy and physical vampires, but she made a point that werewolves and vampires are not mortal enemies as Hollywood would like you to believe in the *Underworld* series of films.

The Blood Cults

On January 7, 2009, a gathering of hundreds of Shiite men unsheathed their daggers and slashed the scalps of boys in the annual ritual of Ashura, a public display of blood shedding to commemorate the death of the Prophet Muhammad's grandson Imam Hussein at the battle of Kerbala in the seventh century. The annual rite is known as "tatbeer," and after receiving the wounds from the daggers, the boys march through the streets, spilling their blood, as they make their way to a shrine in northern Baghdad.

While many Shiites protest the rite of tatbeer as barbaric and in violation of Islam's prohibition of intentionally bringing harm to the body, those young boys who participate in the bloodletting attest that they feel no pain because they are committing the act for the love of Imam Hussein.

Blood sacrifice, whether of humans or animals, is the oldest and most universal propitiatory act of the pious seeking favor from a benevolent or a wrathful god. An ancient Hittite cylinder seal from the second millennium B.C.E. depicts a human sacrifice in intricate detail.

The God of the Hebrews strictly prohibited his followers from imitating their neighbors in the offering of human sacrifices (Lev. 20:25; Deut. 18:10). The one God placed a high value on human life and forbade this practice (Lev. 20:2–5; Jer. 32:35).

While the Hebrew God on the one hand repeatedly emphasized that He, as Spirit, did not need or require food and that the true gift that He required was that of man's love, commitment, and service, the Laws of Moses did require the blood of animals and the sacrifice of grain to God. These sacrifices were conducted for three basic reasons: Consecration, to dedicate oneself; Expiation, to cover one's sin or guilt; Propitiation, to satisfy Divine anger.

Consecration sacrifices were vegetable or grain offerings, but they could not be brought to God unless they had been preceded by an expiatory offering of a blood sac-

There seems to be a compulsion in various cults and sects to seek to appease the Dark Gods by the offering of the blood of willing—or unwilling—members (illustration by Ricardo Pustanio).

rifice. There was no consecration or commitment to God apart from expiation. According to the law, man could not approach God and be right with Him without the shedding of blood. The sacrifice itself could only be carried out by a High Priest under the strictest obedience to the law. The High Priest himself had to be consecrated before entering the innermost part of the temple or Holy of Holies where the sacrifice was offered to God.

In the Christian cosmology, the surrender of Jesus to submit to the will of the Father and to accept the ignoble death of crucifixion was to serve as the final sacrifice and was forever to put the issue of blood sacrifice to rest.

The *Upanishads* of the Hindu sages, the *Bhagavad-Gita* of Lord Krishna, the Qur'an of Muhammad, the utterances of Zoroaster, the sayings of Confucius, the teachings of the Buddha—all contain central themes very similar to the preaching of Jesus, admonishing their followers to resist the demands of the flesh and to offer God works of the spirit rather than sacrifices of blood.

Regardless of the prohibitions against human sacrifice by major religious groups, there seems to be an atavistic compulsion in various cults and sects to seek to appease the various facets of divinity by offering the blood of their willing members or, in many cases, the blood and flesh of their very unwilling victims.

The Leopard Men

For many centuries a leopard cult has existed in West Africa, particularly in Nigeria and Sierra Leone, wherein its members, believing that they have shape-shifted into leopards, kill by slashing and mauling their human prey with steel claws and knives. Later, they drink the blood and eat the flesh of human victims as if they were truly in the form of leopards.

Initiates who aspire to become members of the cult must return with a container of their victim's blood and drink it in the presence of the assembled members. The cultists believe that a magical elixir known as *borfima*, which they brew from boiling their victim's intestines, grants them superhuman powers and enables them to transform themselves into leopards.

Misfortunes such as illness or crop failure would be sufficient to demand a human sacrifice. A likely victim would be chosen, the date and time of the killing agreed upon, and the executioner, known as the *Bati Yeli,* would be selected.

The Bati Yeli wears the ritual leopard mask and a leopard skin robe. It is customary that the sacrifice be performed at one of the Leopard cult's jungle shrines, but if circumstances demand a more immediate shedding of blood, the rite may be conducted with the ceremonial two-pronged steel claw anywhere at all.

It should be noted that in ancient Egypt the leopard was esteemed as an aspect of divinity and associated with the god Osiris, the judge of the dead. For many African tribal members, the leopard is a powerful totem animal that is believed to guide the spirits of the dead to rest. The vast majority of those individuals who revere the leopard as their totem are not killers. Those who believe that they can shape-shift into leopards by drinking human blood and eating human flesh have fallen victim to spiritual parasites that require human sacrifice.

In Nigeria and Sierra Leone some believe in the shape-shifting leopard people.

The first serious outbreak of leopard-cult murders in Sierra Leone and Nigeria occurred shortly after World War I. Many of its members were captured and executed, and the white administrators believed that they had crushed the cult. However, the leopard men simply went underground, continuing to perform ritual murders sporadically every year over the next two decades.

In the 1940s, the leopard men became bold, and there were 48 cases of murder and attempted murder committed by the leopard cult in 1946 alone. It soon became obvious from the nature of the slayings that the leopard men had begun directing many of their attacks against whites, as if to convince the native population that the cult had no fear of the police or of the white administrators. The sacrifices continued during the first seven months of 1947, when there were 43 known ritual killings performed by the leopard cult.

Early in 1947, when District Officer Terry Wilson discovered that leopard men had begun killing young women in his jurisdiction, he raided the house of a local chief named Nagogo. In the chief's dwelling, Wilson found a leopard mask, a leopard-skin robe, and a steel claw. Acting on a tip from an informer, Wilson ordered his police officers to dig near the chief's house, where they found the remains of 13 victims. The chief was put in prison to await trial, and Wilson set out on a determined mission to squelch the leopard men's reign of terror.

There were several more murders during the weeks that followed, including the wife and daughter of Nagogo, the imprisoned chieftain. When Nagogo saw the bloodied corpses of his wife and daughter and realized how viciously his fellow leopard men had betrayed him, he collapsed and died of heart failure.

Wilson requested and received 200 additional police officers as reinforcements, but the leopard men became increasingly bold in their nocturnal attacks. One night they even sacrificed a female victim inside the police compound.

After that grisly defiant gesture, the cult committed several murders in broad daylight. The native inhabitants of the region lost all confidence in the police and their ability to stop the killings by the powerful leopard men. Even some of Wilson's men had come to believe that the cultists truly possessed the ability to shape-shift into leopards and to fade unseen into the shadows.

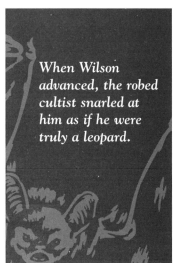

When Wilson advanced, the robed cultist snarled at him as if he were truly a leopard.

One night in mid-August 1947, Wilson had one of his best men walk on the path to a village where several slayings had taken place. Hoping to set a trap, Wilson and a dozen men hid in the jungle.

Suddenly, with the blood-curdling shriek of an attacking leopard, a tall man in leopard robes charged headlong at the officer, swinging a large club. The young constable struggled with the man, but before Wilson and the other officers could arrive on the scene, the cultist had smashed in the officer's skull and fled into the bushes.

District Officer Wilson had lost one of his best men, but as he was about to have some officers take the constable's body to the compound he had a sudden hunch that the attacker might return to the scene of the crime. When the other officers left to search the neighboring villages, Wilson hid himself behind some bushes overlooking the trail.

Around midnight, a nightmarish figure crawling on all fours emerged from the jungle, leaped on the young constable's corpse, and began clawing at his face like a leopard. Wilson caught the glint of a two-pronged steel claw in the moonlight. The leopard man had returned to complete the cult ritual of sacrifice.

When Wilson advanced, the robed cultist snarled at him as if he were truly a leopard. When he came at him with the two-pronged claw, Wilson shot him in the chest.

Wilson's act of courage provided the natives of the region with proof that the leopard men were not supernatural beings that could not be stopped. They were, after all, men of flesh and blood—savage, bestial, and vicious—but men, nonetheless. Witnesses began to come forward in great numbers with clues to the identity of cult members and the possible location of a secret jungle shrine.

The shrine itself was found deep in the jungle, hidden and protected by a large boulder. The cult's altar was a flat stone slab that was covered with dark bloodstains. Human bones were strewn over the ground. A grotesque effigy of a half-leopard, half-man towered above the gory altar.

In February 1948, 73 initiated members of the cult were arrested and sent to prison. Eventually, 39 of them were sentenced to death and hanged in Abak Prison.

Their executions were witnessed by a number of local tribal chiefs who could testify to their villages that the leopard men were not immortal.

Although the defiant strength of the leopard men was broken in 1948, inhabitants of the region are well aware that the cult still exists as a secret society with a shrine hidden in the jungle. Individuals who go missing and whose bodies are never found are feared to have been offered as sacrifices to the dark gods of the leopard men.

Isawiyya

Founded in the early sixteenth century by the fakir and mystic Sheikh Abu Abd Allah Sidi Muhammed ben Isa as-Sofiani al Mukhteari (Ibn Isa), the fanatical Muslim sect known as the Isawiyya have adherents spread out across North Africa, the Middle East, and the Sudan. Because Ibn Isa was believed to have the ability to communicate with all creatures, the religious gatherings of the sect require that each individual member wear a mask that represents one of seven animals—camels, cats, dogs, panthers, jackals, boars, or lions.

Believing himself to be in the lineage of Biblical Esau, Ibn Isa, "the son of the Hairy One, Isa (Esau)" slept and prayed on two panther skins. In the *qasida At-Taiya,* which he composed, Ibn Isa defined his powers by writing that both humans and the Jinns, were all devoted to him, as well as the venomous reptiles and the beasts of the desert.

Before embarking on a pilgrimage, the Isawiyya sacrificed a bull or a calf in honor of Ibn Isa. Before the ritual, the calf or bull is dressed in women's clothing, thus becoming an obvious substitute for a human victim. As the rites progress, the members of the cults work themselves into such a frenzy that the sacrificial animal is torn to bits and its flesh eaten raw. When they begin their journey homeward after the pilgrimage, they dye their hands and feet red to represent fresh blood.

European witnesses to an Isawiyya initiation rite told of watching the initiates dancing and whirling faster and faster until they reached a point of violent ecstasy. Then, as they were writhing in the dust, bowls of live snakes, lizards, toads, and scorpion were set before them. Immediately, the initiates seized the bowls and began stuffing the wriggling creatures into their mouths, biting and tearing at them until there was nothing left but bloodstains.

Santeria

Forced to accept the religious practices of their white masters, the African slaves in Cuba were greatly distressed when they could no longer worship the *Orishas,* their spiritual guardians. Since they were in no position to petition for the right to practice their native religion, the Yoruba and Bantu priests began to notice a number of paral-

A Santeria drum may be used in religious ceremonies that many North Americans don't understand and may even fear.

lels between the old religion of western Africa and aspects of Spanish Catholicism. While paying obeisance and homage to various Christian saints, the Africans found that they could simply envision that they were praying to one of their own spirit beings. Around 1517, a secret religion was born—Regla de Ocha, "The Rule of the Orisha," or the common and most popular name, Santeria, "the way of the saints."

Olorun or *Olodumare*, "the one who owns Heaven," is the supreme deity in Santeria. The lesser guardians, the Orisha, are the entities who are each associated with a different Roman Catholic saint: Babalz Ayi became St. Lazaurus; Oggzn became St. Peter; Oshzn became Our Lady of Charity; Elegba became St. Anthony; Obatala became the Resurrected Christ, and so forth. Priests of the faith are called Santeros or Babalochas; priestesses are called Santeras or Iyalochas. The term Olorisha may be applied to either a priest or a priestess.

While Santeria's rites are controversial in that they may include the sacrifice of small animals, it is essentially a benign religion. Each celebration usually begins with an innovation of Olorun, the supreme deity. Dancing to strong African rhythms continues until members are possessed by various Orisha and allow the spirits to speak through them. The ritual is climaxed with the blood sacrifice, usually a chicken.

Santeria continues to grow among Hispanics in Florida, New York City, and Los Angeles. Some estimates state that there are over 300,000 practitioners of Santeria in New York alone.

While the secret rites remain hidden from outsiders, a few groups have recently emerged which allow their members an opportunity to practice Santeria freely. The Church of the Lukumi Babalu Aye was formed in southern Florida in the early 1970s and won a landmark decision by the Supreme Court to be allowed to practice animal sacrifice. The African Theological Archministry, founded by Walter Eugene King in South Carolina, now reports approximately 10,000 members. The Church of Seven African Powers, also located in Florida, instructs its members how to use spells in their daily lives.

In April 1989, the religion of Santeria was dealt a blow that severely tainted its image in the public consciousness. Police officials digging on the grounds of Rancho Santa Elena outside of Matamoros, Mexico, found a dozen human corpses which had all suffered ritual mutilations. When it was learned that the mother of Adolfo de Jesus Constanzo, the leader of the drug ring responsible for the murders, was a practitioner of Santeria, a media frenzy swept across both Mexico and the United States. Santeria was most often defined by the media as an obscure cult that was a mixture of voodoo and demon-worship.

Constanzo had actually created his own concept of a cult and declared himself its High Priest. He was joined by Sara Maria Aldrete, an attractive young woman, who led a bizarre double life as a High Priestess and as an honor student at Texas Southmost College in Brownsville. Although, on the one hand, the ritual sacrifices were used as a disciplinary tool by the drug boss, it was learned from gang members that Constanzo had promised his followers that they would be able to absorb the spiritual essence of the victims.

Subsequent investigations of Constanzo's grotesque version of a cult of human sacrifice determined that he had combined aspects of Santeria, voodoo, an ancient Aztec ritual known as *santismo,* and combined them with elements of his own bloody cosmology. Mexican police officials had discovered the grisly handiwork of the drug ring by following one of its members to a large black cauldron in which a human brain, a turtle shell, a horseshoe, a human spinal column, and an assortment of human bones had been boiled in blood.

Macumba

The ancient highly respected role of the shaman remains central to Macumba (also known as Spiritism, Candomble, and Umbanda), a religious expression still practiced by a large number of Brazilians. The shaman (most often a male) enters into a trance state and communicates with the spirits in order to gain advice or aid for the supplicants. Altered states of consciousness among the practitioners are encouraged by dancing and drumming, and the evening ceremony is climaxed with an animal sacrifice.

Macumba was born in the 1550s from a blending of the African spirit worship of the slaves who had been brought to Brazil and the Roman Catholicism of the slaveholders. As with the origins of Santeria, the native priests soon realized how complementary the two faiths could be—especially since, unlike the slave owners in the United States, the Brazilians allowed the slaves to keep their drums. From the melding of the two religious faiths, the African slaves created the samba, the rhythm of the saints. The African god, Exu, became St. Anthony; Iemanja became Our Lady of the Glory; Oba became St. Joan of Arc; Oxala became Jesus Christ; Oxum became Our Lady of the Conception, and so on.

Those who participate in a Macumba ceremony enter a trance during the dancing and the drumming and allow a god to possess them. Once the possession has taken place, the shaman must determine which gods are in which dancer so the correct rituals may be performed. The process is assisted by the sacrifice of an animal, and the shaman smearing blood over the cult members. Once the members have been blooded, they take an oath of loyalty to the cult. Later, when the possessing spirit has left them, the members of the Macumba cult usually have no memory of the ritual proceedings.

The Mau Mau

In 1948, police officials in the British colony of Kenya began to receive rumors of strange ceremonies being held late at night in the jungle. These midnight assemblies were said to be bestial rituals that mocked Christian rites and included the eating of human flesh and the drinking of blood. Accompanying these sordid rumors were reports of native people being dragged from their beds at night, being beaten or maimed, and forced to swear oaths of initiation to a secret society called the Mau Mau.

It has been said that no one knows the real meaning of "Mau Mau" other than a Kikuyu (also Gikuyu) tribesperson. The origin of the name is shrouded in ancient African tribal mysteries and covered in blood. As nearly as it can be determined, the Mau Mau was quite likely an ancient Kikuyu secret society that had been reactivated. The Kikuyu tribe was the most populous and best educated in Kenya, but their culture also permitted secret societies to flourish, and there were many such groups that had been in existence since long before the Europeans came to Africa.

The ranks of the Mau Mau increased when they began to force unwilling individuals into participating in their blood oaths. The oath ceremonies began with the new members taking a vow to honor the old religion of their tribal ancestors. There were at least seven stages of oath-taking, which might take several days or weeks to complete and which included the drinking of blood, eating portions of human flesh, cohabiting with animals, and ingesting bits of brains from disinterred corpses. After the seventh stage of the oath-taking had been reached, the members had to repeat the cycle and reinforce their vows by beginning again.

The first murder victim of the Mau Mau was a Kikuyu chief who spoke out against the secret society and berated them for choosing to revert to savagery and bar-

barism. In October 1952, a lone white settler was killed and disemboweled. An elderly farmer was found dead in November. A state of emergency was declared in Kenya as the secret rituals had escalated to the murder of Kikuyu policemen, whose bodies were found mutilated and floating in rivers. White farmers found their cattle disemboweled and the tendons in their legs severed so they could not walk.

In January 1953, two partners who worked a farm were discovered murdered by the Mau Mau. A vicious attack on January 24 claimed the Rucks, a family of English heritage, whose bodies were found so hacked and ripped as to be nearly unrecognizable. Later it was learned that native men and women who had been employed by the Rucks for many years had been foremost in the slaughter of the English family.

What seemed particularly insidious to the white population was discovering to their horror that employees who had been loyal to them for decades were suddenly rising up and butchering them without warning. The Mau Mau insisted that long-standing associations and friendships between black and white were no longer considered something of value.

On March 26, a successful raid by the Mau Mau occurred against the police station at Naivasha. The station was overrun and guns and ammunition were taken away in a truck. Later that same night, the Mau Mau bound the circular huts of the villages of Lari with cables so the doors could not be opened, poured gasoline over the thatched roofs, and set the homes on fire. Most of the men of the village were away serving in the Kikuyu Guard, an anti-Mau Mau force, so the greatest number of the 90 bodies found in the charred remains were those of women and children.

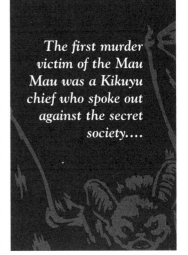

The first murder victim of the Mau Mau was a Kikuyu chief who spoke out against the secret society....

In May 1956, Dedan Kimathi, who was identified as the militant head of the Mau Mau, was captured by a party of Kikuyu tribal police. Soon after Kimathi had been apprehended, the Mau Mau society crumbled from lack of ammunition and arms, internal quarrels in the ranks, and disease brought about by the hardship of existing in the jungle under extremely difficult conditions. Kimathi was executed by the British in 1957 for having ordered atrocities and murders as the leader of the Mau Mau.

By the time the Mau Mau was disbanded, they had slaughtered over 2,000 African tribes people and brutally maimed many thousands more native people. Although the murders of Kenyan civilians of European ancestry were brutal and bloody, the actual numbers of those killed at the hands of the Mau Mau were greatly exaggerated by the media.

Born to Be the Goddess of a Blood Cult

In 1963, the police in Ciudad Victoria, Mexico, announced that members of a cult had sacrificed 12 persons to the Dark Gods. Blood had been drunk from ceremonial goblets passed from member to member. Hearts had been ripped from the bodies of

In 1963, police in Ciudad Victoria, Mexico, arrested Magdalena Solis, a self-proclaimed high priestess, for sacrificing 12 villagers and drinking their blood from ceremonial goblets (illustration by Ricardo Pustanio).

living victims during grisly ceremonies. Others had been stoned to death on orders from a prostitute-turned "goddess."

In Magdalena Solis's eyes, she had been born to be a goddess, not a prostitute who prowled the Monterrey bars for paying customers. In spite of her blonde beauty, she earned only a few pesos from the frequenters of Monterrey's night spots, barely enough to support herself and Eleazor, her skinny, homosexual brother who had pimped and sold her flesh since they had been children.

Then, in the summer of 1962, life changed for Magdalena.

In a few months, she had conducted mass killings offered to ancient Inca gods, operated a sex cult that indulged in orgiastic rituals, and posed as a high priestess who bade her followers to drink from a ceremonial goblet filled with a mixture of marijuana leaves and human blood. It was the Hernandez brothers, Santos and Cayetano, who presented Magdalena and Eleazor with a most unusual proposition. It seemed that the Hernandez brothers needed a god and a goddess to supplement the sex cult that they had established in the village of Yerba Buena.

Cayetano said that the simple farmers of the village had joined their cult for three reasons. They felt the need to belong to something since there was no church in their village; they enjoyed the excitement that the brothers gave their otherwise dull lives; and the brothers offered them a share in the treasure. A treasure? The Hernandez brothers now had Magdalena's and Eleazor's full attention.

"But of course," Santos chuckled. "A marvelous ancient Inca treasure that is worth the ransom of a hundred kings." Magdalena wondered if they had such a treasure, why were they living in a poor village trying to take advantage of the farmers? Cayetano said that was the scam. Of course they had no treasure, but only the promise that they had a hoard of Inca gold.

"Do you think that a bunch of stupid farmers know that the Incas were in Peru, not Mexico?" he laughed.

Santos outlined the scam to Magdalena and Eleazor. For several months, they had been living in a cave, conducting mystic rites and promising the farmers that if they brought them regular offerings of money, they would continue to pray to the cave gods and attempt to convince the deities to give up the treasure that the Incas had buried in the mountains.

At first all had gone well, Santos told them. The farmers brought their money, and he had enjoyed the bodies of the more attractive of their wives. Cayetano had sported with the men, for such was his way. The Hernandez brothers had convinced the villagers that sex with the priests was necessary to rid their bodies of demons.

Next, when the farmers and their wives had desired something more, Santos and Cayetano had initiated a beautiful village girl to serve as a priestess. Her full figure and her nude dances had kept the men's minds off the treasure for several weeks. But recently the villagers had become very impatient. They had begun to complain that they had grown weary of purging their bodies of demons. They were now demanding their share of the treasure.

In a last desperate effort to keep the villagers' minds off the treasure, the Hernandez brothers had promised them the reincarnation of a local faith healer who had been dead for 50 years.

"In the eyes of the villagers," Santos explained, "this woman has become a goddess. We have promised them that she will return to them in the company of an Incan god. Supposedly, even now, we are up on the mountaintop praying for their holy arrival. We decided that it would be to our greater advantage to come to Monterrey to bargain with you."

Cayetano had already aroused Eleazor's interest by his mention of the simple, but muscular, farmers. Magdalena had made no secret of her preference for love-making with her own sex, so Cayetano launched into an elaborate description of the charms of Celina, their local village priestess. With the Hernandez brothers focusing a dual attack on the vanity and the lusts of Magdalena and Eleazor, the prostitute and her pimp eventually succumbed to the lure of sex and money.

Magdalena's frustrated creativity and sense of the dramatic were given full expression with the carefully orchestrated appearance of the reincarnated faith healer and the god before the astonished farmers and their wives. She and Eleazor appeared in the sacred cave in a puff of billowing smoke. When the "holy mists" cleared, the villagers fell in awe before the forms of the goddess and the ancient Inca god.

Magdalena imperiously informed the villagers that before she could once again perform healings or reveal the treasure, there must be a serious purging of their lusts and their bodily demons. Once she had warmed to the idea of being a goddess, Magdalena found that she had a real flair for fashioning impromptu rituals. On the night of the "holy one's" arrival, the farmers and their wives were led through an orgy that included weird chants, bizarre dances, uninhibited sex, and the communal sharing of a bowl that had been filled with chicken blood and marijuana leaves.

The two priests and the two deities settled into comfortable adjustments. Eleazor and Cayetano had the robust farmers on whom to indulge their homosexual yearnings; and in the interest of harmony, Santos surrendered his claim on the beautiful Celina to Magdalena and contented himself with the rustic charms of the farmers' wives.

After a time, however, there were once again rumblings of discontent. Jesus Rubio, a villager whom the Hernandez brothers had taken into their confidence since he was too bright to fall for the scam, came to them with tales of impatience and distrust among the people. Magdalena pacified the potential rebellion with an extra por-

The Inca civilization left behind many artifacts of their religion, such as this figurine of one of their gods.

tion of marijuana leaves in the brew that she dispensed at the ceremonies.

Eventually, the day had to come when marijuana and group sex could no longer distract the poor villagers' thoughts of ending their poverty with the Inca treasure. Jesus Rubio informed the conspirators that the men had grown weary of Eleazor and Cayetano using them for sexual acts that they considered loathsome and unnatural, and their wives had become impatient with the continual purging of demons from their bodies. The villagers wanted to see the glorious gold that they had been promised for so many months. Magdalena told the others that she would handle the problem. Her hardened survival instinct was about to bring the villagers a terrible kind of fear and immerse the cult into new depths of loathsome perversion.

That night she told the group assembled in the cave that, while it was true that most of them had been faithful, there existed among them those who had profaned the priests and the gods. "It is these doubters who are keeping the gold from you," she screamed at them, "not the gods!" Pausing for effect and allowing the murmuring and the nervous side-long glances to subside, Magdalena continued: "It is the gods' wish that you should be happy. But they will not release their ancient gold into the hands of those who doubt. Alas, all of you suffer because of the lack of faith of a few."

A confused babble and wailing arose as the villagers loudly protested their fidelity and their devotion to the gods. At a secretive nod from Magdalena, Jesus Rubio pushed two men into the center of the circle.

"Your Holiness," he shouted above the gasps of surprise and the whimpers of fear. "These pigs have denied the old gods and their priests. They have blasphemed your own holiness. The guilt lies not with the others, O Holy One, but with these dogs!"

Magdalena was swift in her judgment. They must be destroyed. They must be killed or the gods would never release the gold of the ancient kingdom! With cool efficiency, the blonde "goddess" commanded the two men to be stoned and their blood collected in basins for the group communion.

After her grisly orders had been obeyed, Magdalena told the villagers that they must now work even harder to convince the gods of their love and sincerity. And thus it was that Magdalena Solis had created a method by which to guarantee the scam a longer life at the expense of a few villagers' lives. She had discovered that impatient and dissenting followers might be dealt with in that most ancient and heinous method—human sacrifice.

By May 28, 1963, at least eight villagers had been eliminated by Magdalena's primitive manner of cult purification. But also by that time, those men and women who guessed that they might be marked for sacrifice had begun fleeing Yerba Buena. Jesus Rubio reported that the villagers had been pushed as far as they could. It would probably be only a matter of a very short time before some of those who had fled the village would be contacting the Federales.

Cayetano, Santos, and Eleazor all voted to terminate the scam at once and head back to Monterrey before the authorities learned of their cult. Magdalena, however, decided that what the cult really needed to survive was one great and dramatic act on the part of the priesthood. Celina, the lovely village girl, had existed only to serve the cult. In spite of all the perversities that she had witnessed and the unnatural way that her body had been used, she had never lost her faith in the gods and the priests. Now, in Magdalena's demonic mind, it was simply expedient to put the girl to death in an elaborately staged sacrifice.

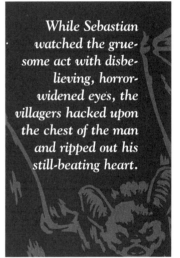

While Sebastian watched the gruesome act with disbelieving, horror-widened eyes, the villagers hacked upon the chest of the man and ripped out his still-beating heart.

Then, in one of those remarkable coincidences that so often halt a career of crime, perhaps the only citizen of Yerba Buena who did not know about the gods and the goddess of the cave, happened to walk by the cave at that terrible time and witness the vicious sacrificial murder of Celina.

Teenaged Sebastian Gurrero was a young man with ambition, and each day during the school year, he rose before dawn so that he might walk the 17 miles to the small, one-room schoolhouse in Villa Gran. With such a schedule to keep, young Sebastian had not even heard a whisper of group sex and ritual sacrifices. But now, all at once, he was witnessing a scene out of humankind's primordial past.

After the girl had been beaten to a bloody, faceless corpse by ceremonial clubbing, a blonde woman in flowing robes put a torch to the pyre at her feet. A man, whom Sebastian recognized, stepped forward and shouted something about how he now wanted the gold at once. The woman in the robes screamed at him for being a doubter and commanded the others to fling him to the ground and to slash out his heart with machetes.

While Sebastian watched the gruesome act with disbelieving, horror-widened eyes, the villagers hacked upon the chest of the man and ripped out his still-beating heart. As if that scene from hell was not enough, the blonde woman stepped forward to catch the man's blood in an earthen bowl. Somehow, Sebastian managed to run, walk, and crawl the 17 miles to Villa Gran in a virtual state of shock.

Patrolman Luis Martinez did not laugh at the boy's wild story. He had been hearing some very strange rumors about a pagan cult flourishing in Yerba Buena. If Patrolman Martinez had not decided to return to the village with the teenager to investigate the story, today Sebastian might well have been a successful doctor practicing among his people. As it was, the cultists fell upon the officer and the boy, hacked them to death with machetes, and added their corpses as sacrifice to the Inca gods.

Inspector Abelardo G. Gomez did not repeat the patrolman's fatal mistake. Although the cultists resisted arrest and fired upon Gomez and his officers, they dropped their weapons and surrendered when their "immortal" priest, Santos, caught a slug from a policeman's rifle and died instantly.

On June 13, 1963, only 11 days after their arrest, Eleazor and Magdalena Solis were brought to trial along with 12 members of the cult. The Mexican state of Tarnaulipas had abolished capital punishment, but each of the 14 cultists brought to trial received the maximum sentence of 30 years in the state prison at Victoria. At the trial it was learned that Cayetano Hernandez, the man who had originally conceived the scheme to milk Yerba Buena for sex and money, had been murdered by Jesus Rubio in a power play within the cult shortly after Patrolman Martinez and Sebastian Gurrero had been murdered.

Blood Sacrifices Continue in Secret

As distasteful as it may seem to many, space age technology and the ancient traditions of blood sacrifice can exist side by side very easily in the crazy quilt patterns of planet Earth. The February 1990 issue of *Omni* magazine's "Explorations" section carried the following extraordinary quote from a self-confessed practitioner of human sacrifice: "If a person *comprehends*, if he's really convinced, and has enough faith to carry out a human sacrifice, only then does good luck really come to him—cars, houses, everything."

The 74-year-old Aymara Indian with the alias "Maximo Coa," described without the slightest indication of guilt or remorse how he cut his victims' throats, filled a crystal goblet with their blood, and presented it to the patron of the sacrifice—and, quite often, to his wife or girlfriend, as well. Proud of conducting at least 12 human sacrifices, Coa offers unique discourses on the Bible which he believes promises hidden knowledge.

Tragically, such an atavistic religious impulse remains unchecked in those who heed the summons of spirit parasites to shed the blood of their brothers and sisters in order to secure what the negative entities have deluded them into believing will attract the favor of the Old Gods. And sometimes human sacrifices are offered only in order to satisfy personal lust and greed.

The Demon-riddled Hysteria of the Middle Ages

I n all the many centuries of spiritual warfare waged against the human species, one of the most masterful and deadly ploys ever engaged by the Sons and Daughters of Lilith and their fellow disciples of darkness was begun at the beginning of the second millennium C.E. and continued for nearly 800 years. During these demon-riddled centuries, the very priests who had sworn to banish human sacrifice ripped the flesh and shed the blood of hundreds of thousands, perhaps millions, of innocent men and women. The very Church that preached the message that Christ had performed the ultimate and final blood sacrifice for the sins of all humankind began a monstrous campaign of gathering fresh sacrifices to be killed on the rack, the wheel, and the stake to atone for demon-inspired sins.

Some call this ghastly period "the time of burning." The Roman Catholic Church called it the Inquisition.

Alarmed with what he believed to be the growing influence of Satan in Europe, Pope Innocent III actively began to condemn heretics as soon as he ascended to the papacy in 1198. The first burnings for heresy may have taken place in about the year 1000 in Ravenna, but the first actual recorded burning occurred at Orleans in 1022, and was ordered by Robert the Pious, King of France. Other burnings were followed by those at Toulouse in 1028 and conducted by Simon de Monfort.

In 1047 "Upir" made its first appearance as a term for a wicked or "blood-sucking person," when a document referred to a Russian prince as "Upir Lichy," or "wicked vampire." The word "vampyre" would not enter the English language until 1734.

In 1196, William of Newburgh's *Chronicles* included several reports of vampire-like beings in England. Executions of those who had fallen from grace with the Church were sporadic and few until 1197 when Pedro of Aragon ordered the burning of heretics who had lapsed in their promises to repent of their sins of doubt and questioning.

In 1198, Pope Innocent declared such individuals as traitors against Christ and condemned them to death by burning.

Defeating Demons by Sacrificing the Innocent

By offering the bodies of their human servants on the pyres of flames to defeat demons, the priestcraft had the creatures of the dark side laughing with delight and hungrily feeding on the soul energy of the innocent victims that the Church so self-righteously offered up to them. Once the burnings had been set in motion, it took little effort to convince those in power that they were only serving the god of their faith by finding more heretics and demon-worshippers to sacrifice.

In 1208, the Cathar sect—also known as the Albigensians—had become so popular among the people in Europe that Pope Innocent III considered them a greater threat to Christianity than the Islamic warriors who were pummeling the Christian knights on the Crusades. Although the Cathars centered their faith around Jesus Christ, they perceived him as pure spirit, like an angel, that had descended from Heaven on the instructions of the God of Good to liberate humankind from the world of matter. According to the Cathars, because Christ was pure spirit, he did not die on the cross and the teachings of the Church were false. To quell his concern, the Pope ordered the only crusade ever launched against fellow Christians by attacking the Cathars who resided in the Albi region of southern France.

The Cathars held out against the armies massed against them until Montsegur, their final stronghold, fell in 1246. Hundreds of the remaining Cathars were burned at the stake—men, women, and children. Pope Innocent III did not live to see his triumph over the heretics, for he died in 1216. Before he died, however, he enacted a papal bull that allowed a judge to try a suspected witch or heretic even when there was no accuser and granted the judge the power to be both judge and prosecutor.

In his report to Emperor Otto IV in 1214, Gervaise of Tilbury reported cases in Auvergne in which men were seen to take the form of wolves during the full moon.

In 1220, Caesarius of Heisterbach described numerous accounts of shape-shifting, pacts with Satan, and the ability of witches to fly through the air.

The Birth of the Inquisition

The Inquisition came into existence in 1231 with the *Excommunicamus* of Pope Gregory IX, who entrusted the office of Inquisitor primarily to the Franciscans and the Dominicans, who, because of their reputation for superior knowledge of theology and their declared freedom from worldly ambition, were deemed well-equipped to expose heretics. Each tribunal was to include two inquisitors of equal authority, who would be assisted by notaries, civil police, and counselors. Because they had the power

The sons and daughters of Lilith began a monstrous campaign against their human foes that lasted for nearly 800 years. Evil whispers provoked the very Church that preached the message that Christ had performed the final blood sacrifice to launch an Inquisition that shed the blood of thousands of innocent men and women (illustration by Bill Oliver).

to excommunicate even members of royal houses, the inquisitors were formidable figures with whom to reckon.

In 1257, the Church officially sanctioned torture as a means of forcing heretics, sorcerers, and shape-shifters to confess their alliance with Satan. The Inquisition became a hideous kind of self-supporting industry. It employed judges, jailers, torturers, exorcists, wood-choppers, and experts to ferret out the evil ones who were threatening the ruling powers.

"Witch persecutors ... were craftsmen with a professional pride," Kurt Seligmann writes in *The History of Magic* (1948). "A hangman grew melancholic when a witch resisted him unduly. That was akin to a personal offense. In order to save face he let the accused die under the torture, and thus his honor was not impaired, for the blame for the killing would then rest on the devil.... The business became so prosperous that the hangmen's wives arrayed themselves in silk robes.... For every witch burned, the hangman received an honorarium. He was not allowed to follow any other profession, therefore he had to make the best of his craft."

The torturers soon discovered a foolproof method for perpetuating their gory profession. Under torture, nearly any heretic could be forced to name a long string of his or her fellow demon worshippers, thereby making one trial give birth to a hundred. Inquisitors boasted that if the judges gave them a sanctimonious bishop, they could soon have him confessing to being a wizard! Cynical clergymen declared that the Holy Inquisition was the only alchemy that really worked, for the inquisitors had found the secret of transmuting human blood into gold.

In 1305, the Knights Templar, who had for centuries been the defense of Christianity against those who would destroy it, were themselves accused of invoking Satan, consorting with female demons, worshipping large black cats, and conducting human sacrifices. While many clergy, including the Pope himself, were reluctant to believe such charges against the Knights Templar, it soon became apparent that the order had become too wealthy and powerful to fit suitably into the emerging political structure of France and the aspirations of its king, Philip the Fair.

After years of persecution, many knights scattered and went into hiding throughout Europe and England. Those Templars who insisted upon presenting a defense were finally brought to trial in 1312; and in spite of 573 witnesses for their defense, at least 54 knights were tortured *en masse*, burned at the stake, and their order disbanded by Pope Clement V.

In 1313, as he was being burned to death on a scaffold especially erected for the occasion in front of Notre Dame, the Templar's Grand Master, Jacques de Molay, recanted the confession that was forced from him by torture and reaffirmed his innocence to both the Pope and the King. With his last breath, de Molay invited his two former friends and allies to join him at Heaven's gate. When both dignitaries died soon after de Molay's public execution, it seemed to the public and a good number of political and religious figures that the Grand Master had truly been innocent of the charges of heresy and Satanism.

The Black Death Decimates the European Population but Increases the Number of Witchcraft Trials

In the fourteenth century, the Christian Establishment of Europe was forced to deal with an onset of social, economic, and religious changes. It was also during this time (1347–1349) that the Black Death, the bubonic plague, decimated the populations of the European nations and greatly encouraged rumors of devil-worshippers who conspired with other heretics, such as Jews and Muslims, to invoke Satan to bring about a pestilence that would destroy Christianity and the West. During most of the Middle Ages, those who practiced the Old Religion and worked with herbs and charms were largely ignored by the Church and the Inquisition. After the scourge of the Black Death, witchcraft trials began to increase steadily throughout the fourteenth and fifteenth centuries.

In 1407, men and women suspected of being werewolves were tortured and burned at Basel. The first major witch-hunt occurred in Switzerland in 1427; and in 1428, in Valais, there was a mass burning of 100 witches.

The Spanish Inquisition Fashions Its Own Rules

In 1478, at the request of King Ferdinand V and Queen Isabella I, papal permission was granted to establish the Spanish Inquisition and to maintain it separate from the Inquisition that extended its jurisdiction over all the rest of Europe. The Spanish Inquisition was always more interested in persecuting heretics than those suspected of witchcraft. It has been estimated that of the 5,000 men and women accused of being witches, less than one percent were condemned to death. The Spanish Inquisition was concerned with trying the Marranos or conversos, those Jews suspected of insincerely converting to Christianity; the converts from Islam, similarly thought to be insincere in practicing the Christian faith; and, in the 1520s, those individuals who were believed to have converted to Protestantism.

The support of Spain's royal house enabled Tomas de Torquemada to become the single Grand Inquisitor whose name has become synonymous with the Inquisition's most cruel acts and excesses. Torquemada is known to have ordered the deaths by torture and burning of thousands of heretics and witches.

The Spanish Inquisition seemed to take special delight in the pomp and ceremony of the *auto-de-fe*, during which hundreds of heretics might be burned at one time. If an *auto-de-fe* could not be made to coincide with some great festival day, it was at least held on a Sunday so that the populace could make plans to attend the burnings.

Prisoners of the Inquisition were held captive under the most abominable conditions, such as this iron-barred cell.

The Malleus Maleficarum—A Hammer for Witches

In 1484, Pope Innocent VIII became so outraged by the spread of witchcraft in Germany that he issued the papal bull *Summis Desiderantes Affectibus* and authorized two trusted Dominican inquisitors, Henrich Institoris (Kramer) and Jacob Sprenger, to develop a new weapon with which to squelch the power of Satan in the Rhineland.

In 1486, Sprenger and Kramer published their *Malleus Maleficarum*, "A Hammer for Witches," which quickly became the official handbook for professional witch hunters. *Malleus Maleficarum* strongly condemned all those who claimed that the works of demons existed only in troubled human minds. The Bible clearly revealed how certain angels fell from Heaven and sought to bewitch and seduce humans, and Sprenger and Kramer issued a strict warning that to believe otherwise was to believe contrary to the true faith. Therefore, any persons who consorted with demons and became witches must recant their evil ways or be put to death.

Interestingly, in his *Witchcraft* (1960), Charles Williams writes that if one were to judge *Malleus Maleficarum* as an intellectual achievement, it is of the first order. While one might suspect a book that detailed prescribed horrible tortures to be administered to suspected heretics to be the efforts of half-mad, sexually obsessed individuals, Williams says that "there is no sign that they were particularly interested in sex. They were interested in the Catholic Faith and its perpetuation, and they were, also and therefore, interested in the great effort which it seemed to them was then in existence to destroy and eradicate the Catholic Faith." Williams is of the belief that the two devout Dominican priests took extreme pains to correct error, to instruct against ignorance, and to direct cautious action. "In spite of all this," Williams says, "the book is one of the most appalling that has ever been written."

Although the authors of the witch hunters handbook may not have been "particularly interested in sex," the Inquisitors directed their tortures toward the private parts of the body and the secret places of the soul. Then, too, the judges of the great tribunals examined, tried, and tortured female witches at a ratio of 10-to-1, 100-to-1, or 10,000-to-1, depending upon the authority cited. Only in the Scandinavian countries were men accused of being witches and sorcerers at an equal or larger percentage than women.

Once an accused woman found herself in prison through the testimony of someone who had allegedly seen her evil powers at work, she might very well be as good as dead. And, sadly, the accusation of witchcraft may have been brought by a neighbor woman jealous of the "witch's" youth and beauty, a suitor angered by her rejection, or a relative who sought her inheritance. And no lawyer would dare defend such an accused witch for fear that he would himself be accused of heresy if he pled her case too well.

The Inquisition demanded that a witch should not be condemned to death unless she convict herself by her own confession. Therefore, the judges had no choice other than to order her torture so that she should be forced to confess so that she might be put to death. Therefore, in order to fully comply with the law, the judges turned the accused witches over to the eager black-hooded torturers. Once the witch had con-

Fears of demons, vampires, werewolves, and witches and the malignant machinery of the Inquisition of the Church keep the torture chambers full and the fires around the stakes of the heretics burning night and day (illustration by Bill Oliver).

fessed, she was now eligible to be reconciled to the Church, absolved of sin, and burned at the stake.

Intellectual Protests Cannot Extinguish the Fire for Heretics

In 1530, Italian scientist Ludovico was burned at the stake for writing *A Treatise on Vampires*, in which he argued that there was a biological cause for vampirism.

In 1563, Johann Weyer (Weir), a critic of the Inquisition, managed to publish *De praestigus daemonum* in which he argued that while Satan did seek to ensnare and destroy human beings, the charges that accused witches, werewolves, and vampires possessed supernatural powers were false. Such abilities existed only in their minds and imaginations.

To counter Weyer's call for a rational approach to dealing with accusations of witchcraft, in 1580 the respected intellectual Jean Bodin, often referred to as the Aristotle of the sixteenth century, wrote *Del la demonomanie des sorciers* (1581), in which he argued that witches truly possessed demonic powers. In the first and second volumes of this monumental work, Bodin offers his proofs that spirits communicate with humankind, and he itemizes the various means by which the righteous might distinguish the good spirits from their evil counterparts. Those men and women who seek to enter pacts with Satan in order to achieve diabolical prophecy, the ability to fly through the air, and the power to shape-shift into animal forms are dealing with evil spirits. Bodin acknowledged that he was well aware of spells by which one might summon incubi or succubi for carnal pleasure.

By his own boast, witch trial judge Pierre De Lancre tortured and burned over 600 men and women accused of consorting with demons. In his books *Tableau de l'inconstance des mauvais anges* (1613) and *L'Incredulité et mescréance du sortilege* (1622), De Lancre defended the belief in demons, black magic, and witchcraft. In his opinion, even to deny the possibility of witchcraft was heresy, for God Himself in the Holy Bible had condemned magicians and sorcerers. De Lancre was not a member of the clergy, and his concerns were social, rather than theological. He believed that sorcerers and witches were a well-organized anti-social force that sought to overthrow the established order.

The judges of the Inquisition assumed that all Jews were demon worshippers and sorcerers. De Lancre was no exception, stating that God had withdrawn His grace and promises from the Jewish people. De Lancre also claimed to have it on great authority that many Jews had the ability to shape-shift into wolves by night. De Lancre, like so many of the trial judges, became fixated on the details that the witches provided of their carnal encounters with demons. De Lancre decided that incubi and succubi, those demonic seducers of men and women, had as their mission the infliction of a double injury to their victims, attacking them in both their body and their soul.

The great irony in the works of De Lancre and others lies in their justifiable concern about the supernatural beings that sought to enslave humans by possessing their bodies and their souls. But by the torture and slaughter of their victims, they only made the true demonic entities stronger and more confident of their victory over a species so easily deluded by misplaced evangelical efforts.

In 1630, Prince-Bishop Johann Georg II Fuchs von Dornheim, the infamous "Hexenbischof" (Witch Bishop) constructed a special torture chamber which he decorated with appropriate passages from scripture. He burned at least 600 heretics and witches, including a fellow bishop he suspected of being too lenient.

In 1645, Leo Allatius completed authorship of the first treatment of vampires, *De Graecorum hodie quirumdam opinationabus*. With Allatius's monumental work to guide him, Fr. François Richard linked vampirism and witchcraft in 1657. And in 1679, Phillip Rohr wrote *De Masticatone Mortuorum*, a German text on vampires. It is likely that such works as Allatius's, Richard's, and Rohr's may have had considerable influence on the wave of vampire hysteria that shuddered Istra in 1672 and swept through East Prussia in 1710 and, again in 1725.

While the Protestant states in Germany abandoned the persecution of witches a generation before those states under Roman Catholic dominance, the uncompromising doctrines of the Lutheran and Calvinist doctrines continued the witchcraft trials until around 1660. The witchcraft trials in Germany ended in 1684.

By the middle decades of the sixteenth century, when the Protestant Reformation began to restructure nearly all of Europe politically, as well as religiously, witches were largely overlooked by the rulers of Church and State who now struggled with the larger issues of the great division within Christianity. Then, after a time of relatively little persecution, the period of the great witchcraft craze or hysteria that many practicing witches and students of witchcraft today refer to as the "Burning Times," occurred from about 1550 to 1650.

A memorial erected to reflect on the witch burnings conducted in Dunning, Scotland, in 1657.

In the period from about 1450 to 1750 somewhere around 40,000 to 60,000 individuals were tried as witches and condemned to death in Central Europe. Of that number, as high as three-quarters of the victims were women.

For many years and in dozens of books and articles on witches and Wicca, the number of innocent people executed for the practice of witchcraft during the four centuries of active persecution has been estimated as high as nine million. Wiccan author and scholar Margot Adler has noted that the source of the oft-quoted nine million witches put to death was first used by a German historian in the late eighteenth century who took the number of people killed in a witch hunt in his own German state and multiplied by the number of years various penal statues existed, then reconfigured the number to correspond to the population of Europe.

In 1999, Jenny Gibbons released the results of her research in the Autumn issue of *PanGaia* in which she verified that overall, approximately 75 to 80 percent of those accused of witchcraft were women, but to date (circa 1999) an examination of the official trial records of the witchcraft trials indicate that less than 15,000 definite executions occurred in all of Europe and America combined. The period of the heaviest persecutions of witches occurred during the 100 years between 1550 and 1650, Ms. Gibbons reports, and the total number of men and women accused of witchcraft who were actually hanged or burned probably did not exceed 40,000.

One last wave of the witch craze swept over Poland and other eastern European countries in the early eighteenth century, but it had dissipated by 1740. The last legal execution of a witch occurred in 1782 in Glarus, Switzerland—not far from where the witch craze had begun in 1428. The last known witch-burning in Europe took place in Poland in 1793, but it was an illegal act, for witch trials were abolished in that country in 1782.

Satanic Sacrifice

Juan Rivera Aponte had been born in Puerto Rico and reared on a blend of Christianity, black magic, voodoo, and Santeria. Ever since his childhood he had heard the old witch doctors tell of a legendary formula that could give a man complete sexual control over women. There was one great impediment to the implementation of this successful formula: It involved a sacrifice to Satan of an innocent young boy.

When he came to the United States, Aponte got a job on a chicken ranch on the outskirts of Vineland, New Jersey. After he had completed his chores on the farm, he would spend the evenings searching the old volumes that he had brought with him for the magical love potion. Although such nights were rather bleak and dismal, he knew in his heart that future evenings would be spent making love with beautiful women.

His fevered mind had focused on one particular girl. A beautiful schoolgirl with dark eyes, jet-black hair, and a maturing body that had come to obsess him. Juan knew that she was too young for marriage, but the magic would compel her to surrender to him.

Again and again he read the passage in the legendary "love slave" potion. Dried bat wings would be easy. The entrails from a lizard presented little problem. But it was the final ingredient that always caused him to close the book: "Sprinkle the potion with the dried, powdered bone meal from a human skull. The powder must be prepared from the skull of an innocent young boy." Although he was momentarily sickened with horror at the dark thing that he must do, he knew that no price would be too great to pay Satan for the right to have any woman he wanted.

On the evening of October 13, 1957, Roger Carletto, a 13-year-old high school student, planned to attend a movie in Vineland with his sister. "A guy owes me a dollar," Roger told his sister. "Wait for me while I go and collect it." He jumped on his bicycle and pumped rapidly down North Mill Road toward the outskirts of the city. When Roger did not return within a reasonable time, his sister complained to their parents—and after a longer interval, the family notified the police. Roger Carletto was never again seen alive.

Following Satan means committing blood-thirsty crimes to appease his desires, and some people are all too willing to do so.

Winter passed, and when the spring thaw came, the rivers and ponds around Vineland were once again dragged for the body of the missing boy. By summer, the police still had no clues. It was as if the boy had simply stepped into another dimension. Then, on the night of July 1, the authorities received their first break in the case. Patrolmen Joseph Cassisi and Albert Genetti answered a midnight call from a chicken farmer on North Mill Road who said that his hired hand had gone berserk.

According to the farmer, his wife had awakened in the night and had discovered their worker, Juan Rivera Aponte, transfixed in their bathroom, standing as if he were a stone statue. He had a club in his hand, which he began swinging at the couple, until the farmer took it away from him. The two police officers were led to Aponte's room over a chicken house. They found him sleeping on a cot, surrounded by several empty beer bottles. The walls of his room were covered with dozens of photographs of pinup girls, movie stars, and starlets.

During the initial interrogations of Aponte, he claimed that his boss, the young farmer, had killed the Carletto boy and buried him in the chicken house. Following the hired hand's instructions, the police dug up the dirt floor of the chicken house and were startled to find the corpse of the young boy. The body was clad only in a pair of shorts, and the upper part of the skull, the left hand, and a foot were missing. Digging deeper, officers disinterred the missing foot and the hand, but they could find no sign of the missing part of the skull.

Detective Tom Jost could not believe the farmer was guilty, stating that he had a reputation as a hard-working man of good character. Captain John Bursuglia wasn't buying the story, either. He ordered a search of Aponte's room, and he hired a translator to tell him what were in all those old books written in Spanish. The young woman who had acted as an interpreter during Aponte's interrogations needed no more than a glance to tell Captain Bursuglia that the volumes dealt with voodoo, black magic rituals, and instructions on how to hex people.

Several days later, she had the police officer's complete attention when she read aloud the ingredients for a special love potion, a potion that required the skull from an innocent young boy. After five hours of questioning by the detectives, Aponte finally broke down and confessed to the slaying of Roger Carletto. Aponte explained how he had needed that love potion so that he could have the girl of his dreams. He had been wondering where he would find an innocent young boy when Roger Carletto had come knocking on his door. He had loaned Aponte a dollar, and he wanted him to pay it back.

"I needed the powdered skull bone," Aponte said matter-of-factly. "I would have killed any boy to get it. Roger just happened to be the first boy who came by."

The sickened officers listened in silence as Aponte described how he had beaten the boy, choked him with a rope, then buried his body under the dirt floor of the chicken house. Aponte had kept watering the grave to keep the body from sinking in the earth. He didn't want his boss to see a depression in the dirt and get suspicious.

After a few months, he had dug up the body and cut off the top of the head with a knife. After he had refilled the grave, Aponte fastened some wires to the skull and hung it beside the stove in his room. He wanted it to dry rapidly so he could complete the love potion. Psychiatric tests indicated that Juan Aponte knew the difference between right and wrong. At his trial, the satanic murderer entered a plea of no defense and was sentenced to life imprisonment.

Aponte's only complaint was that he never got to complete his love potion. He told a cell mate that he knew that Satan would have given him any woman he wanted because he had performed the sacrifice according to the instructions in the book. Aponte died in prison after many years of confinement.

Following Satan Gave Him the Right to Snuff People Out

On June 3, 1970, a hitchhiker found the body of Mrs. Florence Nancy Brown in a shallow, leaf-covered grave off Highway 74 midway between San Juan Capistrano and Elsinore, California. Mrs. Brown, a 31-year-old school teacher in Mission Viejo and mother of two young children, had been repeatedly stabbed in the chest. Hardened police officers, conditioned to scenes of terrible violence, were puzzled by the grisly fact that her right arm had been severed at the shoulder and her heart and lungs had been removed from her body. As if that were not enough gruesome desecration of the corpse, three of the victim's ribs had been removed and a large strip of flesh had been sliced from her upper right leg.

Toward the end of June, three young men were arrested as suspects in the murder of a gas station attendant in Santa Ana, and one of them, Steven Hurd, reportedly confessed to the mutilation slaying of Mrs. Brown. Although Hurd later pleaded innocent at his arraignment on July 9, by then the press had revealed that the worship of Satan and a belief in human sacrifice were likely potent ingredients in the killing of Mrs. Brown. According to Hurd's later testimony, the victim's right arm, heart, and lungs had been removed to carry out a sacrifice to Satan.

Hurd, in his cold, compassionless recounting of the crime, stated that if he had had his way, the woman's entire body would have been sacrificed to his Satanic Majesty. Hurd was defiantly proud of being a member of a secret Satanist cult that believed it was their right to "snuff people out." They obtained this grim "right" by sacrificing a portion of the victim's body to Satan.

Hurd's attorney, William K. Gamble, revealed the contents of two letters that the self-avowed devil worshipper wrote while he was in Orange County jail: "What's wrong with me?" Hurd asks, perhaps rhetorically. "Maybe if I stopped believing in the Devil I'd be all right. But I can't. Because when I'm alone here he shows me what [people] are trying to do. He talks to me."

Satanism—The Oldest of the World's Religions

Many people today would say that a worship of Satan and ritual sacrifice to his Satanic Majesty belongs within that special province of human experience overseen by psychiatry. On the other hand, accounts of satanic sacrifice carry intriguing aspects that lie more in the domain of the theologian and those who warn of spirit parasites.

Satanism, according to some scholars, is the oldest of all world religions and is the one and only that by doctrine lays claim to having its origin in the Garden of Eden. Adam's firstborn son Cain celebrated the first Satanic sacrificial Mass, and today, any lone Satanist can celebrate a valid sacrificial Mass if the occasion arises. In the case of Satanic cults, a priest performs the office of the liturgy. Satanism, these same scholars maintain, is also the oldest form of worship. As proof, they point to discoveries made by archaeologists, who have found drawings of the Horned God (Satan) in caves of Europe going back into prehistoric times.

The Satanic Sacrifice Hysteria of the 1980s and 1990s

In the 1980s and 1990s, a widespread fear swept across the United States that there were dozens of secret satanic cults involved in sacrificing hundreds of babies, children, and adults. Television and radio talk shows featured people who claimed to be former members of demonic cults and those who had allegedly recovered memories of satanic abuse.

Even at its most alarming peak of belief, however, few accused religious Satanists, such as members of Anton LaVey's Church of Satan or Michael Aquino's Temple of Set, as condoning ritual human sacrifices. After exhaustive police investigations on both local and national levels failed to produce any hard evidence to support such frightening accounts of large scale attacks on the populace by religious Satanists, the kind of gruesome satanic sacrifices committed by the likes of Steven Hurd were deemed to be those perpetrated by free-form Satanists and cultists.

There is no question that a number of serial killers have claimed to be Satanists, but police investigations have revealed that the murderers were not actually members of any of satanic religious groups. Even such a high-profile disciple of Satan as Richard Ramirez, the infamous "Night Stalker" of Los Angeles, who committed a series of brutal night-time killings and sexual attacks, was not a member of any formal satanic group, such as the Church of Satan or Temple of Set. Although Ramirez scrawled an inverted pentagram (a symbol traditionally associated with satanic rituals) in the homes of some of his victims and shouted "Hail, Satan!" as he was being arraigned on charges of having murdered 14 people, he was strictly a lone-wolf worshipper of evil.

There are many kinds of free-form Satanism, ranging from the kind that is merely symptomatic of sexual unrest and moral rebellion among young people to those mentally unbalanced serial killers who murder and sacrifice their victims to their own perverse concept of satanic evil. The vast majority of teenagers and young adults who dress in dark Goth outfits and paint their fingernails and their lips black are quite likely merely role-playing and protesting the conformity that they wish to resist as long as possible. Other young people may be drawn into an attraction toward Satanism by a number of heavy-metal bands, who play the role of practicing Satanists primarily to provoke publicity in the highly competitive field of contemporary music.

The Differences between Satanism, Witchcraft, and Wicca

According to some scholars, Adam's firstborn son Cain celebrated the first Satanic sacrificial Mass. Archaeologists have found drawings of the Horned God (Satan) in caves of Europe going back into prehistoric times (illustration by Ricardo Pustanio).

Although Satanism and witchcraft have become synonymous in the popular mind for many centuries, they constitute two vastly divergent philosophies and metaphysical systems. Generally speaking, witchcraft, the Old Religion, has its origins in primitive nature worship and has no Devil or Satan in its cosmology. Satanism—although manifesting in a multitude of forms and expressions and having also originated in an ancient worship of a pre-Judeo-Christian god—is essentially a corruption of both the nature worship of witchcraft and the formal Christian church service, especially the rites of the Roman Catholic Church.

Since the Middle Ages, witchcraft, the "old religion," or Wicca, the "ancient craft of the wise," have been used interchangeably to name the followers of a similar nature religion. However, even those men and women who practice Wicca or witchcraft have difficulty reaching a consensus regarding whether or not Wicca can truly be traced back to ancient times or whether it developed as a new natural religion in the early nineteenth century and gained momentum in the mid-twentieth century.

One definite assertion that may be made about Wicca is that practitioners of the religion are not Satanists. They do not worship the Devil or glory in the exaltation of evil. Generally speaking, Wiccans believe that the sources of good and evil lie within

While those who practice the Wiccan belief system study magic, their goal is always to achieve benign and peaceful purposes.

each individual, thus universally agreeing with the eight words of the Wiccan Rede: "If it harm none, do what you will."

Gerald Brosseau Gardner (1884–1964) is considered the father of all contemporary expressions of Wicca, and he became a well-known practitioner of the craft due to the many books that he published on the subject after the laws against practicing witchcraft were repealed in England in 1951. Gardner claimed to have been initiated into the famous New Forest Coven in 1939 by a traditional and hereditary witch named Dorothy Clutterbuck. In 1954, Gardner published *Witchcraft Today*, which continued the thesis espoused by Margaret Murray that witchcraft had existed since pre-Christian times but had gone underground to escape persecution.

The person responsible for the introduction and growth of modern witchcraft/ Wicca in North America was Raymond Buckland, an Englishman who had immigrated to the United States in 1962. In 1963, Buckland traveled to Perth, Scotland, to be initiated into Wicca by Gardner's High Priestess Lady Olwen and to meet Gardner. In 1966, Buckland established a museum of witchcraft in Long Island, New York. A prolific author of over 30 books on Wicca and related subjects, Buckland founded Seax-Wica, a new branch of the craft, in 1973.

Gavin and Yvonne Frost formed the first Wiccan Church in 1968 and in 1972 gained federal recognition of witchcraft as a religion. In 1985, they convinced a federal appeals court that Wicca was a religion equal to any other.

According to the United States Census, the number of individuals professing to be Wiccans rose from the 8,000 reported in 1990 to 134,000 self-proclaimed witches in 2001. A study released in November 2001 by the Graduate Center of the City University of New York found that the number of adults who subscribe to a Pagan religion was over 140,000.

Some scholars argue that the Church itself "created" the kind of Satanism it fears most through the excesses of the Inquisition, which made an industry out of torturing and killing men and women accused of being doctrinal heretics and those practitioners of the Old Religion who were condemned for worshipping the Devil through the practice of witchcraft. It was such loathing for the unprincipled practices of the Church that led one of its most devout leaders, Gilles de Rais, to become a monster who may have sacrificed as many as 500 to 800 young boys and girls to Satan.

Gilles de Rais

In 1415, as a lad of 11, Gilles Mortmorency de Laval, Baron de Rais, attained one of the greatest fortunes in France by inheriting vast domains from his grandfather, Jean de Craon, and his father, Guy de Laval. At 16, he greatly increased his wealth by marrying Catherine de Thouars, who had herself inherited a vast fortune. Later that same year, young Gilles made a reputation for himself as an accomplished warrior in the wars of succession to the duchy of Brittany. Seven years later, he also distinguished himself in battle against the English, fighting on behalf of the Duchess of Anjou. Because of his prowess on the battlefield and his piety, Gilles was assigned to Joan of Arc's special guard when her "voices" directed her to save France. At the Maid of Orleans's side, he fought with such fierce merit that King Charles the VII awarded Gilles the title of Marshal of France.

Although it was undoubtedly an affair of the heart that was conducted entirely on a spiritual plane, Gilles fell deeply in love with Joan, the strange young mystic. He became her guardian, her protector, but, when Joan was captured and burned by the English, Gilles de Rais became transformed into a Satanic fiend of infamous and unholy proportions. The life of this saintly warrior turned monster has been examined in depth by several scholars, and many agree that de Rais's terrible crimes and acts of sacrilege were quite likely inspired by what he considered God's betrayal of His good and faithful servant, Joan of Arc.

Gilles de Rais left his wife, vowed never to have sexual intercourse with another woman, and confined himself in his castle at Tiffauges. Here, he surrounded himself with broken-down courtiers, sycophants, and wastrels and embarked on several rounds of lavish orgies. He continued even when the vast wealth of the de Rais estate began to show a dent after one marathon debauchery after another.

When, in 1435, the King denied him the right to mortgage any more of his land, Gilles decided to try his hand at alchemy as a means of replenishing his fortune. Within a short time, he had converted an entire wing of his castle into a series of vast alchemical laboratories. Alchemists and sorcerers from all over Europe flocked to Tiffauges, seeking the legendary Philosopher's Stone that would transform base metals into gold. Although de Rais himself joined the alchemists and magicians in work sessions that went nearly around the clock, all of their experiments counted for naught.

It was the sorcerer Prelati who told him that mortal man could not hope to achieve the transmutation of base metals into gold without the help of Satan. And, Prelati emphasized, the serious alchemist could only hope to arouse Satan's interest by dedicating the most abominable crimes to his name. Under Prelati's direction, de Rais lured a young peasant boy into the castle, slashed the lad's throat, plucked his eyeballs from their sockets, ripped out his heart, and caught the blood in inkwells so that he might utilize it for the writing of evocations and formulas.

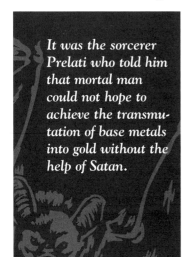

It was the sorcerer Prelati who told him that mortal man could not hope to achieve the transmutation of base metals into gold without the help of Satan.

Satan did not appear and no base metals were transmuted into gold, but Gilles de Rais no longer cared. He had discovered an enterprise far more satisfying than the alchemist's quest. He had discovered the sadistic satisfactions and pleasures which lay in the torture and murder of children.

In their *Sex Crimes in History*, R.E.L. Masters and Eduard Lea tell of de Rais's own testimony of how he liked to dramatize his murders. He would have one of his servants kidnap a child, carry him off to the castle, then truss him up and leave him in a room. Sometime later, Gilles would enter the room, feign shock and surprise at seeing the lad so woefully treated and cut him free from his bonds. He would hold the child on his knees, speak softly to him, dry his tears, win his confidence, assure him that all would be well and that he would soon be back in his mother's arms—then he would slit the child's throat in one swift movement and violate the spasmodically twitching corpse.

Etienne Corillaut, one of Gilles's personal servants, later testified at his master's trial when the Marshal of France was accused of having slain more than 800 children. According to Corillaut, Gilles de Rais would often "… take his rod in his hand, rub it so it became erect … and then place it between the thighs or legs of the … children, and rub his … virile member on the belly of the boys or girls with much libidinous excitement, until he emitted his sperm on their stomachs."

After de Rais had obtained sexual gratification in this manner, the children were murdered, dismembered, and certain of their remains put away to be utilized in magical rituals. Corillaut also testified that his master took special pleasure in masturbating on a child's stomach while the boy or girl was being decapitated. The monster kept the heads of handsome boys or beautiful girls on upright rods and employed a beautician to curl their hair and rouge their lips and cheeks. When he had accumulated enough heads, he would summon the entire castle and conduct a perverse kind of beauty contest; demanding that everyone present in the castle vote on which child's head was the most beautiful.

Because of his high position in the court of France, Gilles de Rais was granted the mercy of being strangled before being burned. The tribunal conveniently looked the other way after his execution, however, and the de Rais family was permitted to remove his corpse after it had been singed. The mass murderer of hundreds of innocent children was interred in a Catholic ceremony in a Carmelite churchyard. The fiendish Prelati and the other professing Satanists were given, at most, a few months in prison for their part in the murders.

"It is thought likely by some historians that this was their reward for testifying against their master," Masters and Lea reflect, "and that both ecclesiastical and civil authorities were far more interested in obtaining Gilles's money and properties, which were still considerable, than in punishing him for his crimes."

Satanism as a Bloody Indulgence for Jaded Aristocrats

It was during the sixteenth and seventeenth centuries that the mold became set for the ritual patterns which many today commonly think of as Satanism. It was then that the practitioners of the Old Religion went completely underground with their worship ceremonies while the decadent aristocracy seized upon the Black Mass as a kind of hedonistic parlor game in which one might express his sexual fantasies on living altars and cavort about in the nude. Unrestrained immorality was the order of the day as Parisians followed the hedonistic example of their Sun King, Louis XIV.

Satanism was perhaps developed to its highest estate as the jaded aristocrats began to adapt witchcraft rituals to suit their own sexual fantasies. The enlightened sophisticates' mockery of the primitive customs had been converted to a serious interest by the tension and insecurity of the times. Although the fires of the Inquisition still consumed its quota of witches, the France of King Louis XIV was a high-living, low-principled era, and Lords and Ladies began to pray in earnest to Holy Satan to grant them high office and wealth. Whether or not their wishes for elevation in the society of their day was granted, it would seem that the majority of these high-born Satanists paid cursory homage to the Horned God only as a means of indulging their baser passions.

To fully understand the power of Satanic worship, we must go back to mid-sixteenth century when Paris was one of the major cities of the world.

A statue of Louis XIV in Versailles, France. During his reign hedonistic rituals were commonly practiced by the decadent aristocracy.

Catherine Montvoisin

In 1658, Catherine Deshayes, a 20-year-old orphan who had been abandoned in the gutters of Paris and raised in the streets, married Antoine Montvoisin. The bridegroom was a shiftless, amiable wine drinker and street brawler with few hopes of supporting his bride. Catherine was one of the few newlyweds who was unperturbed about her future financial security. She was an accomplished fortune teller and palm reader, proficient in the arts of prognostication, and had a vast and loyal clientele.

An hour after the nuptials had been exchanged, Catherine Montvoisin was back on the sidewalk in front of her shop, shouting a list of her services to a crowd of curious Parisians. Not only was she a prophetess and could predict the future, she was also considered to be the most expert midwife in all of Paris. In addition, she was an accomplished abortionist, an herbalist, and a beautician who knew the secrets of the ancient queens of the Nile.

According to some Parisians, Catherine Montvoisin also offered a magic elixir, which, if one took the portions recommended, he or she could live to be as old as the ancient men in the Bible. The magic potion turned old men into young strapping lads. It transformed tired, weary old women into lusty young beauties. In addition to her devil's cupboard of dark, smelly herbal remedies, Catherine Montvoisin also dabbled in the deadly art of poison. She once boasted to her husband, perhaps a veiled warning against infidelity, that if she should dump all of her poison into the River Seine, there would be enough of the deadly fluids to kill half of Paris.

Fortunately for the people of Paris, Catherine Montvoisin did not pollute the river with her poison, but concentrated on expanding the occult services offered in her shop. She studied astrology and started to cast horoscopes for her clients. She discovered that aristocratic ladies drank tea, so Catherine started to read tea leaves.

She boasted publicly about her "inspired gifts," and she never hesitated to claim that great men, religious leaders, and well-known merchants were her clients. The Church was very powerful in France, and Catherine invented a new tale for her Christian customers. "There are those who believe I am the Madonna," she whispered confidentially. "Others think I am an angel of mercy sent down by God to help in this time of need."

The customers spread the news of the new "miraculous Madonna," and in 1660, Catherine Montvoisin was seized and brought before a tribunal of the Catholic Inquisition. Although wholesale witch-hunts had ceased, the Inquisitors were superstitious of anyone who claimed to have supernatural or satanic powers. They were doubtful that a Paris fortune teller was inspired by anything other than a love of money.

In one of those rare twists of history, Catherine Montvoisin convinced the tribunal of learned theologians and Vicar-Generals that her practices were far removed from Satan. She baffled the Inquisition by quoting Biblical passages to support her practices. The tribunal was composed of learned men who reasoned that Catherine was certainly a charlatan of sorts, but they had no definite proof that she had committed any crime other than separating fools from their money. She was judged innocent.

Following her clearance by the tribunal, Montvoisin returned to her shop in the slum area of Paris. Her new notoriety impressed the gullible, and each morning when she opened her shop, a new crowd of hopeful people were waiting outside the door. Surely, her work had been blessed by the church. Even the holy fathers had been convinced of her unusual powers. Catherine Montvoisin quickly became the most popular occult practitioner in all of France. Merchants, housewives, bored ladies of the king's court, and nobility flocked to her shop for services.

Catherine complained to her husband, who acted as a handyman around her shop, that so many of the nobility were afraid to visit their shabby neighborhood. They should move so they could be more accessible to the aristocrats who would pay large sums of gold to have their problems solved. Within a few weeks, an elderly customer of considerable wealth and a baronial mansion agreed to remember Catherine Montvoisin in his will. The ink had barely dried on the gentleman's will before he was seized with a mysterious malady and died.

La Voisin had undergone a metamorphosis from a cunning street girl into a deadly practitioner of Satanic perversions.

Catherine Montvoisin now became La Voisin, the high priestess of a Satanic cult headquartered in an elegant mansion. La Voisin became the darling of French society. Anyone of nobility who had a problem rushed to her headquarters for a solution. In one way or another, La Voisin gave them assistance for a price. She became known as a woman who had control over the powers of darkness.

La Voisin received her clients as she reclined on a massive, gold-gilded throne that sat at the edge of a darkened chamber. A young attractive woman with an innocent appearance, La Voisin allowed her long, blonde hair to flow loosely over her shoulders. Whenever she met with customers, she wore a red, ermine-lined robe which had two hundred gold coins stitched in silver thread down the edges. Even the most jaded nobleman was awed by the aloof beauty of their Satanic benefactor.

La Voisin had undergone a metamorphosis from a cunning street girl into a deadly practitioner of Satanic perversions. Businessmen and merchants crowded into the mansion seeking Satanic aid to lure the goddess of profits. La Voisin promised that Satan would indeed bless these businessmen in their endeavors, but, they must first show their faith in the Devil's powers. They must attend the secret rites of worship to Satan. They must appease the dark one, and in order to have him look favorably on their request, they must bring a bag of gold to lay before the living altar. The gold would purchase an infant for a living sacrifice to the Prince of Darkness.

Noblemen, aristocrats, and the curious paid dearly for an opportunity to witness the strange rites that were conducted in the basement of the mansion. The Satanic priestess succeeded in convincing Madame de Montespan, the beautiful mistress of King Louis XIV, into serving as a nude, living altar for the sacrifice in one of the obscene rituals. The king's mistress was afraid that His Royal Highness was growing cold toward her, and La Voisin said that such an act would bring Satan's assistance in making the King love her.

Hooded figures gathered in the gloomy chamber as Madame de Montespan removed her garments and walked to the altar in total nudity. The King's mistress lay on her back across the altar, spreading wide her legs and arms. The black-robed audience gasped as Abbe Guilborg, a fat, degenerate priest, appeared from the wings and walked toward the altar.

The perverted Mass that followed was a Satanic version of the Catholic mass. Abbe Guilborg beseeched Satan to receive the sacrificial baby with favor. He read from a prayer book that was bound in human skin. A sulphurous incense burned in the foul air as the priest sprinkled "holy water," actually urine, about the altar.

"Bring forth the offering to Satan," commanded the priest.

A baptized baby was carried into the room by a black-robed acolyte. The crying infant was seized by Abbe Guilborg and held high over the nude body of Madame de Montespan. There was a flash of steel in the air as La Voisin stepped forward and slashed the baby's throat. The child's deathly gurgles were drowned out by the priest's Satanic chants. Madame de Montespan lay rigid on the altar, feeling the babe's warm blood drain down onto her body. "Holy Prince of Darkness! Hear my plea," she moaned. "Let the king's love come only to me. May the Queen be barren and may the Dauphin always be mine."

Human sacrifices are still conducted by Satan worshippers today.

As the King's mistress implored Satan for his favors, La Voisin snatched the bloodless little corpse from the priest's hands. She walked to a corner of the room and tossed the baby's body into the door of a roaring furnace.

After the cult had prospered for many months, word of its nefarious activities finally leaked out and were brought to the attention of a detective named Desgrez, who raided La Voisin's mansion. As the Satanic celebrants were taken into the police station, Desgrez discovered there were several high-ranking officials in the group. He had also seized La Voisin's list of clients. It contained Madame de Montespan's name, hundreds of aristocrats, and scores of government officials. Desgrez and his superiors realized they were holding some of the most explosive documents in French history.

Police officials sought an audience with King Louis XIV, where they explained the whole sickening mess. King Louis XIV knew that decadence of this sort might lead to a revolution. The King's own head might roll if a scandal of that magnitude was revealed. Louis XIV suggested that La Voisin be turned over to the Inquisitors. Aristocrats who had participated in the Satanic rites would be given time to leave the country on "an extended trip."

All of La Voisin's records were burned. The King was taken by carriage to the mansion and personally put the torch to the Abbe's detailed description of what occurred when the baby was sacrificed for Madame de Montespan, his mistress. The King also informed the Inquisitors that La Voisin could be tortured—but it would be quite appropriate if the torturers were gentle. His Highness wanted to be certain that all of the aristocracy who might be involved had enough time to escape abroad before she was tortured harshly and confessed all the details of their involvement.

History records that a wholesale migration of noblemen and their wives occurred after La Voisin's arrest. Some sought exile in Italy, preferring the freedom of Rome to the possible death at the stake in Paris. Others visited cousins in Germany, England, or Spain. When the last of the aristocrats were safely out of the country, King Louis encouraged the inquisitors to put La Voisin to extreme torture. She confessed to sacrificing 2,500 babies to Satan as High Priestess of the cult.

Four days after her confession, on February 23, 1680, La Voisin was marched from the torture dungeons of the Inquisition and led to a stake in a public square. As straw was piled around her bound body, La Voisin's face darkened with unrepentant fury. She sang bawdy songs and kicked burning sticks at the crowd until she at last succumbed to the flames and the smoke curling around her.

Beliefs of Contemporary Organized Religious Satanists

In contemporary times, many of those who openly claim to be members of organized religious Satanist groups insist that they do not worship the image of the Devil condemned by Christian and other religions, because the word "Satan" does not specify a being, but rather a movement or a state of mind.

What Satanists do worship, these individuals explain, is a Spirit Being commonly known as Sathan in English and Sathanas in Latin. They do not believe Satan to be the Supreme God, but they believe him to be the messenger of God in that he brought to Eve the knowledge of God. Satanists believe that there is a God above and beyond the "god" that created the Cosmos. The most high God takes no part in the affairs of the world, thus Satanists believe their faith to be the only true religion, insofar as revealed religion to mortals can be understood.

Satanism as an actual religion is composed of a few small groups, which according to census figures in the United States and Canada probably number less than 10,000 members.

Human Sacrifice Continues in Small Secret Cults

All over the world, small cults of free-form Satan worshippers meet in secret and some still conduct human sacrifice.

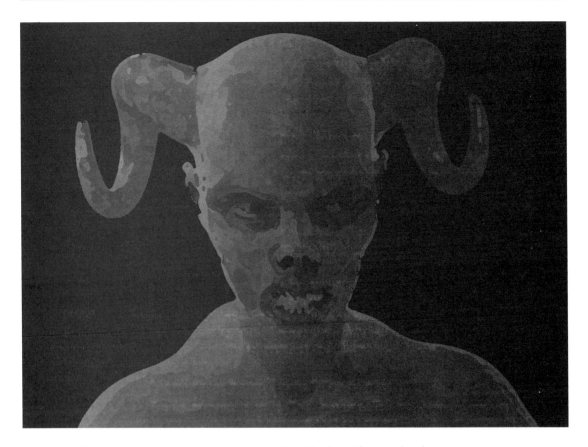

Satanists believe in and worship the horned god, making blood sacrifices to this demon.

A few years ago, I learned of a former British policeman (we will call him Robert) who had joined such a group for kicks. He had grown weary of living life on the straight and narrow as preached by his parents, and he thought that by joining a group who said they worshipped Satan would be a neat way of engaging in acts considered loathsome and foul in the minds of all "ordinary" folk. He admitted that he initially thought joining the group would be largely about having a lot of sex.

Indeed, Robert said, there was the sex, but once he had become a full-fledged coven member, he found himself standing with the others performing extremely distasteful rites beside graves that had been secretly and unlawfully opened at midnight. To his shame, Robert acknowledged that he had surrendered himself body and soul to the worship of evil. He had reveled in the wildest orgies and rituals, attended by men and women equally as depraved as he.

Robert admitted fully enjoying every form of debauchery and licentiousness that the coven handed out, until one night a particularly depraved ritual performed on an Orkney hillside brought him back to his senses. "It was a human sacrifice," Robert named the horror. "And it was so vile as to be indescribable."

The ritual was held on a night deemed sacred in Satan's calendar. A teenage girl was offered by her own parents as the sacrificial innocent. The lovely young woman was led to a lonely hillside, stripped naked, and bound spread-eagled to a tree.

"A few yards away," Robert said, "was a specially trained ram straining at a rope." When the moon had reached its height, a tall figure in a white robe stepped forward and released the maddened ram with a quick slash at the rope. "There was a scream," Robert said, reliving the horror, "then deadly silence. And the girl's blood flowed into the heather."

To the Satanists, it was as if the horned god had truly materialized in order to claim the virginity of the young woman who had been offered to him in propitiation. Robert found himself completely revolted by the cruel and painful debasement of the young girl. And when he observed how calmly her parents had accepted the brutal death of their daughter, he began to gag and to vomit. Within another moment or two, he found himself running from the scene "like a foul monster into the night."

Because of his decision to sever all ties with the Satanists and his intentions to tell his story in print, Robert claimed that he had been threatened with death. He was receiving eerie, frightening messages warning him not to betray his Satanic Majesty.

Although defiant, Robert stated that he took the messages seriously. One such epistle had come wrapped around the ring which had been on the finger of Robert's great-grandfather when the old man was buried.

Chupacabras: A Bizarre Vampiric Monster

With its penchant for seizing goats and sucking their blood, the Chupacabras ("goat sucker") fascinated the public at large and created another night stalker to fear when it first emerged from the shadows in Puerto Rico in the summer of 1995. From August of 1995 into the twenty-first century, the monster has been credited with the deaths of thousands of animals, ranging from goats, rabbits, and birds to horses, cattle, and deer. While some argue that the creature is a new monster, perhaps even created in some scientist's clandestine laboratory, others point out that such vampiric entities have always existed and have been reported by farmers and villagers in Puerto Rico and Central and South America.

Numerous eye-witnesses have described Chupacabras as standing erect on powerful goat-like legs with three-clawed feet. The creature is often described as slightly over five feet in height, though some reports list it as over six and a half feet. Its head is oval in shape with an elongated jaw, a small, slit mouth, and fangs that protrude both upward and downward. Some witnesses have claimed to have seen small, pointed ears on its reptilian-like head and red eyes that glow menacingly in the shadows. Although its arms are thin, they are extremely powerful, ending in three-clawed paws.

Chupacabras appears to have the ability to change colors even though the creature is most often reported to have strong, coarse black hair covering its torso. Through some chameleon-like ability, the creature seems to be able to alter its coloration from green to grayish and from light brown to black, depending upon the vegetation that surrounds it. Another peculiarity of the beast is the row of quill-like appendages that runs down its spine and the fleshly membrane that extends between these projections, which can flare or contract and also change color from blue to green or from red to purple.

There have been reports that the Chupacabras can fly, but others state that it is the beast's powerful hind legs that merely catapult it over one-story barns or outbuildings. It

The "goat-sucker," the Chupacabras emerged from the shadows of the forests of Puerto Rico to be credited with killing thousands of animals, ranging from goats, rabbits, and birds to horses, cattle, and deer (illustration by Ricardo Pustanio).

is those same strong legs that enable the creature to run at extremely fast speeds to escape its pursuers.

Within a short time after the night terrors began in Puerto Rico in 1995, reports of Chupacabras began appearing in Florida, Texas, Mexico, and in Brazil's southern states of São Paulo and Parana. In Brazil, the ranchers called the monster, "O Bicho," the Beast. The descriptions provided by terrified eye witnesses were also the same—a reptilian creature with thin arms, long claws, powerful hind legs, and dark gray in color.

On May 11, 1997, the newspaper *Folha de Londrina* in Parana State, Brazil, published the account of a slaughter that had occurred at a ranch near Campina Grande do Sul when in a single corral 12 sheep were found dead and another 11 were horribly mutilated. From April to September 2000, over 800 animals were slaughtered by the bloodsucker in Chile, and some witnesses to the bloody rampages of the creature described it as a large rodent, others as a mutant kangaroo, still others perceived it as a winged, apelike vampire.

A number of authorities even began to theorize that the Chupacabras had been manufactured by a secret government agency for some nefarious purpose. Clergymen issued pronouncements stating that the demonic creatures were heralding the end of the world. UFO enthusiasts theorized that the monsters had been brought here by extraterrestrial aliens to test the planet's atmosphere preparatory to a mass invasion of Earth. Anthropologists and folklorists reminded people that tales of such mysterious, vampire-like monsters had been common in Central America for centuries.

A widely circulated story stated that Chilean soldiers had captured a Chupacabras male, female, and cub that had been living in a mine north of Calama. Then, according to the account, a team of NASA scientists arrived in a black helicopter and reclaimed the Chupacabras family. The creatures, so the story went, had escaped from a secret NASA facility in the Atacama Desert of northern Chile where the U.S. Space Agency was attempting to create some kind of hybrid beings that could survive on Mars.

On August 30, 2000, Jorge Luis Talavera, a farmer in the jurisdiction of Malpaisillo, Nicaragua, had enough of the nocturnal depredations of Chupacabras. The beast had sucked the life from 25 of his sheep and 35 from his neighbor's flock, and he lay in wait with rifle in hand for its return. That night, Talavera accomplished what no other irate farmer or rancher had been able to do. He shot and killed a Chupacabras.

Scott Corrales, Institute of Hispanic Ufology, reports that a specialist of veterinary medicine examined the carcass and acknowledged that it was a very uncommon creature with great eye cavities, smooth bat-like skin, big claws, large teeth, and a crest sticking out from the main vertebra. The specialist said that the specimen could have been a hybrid animal made up of several species, created through genetic engineering.

On September 5, 2000, the official analysis of the corpse by the university medical college was that Talavera had shot a dog. A furious Luis Talavera declared that the officials had switched carcasses. "This isn't my goatsucker," he groused as the college returned the skeleton of a dog for his disposal.

As we enter the twenty-first century, Chupacabras reports continue unabated from nearly all the South American countries, Puerto Rico, and the Southwestern United States; and frightened and angry people complain that whatever Chupacabras are, they continue to suck the blood from their livestock.

Chubee: The Teenaged Chupacabras

On June 13, 2008, Paul Dale Roberts, an experienced paranormal investigator, headed out to interview a young man with a very bizarre claim. In Paul's words:

I met Chubee at a Starbucks downtown. His story is very incredible. His speech pattern was hard to understand, because his tongue is deformed. He showed me his tongue, and it almost seemed tubular. He claimed that when he was a Chupacabras, he was able to inject his tongue into a goat's throat and drain its blood. His tongue was his feeding device.

Chubee said that he is a hybrid. Half alien Gray and half human. I did notice that his eyes were somewhat slanted and large. He does have an unusual appearance. He claims he was raised in an underground base in Puerto Rico where the government is working alongside the Grays to create an army of super soldiers. He told me that there are many such underground secret bases. Experiments were done on Chubee by the Grays and military scientists, during which he developed a strong craving for blood. The military allowed him under observation to comb the landscape of Puerto Rico to seek out food.

Chubee said that at that time his skin was scaly, and he had spines that went from the top of his head and down his back. He could leap a great distance and would hunt out dogs, cats, [and] goats to drink their blood. The military observed his movements and kept a tracking device on him. They used this information to assess his ability to attack and to be agile on a battlefield. Chubee said that the experiments that were conducted on him lasted from the age of 12 to the age of 19. He claimed that the military is experimenting with DNA manipulation and that they learned these techniques from the Gray aliens.

Chubee was rejected from the military's experiments because his human DNA started to override the manipulative process. His spikes began to fall off; his scales fell

The El Yunque rain forest in Puerto Rico, the wild lands that are home to Chupacabras (photo by permission of Nick Redfern).

off; and tissue that resembled human skin began to spread over his body. He became more human-like, and his craving of blood decreased. His agility lessened, and the military had no more use for him. Through a series of "mind warpings," the military felt they had erased his years with the secret underground base, and they allowed him to go into society with false memories of being raised in Puerto Rico by normal parents and having a normal childhood. He was constantly assisted by strangers (that he now feels were the military) in obtaining jobs, finding an apartment, and so forth.

Chubee claimed that I am the first person to learn this story. He discovered his past life with the military and the Grays through a series of dreams. Now the dreams have stopped and a flood of memories of what he used to be has invaded his consciousness. Chubee, now 23 years old, resides in a town in Northern California and is making a living driving a truck. He claims friends brought him to Northern California and found him a job as a truck driver. His "friends" he believes are members of the secret military. He said that all he wanted to do was to tell his story, and to inform people that there is so much more going on with our world and universe than we can even imagine.

Welcome to Blood Island

Nick Redfern runs the US Office of the British-based Center for Fortean Zoology. His books on cryptozoology and strange creatures include There's Something in the Woods, Memoirs of a Monster Hunter, Man-Monkey, *and* Three Men Seeking Monsters. *He can be contacted at his website: nickredfern.com. This is Nick Redfern's account of his search for Chupacabras in Puerto Rico.*

For most people, any mention of the emotive word "Vampire" invariably and inevitably conjures up stark imagery of either (a) the classic blood-suckers of bygone years as portrayed on-screen by the likes of Bela Lugosi and Christopher Lee; or (b) today's pale-skinned, and black-garbed, Marilyn Manson-like creatures of the night, with which the world of Hollywood is seemingly so obsessed.

There is, however, another breed of vampire that lurks among the shadows and the dark places, and that after the sun has set, surfaces from its lair to feast upon the blood of the living. It haunts the forests, the woods and the isolated farms and villages of the island of Puerto Rico. And it strikes absolute terror into the very hearts of all those that have been unfortunate enough to cross its diabolical path.

Since at least the mid-1990s—but possibly as early as the mid-1970s, as will shortly become apparent—dark and sinister tales have surfaced from the island that tell of a hellish creature roaming the landscape in search of liquid nourishment, and that is typically described as possessing a pair of glowing red eyes; powerful, claw-like hands; razor-sharp fangs; a body not unlike that of a large monkey; and, occasionally, huge and leathery bat-like wings. Yes, Puerto Rico and its people have a vampire firmly in their midst. And it goes by the legendary name of the Chupacabras. A Latin term meaning "goat-sucker," the Chupacabras's name is derived from its apparent particular liking for the fresh blood of goats—not to mention that of pigs, chickens, dogs, and even cows. And according to some very controversial rumors, quite possibly that of people, too.

I have personally now been on two expeditions to Puerto Rico, seeking to once and for all determine the incredible truth about what may very well be the world's most famous monster-vampire. And I can say one thing for certain, and without any hesitation whatsoever: it has been a wild, surreal and infinitely disturbing ride of truly roller-coaster proportions.

My first trip to the island was in the summer of 2004 with fellow crypto-zoologist and good friend, Jonathan Downes, who runs the British-based Center for Fortean Zoology, the world's only full-time organization dedicated to hunting for monsters. For seven days and six nights we roamed the lowlands, the highlands, and just about everywhere else as we sought out both our monstrous quarry and those whose lives had been touched and forever changed and blighted by its vile presence.

One of those people was a farmer named Noel, who lived in a little town on the fringes of the sprawling El Yunque rainforest, and whose main source of income was derived from breeding chickens. As Jon and I stood in the backyard of Noel's home in the sweltering heat of the midday sun, he told us how, only several months previously, he had awoken one morning to an absolutely shocking sight: every single one of his chickens were dead in their cages.

Not only that: to his everlasting horror, Noel could see two distinctive puncture marks on their necks. And, as an examination by a veterinarian soon demonstrated to one and all, their bodies had been totally drained of blood. Noel told us that the incident had forever plagued him since that fateful day, and he wished us well—and quietly advised us to tread very carefully, too—as we headed onwards in search of the unknown.

Also on our agenda was a visit to the home of a man who kept peacocks. He, too, told us how just a few weeks earlier all of his prized birds were found slaughtered in a fashion identical to that described to us by Noel. Rather significantly, in this particular case, a representative of Puerto Rico's Civil Defense Department had visited the man's home and duly conducted an in-depth investigation of the incident. Clearly, the matter was being taken very seriously at an official level. Not only that: the killings and the carnage had left a deep impression on the man's neighbors, and an overwhelming sense of paranoia and fear seemed to envelope the area after sunset. Such is the graphic effect that the presence of the Chupacabras has on the people of the island.

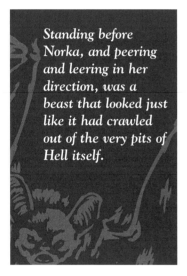

Standing before Norka, and peering and leering in her direction, was a beast that looked just like it had crawled out of the very pits of Hell itself.

And then there was an elderly lady named Norka, who had a very close and personal encounter of the Chupacabras kind way back in 1975. Norka lived in a beautiful and large home that sat high in the hills, overlooking the mysterious rainforest. Jon and I sat on Norka's balcony sipping cold drinks as she related her strange and alarming tale. Late one night, after dining with friends, Norka told us, she was driving home when she was forced to literally bring her car to a screeching halt in the middle of the winding road that cuts an intricate swathe throughout El Yunque.

Standing before Norka, and peering and leering in her direction, was a beast that looked just like it had crawled out of the very pits of Hell itself. As was the case in so many reports we uncovered during the course of our expedition, Norka described the beast as having the ubiquitous glowing red-eyes, elongated nails or claws that flicked ominously in her direction and that looked like they could inflict a huge amount of damage, and giant, membranous wings of a distinctly bat-like nature.

A petrified Norka could only look on with absolute fear as the Chupacabras stared intently back at her—before suddenly making for the shadows of the thick trees at the side of the road. Trembling and terrified, Norka wasted no time in getting home and locking all the doors. Nearly 30 years after her experience, the emotion in her voice as she spoke to us was more than apparent—as was the fear of what might still be lurking within the bowels of El Yunque to this very day.

Of course, one of the most important questions facing Jon and I was: where on the island could the blood-sucking beast be found? Time and again, we were told tales of sightings of the Chupacabras near many of the large caves, caverns, and natural tunnel systems that can be found all across Puerto Rico.

Thus it was that we embarked on an ambitious operation to investigate some of these dark and mysterious underground locales. And, certainly, having done so, we could only conclude that if the Chupacabras wished to carefully conceal its presence, such underground locations would provide the beast with the perfect hiding places.

Chupacabras find refuge in large caves and caverns (photo by permission of Nick Redfern).

Perhaps the most disturbing stories we came across during that bizarre week in Puerto Rico came from several farmers who told us, quite independently of each other, that they had heard tales and rumors of two American tourists whose bodies were said to have been found in the El Yunque rainforest in early 1997 with their throats torn out and, again, their corpses drained of all blood.

Try as we might, Jon and I were never able to verify these rumors; however, this was not surprising to us, since we were also informed that an effective cover-up was reportedly put into place by local authorities, as they sought to prevent widespread panic from erupting all across Puerto Rico. But it was certainly both sobering and disturbing to muse upon the possibility that as well as focusing its attacks upon the animals of the island, the Chupacabras occasionally considered human blood to be a distinctly tasty treat, too. "Perhaps," I said to Jon in complete seriousness, "we should have brought a plentiful supply of wooden-stakes and garlic with us." He nodded gravely, and we continued on our quest.

By the end of the week, we had interviewed around 15 or more people ranging from farmers to Civil Defense employees, and from police officers to members of the public. All were utterly unanimous in their conclusions and opinions: the Chupacabras was both very real and utterly deadly in nature. As I flew back to the United States one week after we arrived, I made a mental note to return to Puerto Rico as soon as possible—which I duly did, a little more than 12 months later, with Canadian researcher and filmmaker Paul Kimball.

One of the many highlights of this particular trip was the discovery of several stories pertaining to black-magic activities, and a whole variety of dark rites and rituals that were said to have been utilized deep within the El Yunque rainforest to, quite literally, summon up the Chupacabras from some horrifying netherworld. Indeed, the possibility that the Puerto Rican vampire has paranormal or supernatural origins was one that was viewed with both a high degree of seriousness and major concern by many of the island's inhabitants.

My next experience with the Civil Defense Department also proved to be highly valuable. Miguel had worked with the CDD on several Chupacabras investigations in the 1990s; and, just as was the case in the previous year, I was told story after story by Miguel of how he had come across several incidents that bore all the classic hallmarks of definitive vampirism. Certainly, the absolute highlight for me was the story of Pucho, who lived in a tiny village near El Yunque. One evening in February 2005, Pucho stated as we stood and chatted near his home, he was walking past a place of worship in the village—known as the Church of the Three Kings—when he was shocked to the core by what he described as a "loud roar" coming from the heart of the dense trees that sat adjacent to the church.

Without any warning whatsoever, a large, winged beast that was described to me as being part-bird and part-bat, loomed out of the foliage and took to the skies, gliding silently down the hillside that sat on the opposite side of the church, and towards a nearby farm. Interestingly, Pucho added, several days later the farm in question was hit, during the early hours of the morning, by a series of horrific attacks that left countless livestock dead, injured, and violently mutilated. Once again, Puerto Rico's bloodsucker of the night had struck—and devastatingly so, too.

Having now traveled the island of Puerto Rico extensively in search of its very own vampire, I am often asked for my opinions and thoughts on what is, or may well be, taking place. Granted, making an absolute, positive identification of the Chupacabras is something that still unfortunately frustrates me, I have to confess. I can say, however, that the beast is no mere myth, hoax or cynically-created tourist attraction. Rather, something very strange, highly elusive, seemingly cunningly intelligent, and utterly lethal is loose on the island.

Its trademark calling-cards of (a) two puncture-wounds to the jugular vein, and (b) bodies completely drained of blood convince me that we are dealing with a very real, flesh-and-blood entity. But whether the creature is some form of giant vampire bat—as was suggested to me by several sources; a creature of definitely extraterrestrial origins—as was also repeatedly offered as a theory; or something far stranger that may very well have been conjured up via ancient and archaic rite and ritual from a realm of existence quite unlike our own, I freely admit that I do not know.

But, of one thing I am absolutely certain: as one of our interviewees concisely told Jon Downes and me in the summer of 2004, "Puerto Rico has vampires." And, should you ever travel to the island and dare to seek out the nightmarish beast for yourselves, I hope you will remember that statement, and you will consider taking along a trusty wooden-stake or two, and perhaps even several cloves of garlic. It is far better to be safe than sorry, and infinitely more preferable to be the hunter instead of the hunted.

Vampiric and
Cannibalistic Murderers

In January 2009 in Mexico City, Mexico, Santiago Meza Lopez asked forgiveness from the families of the 300 victims that he turned into "stew" for a Mexican drug lord. For $600 a week, Meza dissolved in vats of acid those unfortunate people who were suspected of betraying his boss or who owed him money. Mexican police were hopeful that the "Stewmaker" could identify some of his victims in order to give at least some kind of closure to friends and relatives of individuals who had disappeared after their dealings with Meza's boss.

Sondra London, my friend and fellow author of the macabre, sent me a news clipping about the ghastly stewmaker with her comments:

> In my book *True Vampires* (Feral House, 2004), I explain how this kind of ongoing criminal enterprise is literally vampiric on a higher order of magnitude. This is why it is the ultimate evil. The whole body politic is attacked, and the vital essence is sapped.
>
> The individuals who keep it all going are bound to be used by this cartel, possessed and undead, serving their masters' will. This vampiric dynamic is thus attached to the whole body politic of that area. To focus on the criminal acts of one of them because they have an especially ghoulish "ick" factor, is to fail to see the enormity of the malignance.

Sondra makes an excellent point. An attack on any one of us by those who have in one way or another allowed their spiritual essence to become possessed by the undead or the never-dead entities from other dimensions of reality is truly an attack on the sovereignty of all human beings. The "vampiric dynamic" may truly become a malignant growth that affects each of us.

Some who have allowed their spiritual essence to become possessed by the undead or by spirit parasites commit ghastly crimes believing that they, themselves, are members of the undead (illustration by Ricardo Pustanio).

Yours Truly, Jack the Ripper

In many ways, the prototypical/archetypical vampire-cannibal murderer is the notorious Jack the Ripper. The fact that his true identity has evaded the efforts of police and historical researchers for well over 100 years makes Jack even more potent as an inspiration for those who feel they must answer a primitive quest for the blood of their brothers and sisters. Jack the Ripper is an icon for those who yield to the seductive whispers of the Children of Lilith and who admire Cain as their true spiritual sire. If Jack was telling the truth in his taunting letters to the London police, he did indulge his bestial hungers by drinking the blood and flesh of some of his victims.

The number of deaths attributed to the Ripper have been as high as 15. While there is some debate over the number of his victims, there is a consensus that the series of slayings began with the murder of Mary Ann Nichols on the night of August 31, 1888, and ended nine weeks later with the gruesome slaughter of Mary Kelly.

Mary Ann Nichols was found lying across a gutter, repeatedly slashed by someone with a long-handled knife and a general knowledge of anatomy. A week later, Annie Chapman was found in a backyard, her head nearly severed from her neck. Certain other "horrible mutilations" were hinted at in the papers. The Ripper had taken two brass rings from her pockets and carefully arranged them at her feet.

The Ripper was interrupted in his attack on Long Liz (real name, Elizabeth Stride) by a man who drove a pony cart into the yard. The pony shied at the fleeing figure of Jack, and the driver jumped down from his seat to lift the woman's head. The blood poured from the open wound in her throat, and it was evident that she was beyond help. Apparently, the intrusion so irritated the Ripper that within an hour he had lured Catherine Eddows into a lonely alley. After the preliminary slashing of the throat, Jack extracted the left kidney, certain other organs, and wiped his hands and knife upon her apron.

The London newspapers ran countless stories speculating about the Ripper's true identity. Perhaps he was a demonic butcher, a Polish Jew, an American sailor, a Russian doctor, and a host of other suspects—anyone, it seemed, so long as he was not native born. Jack, who was obviously following his press quite carefully and enjoying every inch of ink in the papers, countered with this famous quatrain which he sent to the *Times*:

I'm not a butcher; I'm not a Yid,

Nor yet a foreign skipper;

But I am your own true loving friend,

Yours truly—Jack the Ripper.

The Ripper also corresponded with Scotland Yard in a manner that while monstrous was also darkly humorous. He once wrote that after his next murder, he would clip off the lady's ears and send them to the police to enjoy. To a particularly persistent police officer, he sent part of a human kidney, informing him in an accompanying note that he had fried and eaten the other part.

Mary Kelly was the only victim killed indoors. She had been heard by someone singing "Sweet Violet" during the evening and she had seemed to be in high spirits. Her horribly mutilated corpse was discovered the next morning by a passerby who could look directly into her ground-level apartment.

Sir Melville Macnaghten, a Scotland Yard official, reported that the Ripper must have spent at least two hours over his hellish work. The madman made a bonfire of some old newspapers and of his victim's clothes, and, apparently by this dim light, had scattered most of Kelly's internal organs about the room.

The only description of Jack the Ripper that seemed of potential value to the police came from someone who saw Mary Kelly in the company of a man who may well have been the monster himself: "A man about 35 years old, five-feet six inches tall, of a dark complexion, with a dark mustache turned up at the ends."

Abruptly, the murders ceased. Theories about the true identity of the Ripper continue to this day. Someone with a knowledge of surgery always ranked first in the theoretical list of suspects. The second favorite was a midwife who had both familiarity with her victims and an elementary knowledge of surgery.

Third on the list of frequent speculations was that Jack was a seaman, handy with a knife, perhaps even a ship's doctor, who simply got back on his ship and sailed away to continue his slaughter in other countries. A journalist reported the death of a diabolical doctor in Buenos Aires who allegedly made a deathbed confession that he had been Jack the Ripper, but his claim was impossible to document.

According to a popular bit of Ripper folklore, the notorious Dr. Neill Cream, convicted for poisoning four women, shouted, "I am Jack the …" just as the executioner pulled the lever on the hangman's platform and dropped the doctor to the end of

Jack the Ripper, a prototypical vampire-cannibal murderer, terrorized London in the 1880s.

his rope. Eager devotees of the Dr. Cream/Jack solution to the Ripper legend were disappointed when their investigation yielded the results that Cream had been in Joliet prison in Illinois throughout the period of the East End murders.

More recent theories to Jack's identity have even included HRH Prince Albert Victor, Duke of Clarence, the grandson of Queen Victoria. And then there are those who say that Jack the Ripper is still among us—traveling first in one country to rip and to slash, then traveling to another to ply his grisly work.

If Jack is truly some kind of supernatural being, some vicious Incubus who takes delight in terrible murder, these theorists may be correct. If that theory should not be so, there are more than enough Disciples of Spirit Parasites to take Jack's place.

Elifasi Msomi, Seized by the Tokoloshe

Beginning in August 1953 and continuing for nearly two years, Elifasi Msomi, a witch doctor in Richmond, Natal, killed 15 men, women, and children while under the control of the Tokoloshe, a South African spirit parasite. When Msomi wished to become a more powerful witch doctor, he summoned the demon. The Tokoloshe informed his new student that it would require the flesh and blood of humans in order for Msomi's magic to be powerful.

To prove to the demon his willingness to obey the conditions of his new position, Msomi summoned his mistress, then before her terrified eyes, he raped and stabbed a young girl to death. Rather than being impressed by his prowess in magic and in his ability to command the spirits, the woman ran straight to the police, who immediately arrested Msomi. But if his mistress was repulsed by Msomi's sudden act of violence, the Tokoloshe had been favorably impressed by Msomi's obedience to its demands, and the entity, in Msomi's view, enabled him to escape from police custody.

In April 1955, after the stabbing deaths of at least five children were attributed to his bloody handiwork, Msomi was once again arrested and placed in custody. But almost as soon as he was behind bars, he had again made his escape due to the power of the Tokoloshe.

A month later, he was recaptured with some of his victims' property in his possession and the same bloody knife that had by now claimed the lives of 15 men, women, and children. Msomi did not hesitate to show the police where he had buried some of the bodies that remained undiscovered, for he had confidence that the Tokoloshe would once again set him free. This time, however, it appeared that the blood-thirsty spirit parasite had grown weary of using Msomi's body. In September 1955, the court sentenced Elifasi Msomi to death.

Such was the reputation of the witch doctor's power of channeling the Tokoloshe that prison authorities granted permission to a deputation of tribal chiefs and elders to view Msomi after he had been hanged on February 10, 1956. These men were thus able to return to their respective tribes and proclaim that the witch doctor was really dead and that the Tokoloshe had left him to seek out another host body.

Zodiac—He Killed to Create Slaves for the Afterlife

"My name is Zodiac! I've killed ten people. I will kill more!"

With these chilling words, a vicious killer flaunted his grisly murders to the San Francisco police. For more than three years, this phantom killer committed what appeared to be monstrous murder-by-chance, selecting his victims at random in the San Francisco Bay area.

If ever there was a serial killer well-versed in the occult and immersed in human sacrifice, it was the mysterious Zodiac. This disciple of darkness so terrified the residents of the San Francisco area that even after more than 40 years without his declaring another victim, the memory of his crimes still haunt northern California. From time to time, my wife and I receive a call from a police officer in a major U.S. city asking us to review a serial killer's modus operandi to learn whether or not Zodiac has surfaced in their city. Thankfully, it does appear that he has returned to whatever nightmare dimension released him.

Zodiac's first murders to come to the attention of the authorities occurred on the night of December 20, 1968, when Bettilou Jensen, 16, and her companion, Thomas Faraday, 17, both of Vallejo, parked near a lake reservoir about 11:00 P.M. after attending a concert in San Francisco. Faraday had been shot through the head. Bettilou had apparently attempted to flee. Her body was found about 30 feet from the car. She had been shot five times in the back.

After an investigation, the police reported that there wasn't a single clue as to who killed them, nor was there anything to indicate any kind of motive for their deaths. It would not be long, however, before the police learned that they were dealing with a vicious, occult-oriented mass murderer. With the double murder of the teenaged couple as his gory debut into public consciousness, Zodiac began to terrorize the Bay area with senseless acts of inhuman butchery.

On the evening of July 4, 1969, a 22-year-old waitress and her boyfriend parked beside the shores of Lake Herman, near Vallejo. The young woman was killed when a fusillade of bullets suddenly ripped into the parked car. Her date, a long-time friend, was wounded by four 9mm bullets. After

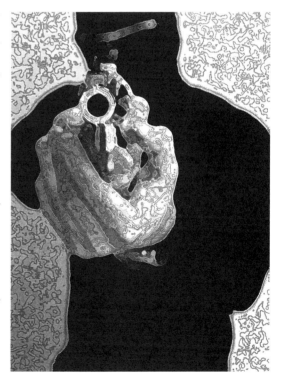

The Zodiac killer—a satanic murderer if there ever was one—slaked his blood lust by shooting innocent women in San Francisco during the 1960s.

many weeks of critical surgery, he survived. Zodiac taunted the authorities by telephoning the Vallejo police shortly after he had attacked the couple and told them where they would find the bodies riddled with his 9mm bullets. Again and again, the authorities heard Zodiac's diabolical laughter as the phantom killer telephoned information about his grisly slayings.

Once, in a letter to the *San Francisco Chronicle,* Zodiac wrote that he had decided that school children would make awfully nice targets. He was strongly considering shooting out the tires of a school bus some morning, then picking the children off one by one as they fled out of the vehicle. Officially, the authorities credited five deaths to Zodiac during his murderous rampage. Unofficially, there was the killer's own boast of 10 slayings.

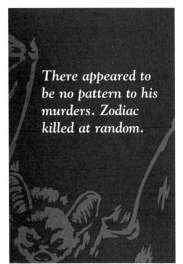

There appeared to be no pattern to his murders. Zodiac killed at random.

There appeared to be no pattern to his murders. Zodiac killed at random. Some investigators once suspected that his murders were being scheduled according to astrological signs. Some local astrologers were asked to draw up horoscopes based on certain clues, but that approach was not successful. According to psychiatrists consulted, the cunning San Francisco madman stalked his human prey because he enjoyed playing God, holding the life or death of his intended victims in his hands.

The satanic killer taunted his pursuers by sending coded messages to the newspapers. His "signature" or insignia was a cross within a circle, a glyph taken directly from the Egyptian *Book of the Dead,* where it was used as a symbol of death. Zodiac claimed that he was killing people who would be his slaves in the afterlife. Such a motive is immediately recognizable as a page right out of the Ahrimanes's playbook, a dictate directly from the Nephilim's unholy scripture.

In many of his messages to the police or the newspapers, Zodiac gave evidence not only of a great knowledge of the occult, but also of cryptography. In addition to letters from the Greek alphabet, some of his coded messages also contained hieroglyphics from South American Indian cultures and dead civilizations in Asia and Africa. It was evident that he had an excellent knowledge of mythology and ancient history.

Eventually, Zodiac was seen committing some of his terrible crimes, and witnesses were able to come up with a partial description. Zodiac was said to be a Caucasian male of medium height with red hair worn short in a crew-cut style. He was huskily built, about 200 pounds, and appeared to be about 35 to 40 years old. Many witnesses also said that he wore thick, black horn-rimmed glasses. Some witnesses said that they had heard his voice, and they remembered it as slightly high-pitched.

A twist in the case occurred when police were able to link the cruel night stalker with the brutal slaying of a college coed in Riverside, California, which had occurred two years before the homicidal outburst in San Francisco. On the night of August 30, 1966, beautiful, 18-year-old Cheri Jo Bates left her study session in the campus library at Riverside College. She was abducted from her car which had been sabotaged so it would not run, savagely beaten, and stabbed. Her mutilated body was then tossed into a ditch.

Shortly after the senseless slaughter of Cheri Jo Bates, a newspaper in Riverside received a typewritten confession of the crime. Pounded out in capital letters, this letter appeared to be Zodiac's first public disclosure of his murderous career. A detailed confession ended with the warning: "Beware, I am stalking your girls."

A month after the letter was received, another clue relating to the killer of the coed was found by a janitor in the college library. At first it appeared to be a meaningless poem scrawled by some vandal on the top of an old desk, but the police thought otherwise. The poem included the lines: "Blood spurting, dripping, spilling; all over her new dress. Oh, well, it was red anyway."

Police authorities checked the handwriting on the earlier poem in Riverside with later messages from Zodiac in San Francisco. The poem had been signed with the letters "RH." Police authorities wondered if that could be the initials of Zodiac's name or if his vampiric preoccupation with the blood of his victims led him to write "Rh" for the "Rh factor" in blood? Eerily, the evidence that linked the killing of Cheri Jo Bates with Zodiac meant that the confident, boastful murderer had already eluded police for two years before he began his rampage against the women of San Francisco.

Crafty, cunning, a diabolical genius, Zodiac openly left a trail of intriguing clues to his true identity. To date, more than 40 years later, no one has deciphered their meaning or captured the monster in his lair. Could Zodiac have decided to halt his crimes of his own accord? That seems unlikely. He enjoyed the game of killing too much. Perhaps the spirit parasite that had held him in thrall had grown weary of the hunt in San Francisco and moved on to possess another student of the occult in another city.

Stanley Baker—This "Jesus" Drank Blood and Ate Human Flesh

In July 1970, tall, bearded Stanley Dean Baker contacted Monterey County (California) Detective Dempsey Billey and the resident FBI agent at the substation and convinced the astonished officers that he had a rather unique problem.

"I am a cannibal," Baker admitted.

Baker went on to explain how he had killed and dismembered a young social worker, James Schlosser, who had made the fatal mistake of giving him a ride outside of Yellowstone Park. He confessed to murdering Schlosser while he slept, then cutting out his heart and eating it.

Baker, who called himself "Jesus," and testified that he was a witch and an occultist, also stated that he had eaten one of Schlosser's fingers and had taken the finger bones with him. Detective Sergeant John McMahon, who took a statement from Baker, said that he could hardly stand to listen to him. Even after 21 years of police work in California, Baker's testimony made him sick.

Investigating officers responded to a fisherman's discovery of a blood-stained survival knife near a river bank and noticed a patch of ground saturated with blood. To

Stanley Baker was a blood-drinking cannibal who called himself "Jesus."

their disgust, the officers found what appeared to be human bone fragments, pieces of flesh, teeth, and what seemed to be the remains of a human ear.

Informants came forward to relate ghastly accounts of Baker's demonic activities around his home base of Sheridan, Wyoming. A teenaged boy told of devil worshipping rites that had occurred in the Big Horn Mountains. He testified that small wild animals had been eaten alive and human blood had been drunk.

A Sheridan College coed claimed that she had watched Baker drink a mug of blood at a beer-and-pot party in the Tongue River Canyon. "With all that hair hanging down to his shoulders, his flashing, evil-looking bright eyes and his half-laugh, half-sneer … well, he was really scary," she stated.

Daniel Rakowitz—Creator of a New Cannibalistic Religion

On September 18, 1989, police officers arrested Daniel Rakowitz, who claimed to be the creator of a new religion, when they discovered a five-gallon bucket that contained the skull and bones of his 26-year-old girlfriend, Monika Beerle, a Swiss dancing student. The grisly discovery ended a two-week search and confirmed rumors that had been circulating in New York's Lower East Side about a human body that had been dismembered and boiled. According to some of the homeless in the Tompkins Square Park area, Rakowitz had walked among them with a kettle of soup, offering generous helpings to the hungry drifters. Slowly, word spread that the soup had been made of Rakowitz's murdered girlfriend.

The son of a deputy sheriff in Edna, Texas, Rakowitz, 28, with his Lone Star drawl, openly sold marijuana and amphetamines in the East Village. Described as a lanky man with scraggly hair and piercing blue eyes, he was known to his acquaintances by the live rooster he carried with him and by his long, disjointed speeches about crucifixion, reincarnation, and the power of Satan.

Chris Karma, a busboy and musician, spoke to the investigating officers about Rakowitz's interest in past lives and in the formation of the Church of the 966. Rakowitz, who, according to Mr. Karma (a remarkably appropriate name), sometimes believed that he was God, the new Messiah, and explained that Satan was represented in the Bible by the number 666. In 1989, Rakowitz was certain, Satan had metamorphosed and was now represented by the number 966.

Not surprisingly, Rakowitz's girlfriend, Monika Beerle, a native of St. Gallen, Switzerland, who had been studying at the Martha Graham School of Contemporary Dance, eventually grew weary of such bizarre theological prattle and asked him to move out of her apartment with his rooster and his new religion. Angered by her lack of religious tolerance, he killed her on August 19 by "punching her as hard as he could in the throat." He then dismembered her body, methodically boiled away the flesh, and retained her skull and bones as mementos of their relationship.

Deputy Chief Ronald Fenrich, commander of detectives in Manhattan, stated that an investigation had begun on September 8 after the police had heard rumors about the dismemberment of a body in an apartment on East Ninth Street. On September 13, investigating officers located a woman who claimed to have seen the body. On September 18, Rakowitz was arrested and subsequently disclosed the five-gallon bucket in which he kept Monika's skeletal remains. Rakowitz provided the police with a full, videotaped confession after his arrest, while at the same time proclaiming himself to be the "New Lord" and advocating marijuana use for everyone.

On September 14, 1990, the Texan with the shoulder-length blond hair asked that a judge empanel a jury of marijuana smokers to try him. "That way," he explained, "I could get a fair trial."

Jeffrey Dahmer—Vampire-Cannibal-Werewolf All in One

A very well-known example of a contemporary vampire, werewolf, and cannibal all in one is Jeffrey L. Dahmer, who killed, dismembered, butchered, and ate portions of the flesh of at least 18 human victims. Basically a night stalker, Dahmer would hang around gay bars or shopping malls until closing time, then approach his victim and ask if he would like to accompany him. If the target was somewhat reluctant, Dahmer would not hesitate to offer money as an added inducement. Once he had managed to lure a young man to his apartment, Dahmer would either drug or strangle him, then gradually dismember him.

The 31-year-old Dahmer was arrested on July 24, 1991, when his most recently selected victim, a teenager, managed to escape from the cannibal's apartment and run out into the street, still wearing the handcuffs that were supposed to hold him until Dahmer found the time to carve him with a butcher knife. Investigating police officers who first entered into the ghastly flat at 213 Oxford Apartments, Milwaukee, Wisconsin, discovered nine severed heads—seven in various stages of being boiled; two kept fresh in the refrigerator—four male torsos stuffed into a barrel, and several assorted sections of male genitalia being stored in a pot. Other scraps of human flesh and portions of limbs and bodies were scattered through the apartment. The wretched stench of putrefaction was beyond the experience or the psychological endurance of the most seasoned police officer.

Although generally regarded as a polite and quiet young man, Dahmer had a prior police record of a number of minor sex offenses against children. Even in his high

Probably the most infamous cannibal of recent times is Jeffrey Dahmer, who killed and dismembered 18 people, then ate their flesh.

school days, Jeffrey had been pronounced "a generally weird dude" by his fellow students. In 1989, Dahmer's father requested that his son receive psychiatric treatment. Jeffrey had been released from prison on probation in 1989 after serving time for having abused a 13-year-old boy. Although Jeffrey Dahmer most certainly expressed extremely aberrant behavior, it was argued that he could still distinguish right from wrong. His defense attorney, on the other hand, tried to build a case that maintained that Dahmer had no awareness that he was mentally ill—he just thought on occasion that he did bad things. The State Prosecutor countered by stating that the sadistic cannibal was not possessed of a diseased mind, but a disordered one.

Throughout his trial, Dahmer sat quietly, almost expressionless. He described how he cooked the biceps of one of his victims, seasoned it with salt, pepper, and steak sauce—then, with apparent sincerity, he said that he was at a loss to believe that any human being could have done the things that he had done. Before he was sentenced, he rose to make a kind of public apology. Quoting from his statement to the court:

[I decided to go through this trial because] … I wanted to find out just what it was that caused me to be so bad and evil, but most of all … I decided that maybe there was a way for us to tell the world that there are people out there with these disorders, maybe they can get help before they end up being hurt or hurting someone…. In closing I just want to say that I hope God has forgiven me; I know society will never be able to forgive me for what I have done.

On May 1, 1992, Jeffrey Dahmer was sentenced to life imprisonment on 16 charges of aggravated murder. On November 28, 1994, while he was mopping the bathroom floor in maximum security, Dahmer was killed by Christopher Scarver, a convicted murderer who was on antipsychotic medication.

Dahmer's mother requested that his brain be preserved in formaldehyde for future study, but his father appealed to the court to honor his son's request for cremation. On December 12, 1995, more than a year after Jeffrey Dahmer's death, the county circuit judge ruled in favor of his father's petition and ordered the brain destroyed.

Real Vampires Enter the Contemporary Era

While vast audiences of vampire fans find the sexual symbolism sensually appealing when they observe a sophisticated Count Dracula or a forever-young male hunk emerge from the shadows and gently bite their beautiful victims' bare throats, the bloody accounts of real-life vampires reveal that they seldom operate with such dignity and grace.

The Vampire of Sacramento

Richard Trenton Chase was always being pursued by one demon or another. From the time of his birth on May 23, 1950, it seemed that Richard had been born under an unlucky star. As a child he was a fire starter and a killer of small animals. When he was a teenager, he often became frightened because he thought his heart had stopped beating. In some instances, he was convinced that someone had stolen his pulmonary artery. Because he believed that his cranial bones were moving, he shaved his head so he could watch them, then he held oranges on his naked skull to absorb the vitamin C directly into his brain in an effort to combat the separation.

When he started high school, Chase felt that he had evidence that a Nazi crime syndicate had targeted him and was paying his mother to poison him with a chemical that was turning his blood into powder. As an antidote to keep his blood flowing and his heart beating, Chase began killing and disemboweling small animals, mixing their organs with Coca-Cola in a blender, and drinking the potion.

In 1975, after he injected rabbit's blood into his veins and developed blood poisoning, Chase was committed to a mental asylum. Somehow, the hospital staff learned, Richard was able to capture small birds that landed on his window sill and eat them.

After he had been found with blood smeared over his face a number of times, the staff began referring to him as "Dracula."

Chase was released to his mother in 1976 with a prescription for an anti-psychotic medicine to be taken regularly. The hospital staff had decided that "Dracula" did not really pose a threat to society at large—and his mother decided that her son really didn't need the medication prescribed by the doctors at the asylum.

In mid-1977, Chase was stopped by a tribal agent as he wandered nude on a reservation in the Lake Tahoe area. The young man immediately aroused suspicion because his shirt was soaked in blood, and he had a bucket of blood with a liver in it in his Ford Ranchero.

Unfortunately for his future victims, Richard convinced the authorities that he had been hunting and the blood was that of an animal. On this occasion, it appears that the blood was not the vital fluid of a human victim, and on the first murder that Chase did commit, he would be careful not to get any blood on him. On December 29, 1977, he killed Ambrose Griffin, 51, in a drive-by shooting.

About a month later, January 21, 1978, Chase shot 22-year-old Teresa Wallin three times. He dragged her body into the bedroom of her home where he stabbed her repeatedly, smeared her blood over his hands and face, and used a yogurt cup to catch some of her blood to drink. Two days later, Chase bought two puppies from a neighbor, killed them, and drank their blood. He decided that animal blood did not give him the satisfaction that he gained from drinking human blood.

On January 27, Chase entered the home of Evelyn Miroth, 38, who was baby-sitting her 22-month-old nephew, David. Her friend Danny Meredith, 51, had come over to keep her company. Evelyn's son, Jason, 6, was getting ready to leave the house to go to play at a friend's. Within minutes, Chase had killed all four of them. Chase shot Meredith and Jason in the head, then forced Miroth into the bedroom where he stabbed her many times. When she was dead, he engaged in necrophilia with her corpse. He also removed several organs from her body and from Jason's body and drank his victims' blood from a cup.

While practicing cannibalism on Miroth, Chase was startled by a knocking on the door. It was Jason's friend, coming to check why he had not come to her house as he had promised. When neighbors noticed that no one was responding in the Miroth residence, they became suspicious, knowing very well that the family was home. While someone called the police to investigate, Chase made his escape.

The investigating officers were shocked to discover a charnel house (a repository for dead bodies) in the Miroth residence. The butchery of the innocent mother and child sickened them. It was not until Karen Ferreira arrived asking about her son David that the crime scene investigators were struck with the horror that the monster who had killed three people in the home had taken a baby with him. A bullet hole in the pillow in the crib gave mute evidence that little David had been killed before his body was stolen away.

Amidst the terrible gore that was everywhere in the home, forensic scientists discovered that Richard Trenton Chase had left perfect handprints in blood in several places in the house. When the police raided Chase's home, they were further disgusted to discover that the vampire had already eaten several of the baby's internal organs. It was also evident that he had brought home a quantity of blood to drink at his leisure.

Officers later said that the nauseating, putrid odor of Chase's residence was overwhelming. Nearly everything in his home was stained with blood. Plates, drinking glasses, eating utensils were thick with coagulated blood. When the refrigerator door was opened, they were horrified to find dishes filled with body parts. An electric blender on the kitchen counter was stained and clogged with rot. There were numerous dog collars scattered around various rooms, but no sign of any living pets.

Little David's body was not found until March 24, when a church janitor noticed a box among other stored items that he did not recognize. He was shocked when he opened it to discover the remains of a male baby. Chase was subsequently examined by a dozen psychiatrists. He only once admitted that he was disturbed about killing his victims, but only because he was concerned that their spirits might return to haunt him. He seemed to experience no real guilt for what he had done. He simply needed human blood to combat the many afflictions that he suffered. Blood drinking was therapeutic.

The trial for the Vampire of Sacramento began on January 2, 1979, in Santa Clara County, the requested change of venue. Chase was charged with six counts of murder. The defense argued that Chase's long history of mental illness indicated that none of the murders were premeditated.

Richard Trenton Chase, the Vampire of Sacramento, was charged with killing six individuals in little more than a month. When police investigators entered his home, they found nearly everything stained with blood (illustration by Ricardo Pustanio).

On May 8, the jury rejected the argument that Chase was not guilty by reason of insanity and found him guilty of six counts of first degree murder. It had taken them only four hours to decide that Richard Trenton Chase should die in the gas chamber at San Quentin Penitentiary. On December 26, 1980, a prison guard found Chase dead in his bed. The Vampire of Sacramento had taken his own life just a few days short of the third anniversary of his rampage of death. A coroner determined that Chase had been hoarding his daily dose of Sinequan, a drug to combat depression and hallucination, and had overdosed.

Real Vampires and Proud of It

When he was apprehended in 1977 for the deaths of six victims and the wounding of seven other persons, David "Son of Sam" Berkowitz told investigators that he not only took his orders from a 6,000-year-old entity who relayed commands through his neighbor's dog, but also claimed that he had been poisoned by bloodsucking demons.

Serial killer Ted Bundy admitted during his trial in June 1979 that he had bitten his victims, and he admitted that he felt like a vampire.

In October 1981, James P. Riva II was convicted in Brockton, Massachusetts, of murdering his grandmother and drinking her blood from the bullet holes made by "golden bullets." "Voices" had told James that he was a vampire and that he must feast on human blood.

In February 1991, the lesbian lover of a vampire was found guilty of murder in an Australian court trial. After deliberating for 48 hours, the jury convicted Annette Hall of murdering Charles Reilly in a coastal suburb and sentenced her to life in prison. By her own testimony, Ms. Hall stated that she had stalked and killed Reilly so her vampire lover, Susi Hampton, could drink his blood. She described in detail how her lesbian girlfriend went into a "feeding frenzy" after Reilly had been stabbed over a dozen times. Ms. Hampton, a self-confessed vampire who lived on human blood, had previously pleaded guilty and had been sentenced to life in prison.

Sean Sellers, the Devil Child

When he was 13, Sean Sellers, a self-proclaimed "Devil Child," made a pact with the Devil and sealed it by drinking his own blood. From that time on, he kept a jar of his blood in the refrigerator, hidden behind the eggs. He later told the authorities that he drank a lot of blood, just like a vampire.

Later that year, when he moved with his mother and stepfather, Vonda and Lee Bellofatto, back to Oklahoma from Greeley, Colorado, Sean had begun holding nightly rituals and inviting demons to possess his body. After a while the demons renamed him "Ezurate" and told him his power would grow if he were to kill someone.

On Sunday, September 8, 1985, sometime after midnight, Sean/Ezurate entered the Circle K at Council Road and 122nd Street in Oklahoma City, and selected his first victim, Robert Bower, a 36-year-old night clerk. Although the first slug from the teenager's .38 tore through Bower's face, it did not kill him. A second shot missed the terrified man completely, and Bower made a run to the rear of the store. Hoping to lock himself in the bathroom to escape his attacker, a third bullet penetrated his rib cage and proved to be a mortal wound.

At first, the investigating officers assumed that it was another case of a robbery gone bad, tragically resulting in the murder of the night clerk. Then they noticed that the cash register had not been touched. Could Bower, a drifter from Ohio who had only been working at the convenience store for less than three months have been the victim of a revenge killing? Or had he become the victim of some violent psychopath?

No one, at the time of Bower's murder, could have suspected that the bright, moody student, who wrote weird essays for his English class about being touched by the World of Darkness, might be that psychopath. Sean also wrote that evil had taught him good, that after the Dragon had visited him the love that he had felt for everyone had turned to hate. Sean also proclaimed that he could kill without remorse and that he had become Ezurate.

Although several of Sean's teachers noticed that he experienced mood swings, the nonsense that the teenager had merged with a demon named Ezurate seemed pretty far out for Oklahoma. After a number of discussions, the teachers dismissed their concerns when they learned that numerous students, including Sean, were seemingly obsessed with the popular game "Dungeons and Dragons."

Just a few minutes before midnight on March 14, 1986, Sean stripped down to his black underwear and conducted a demonic ritual while his parents slept one bedroom away. Then, he later told police investigators, the temperature in his room suddenly dropped 10 degrees. Sharp, clawed fingers touched his flesh, and he was surrounded by demons flying all around him in a strange kind of mist. In the next few moments, Sean entered his parents' bedroom and shot them both in the head. He truly loved his parents, he insisted, but he laughed at the blood that poured from their wounds.

On October 2, 1986, Sean Sellers was convicted of first-degree murder. At the age of 15, he became the youngest prisoner on Oklahoma's death row.

A Strange Party Filled with Otherworldly Guests

In early February 2008, Kyle found himself at a most unusual party and the memory has haunted him ever since. Although Kyle admits that he had taken some drugs earlier that evening, he insists that the experience occurred free from any substance that he may have ingested. Kyle tells his story as follows.

Earlier in the week, I was invited to a party by my lab partner, Will. On the night of the party, I was standing outside on the porch of the apartment when I started feeling invisible hands feeling in all my pockets. I also saw my jacket move as if there was something moving it around me. The "hands" then started feeling my genitals. I immediately said, "Whoa, we have to stop that." A guy at the party who wasn't even near me said, "Okay, I'll stop."

It was very weird. I was not scared. I was thinking, "Wow are these some magicians or something else?" There was a game of beer pong that we also played in which some weird things happened. First of all, we were filling up the cups with a beer pitcher, but for some reason, the table would always be clean and dry. Even when I knew there had to be a little beer spilled around it.

The game of beer pong that we played that night had rules that were on a different level. Some people at this party had powers that were just unbelievable. One time when I threw the ball, it went right in the cup. One of the guys handed me another ball and said "throw it"—and it went in the cup almost unrealistically.

When the booze flows, a party can get pretty strange, but Kyle found himself in the midst of the creepiest party of his life.

I said, "This isn't even fun anymore if the ball goes in every time." Someone handed me another ball and said, "Try again." I threw the ball, and it missed horribly, like somebody made it happen. A guy named Brandon said something like, "Things aren't always what they seem."

I asked people at this party to explain this stuff. Will told me to "just leave it to people who know more than you." Someone named Carlos transmitted a thought into my head that I can only describe as total chaos and confusion. He then told me, "See, its unexplainable."

Ever since I entered the apartment where the party was held, there was almost always the feeling of warm hands on my body and genitals. The group wanted me to have sex with one of the girls. Another guy there who looked and acted gay tried to seduce me. Some very young looking girls were there to whom I was extremely attracted, but when they came into the room and tried to seduce me, there was just something not right about it. Also during this time, I was bombarded with thoughts and ideas that felt implanted into my mind. Some of them were jokes, comments, and things like that.

I also felt I was under control of other minds. A common thought that would be implanted would be some kind of mental puzzle. The end result of this would always be "Brandon is the man." I would look at Brandon and we would tap fists. On [another] occasion, I was standing outside on the porch, and Brandon walked out there. A piece of paper taped to the railing caught on fire. I looked at Brandon and he either had glowing red hands or a flame on his hand. I realized that it was he who created the fire. He also made some liquor bottles that were on a shelf start to glow red.

During this same time, I would put my lighter in my pocket or pull it out only to have it completely disappear. I would want to light my pipe, look for the lighter in my pockets and it would be gone. I saw a lighter on a table which I thought I would grab to light my pipe. Some prankster (who I think was Brandon), kept jacking up the flame so that it would singe my eyebrows when I tried to light the pipe. This prank was pulled on me more than a few times.

At no time in the night did I actually have sex. I am not quite sure, but I think I was subconsciously fighting the temptation. All of these events did not scare me too much, because I felt like I was helpless to do anything about them. I felt like I was just there for the experience, and I had to leave faith in the hands of a higher power.

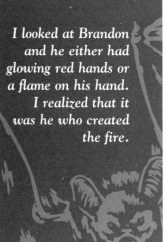

I looked at Brandon and he either had glowing red hands or a flame on his hand. I realized that it was he who created the fire.

Throughout the night, it seemed that people—total strangers to me—knew things about my past that they would bring up to get my reaction. I felt like they could read my thoughts, that they knew things about me that other people didn't know. They could transmit thoughts and ideas into my mind. The music that was being played at that party was something that I have never heard before. The dancing that I witnessed was something that I have never seen before. Time seemed altered. I do feel that these individuals were otherworldly beings. They felt almost god-like in that they could manipulate objects and freely demonstrate psychic abilities.

At one point, a girl asked me if I believed in God. I replied that I didn't, that I was a realist (my biology class at the time had me convinced that there was nothing else in the world). She gave me a high five. The gay guy told me, "Satan lives here," and he pointed to a pentagram drawn on the wall.

Jokingly, I said something like, "I love Satan." It seems very awkward to me now that I think about it. At one point I was possessed and encouraged to kick down a door in the house. This event got me kicked out of the party and booted out into the cold. I tried to sleep in my car and failed, only to drive home around five in the morning.

I have had a rough time the past year. Almost daily since the event, I have questioned my sanity, whether the events I experienced at the party were real. I have come to conclude that they really happened.

Confronting a Real Vampire in the Castle

Two correspondents of mine, Azrahn and Annie, told me how on September 7, 1995, when they were out clubbing in Ybor City, Tampa's Latin Quarter, they actually met a "bona fide vampire." Azrahn admitted that he was up to a bit of mischief that evening. He stands six-foot-six, has long straggly hair, and that night he was dressed in a black leather trench coat, wearing black eyeliner, and sporting a metal claw on his left arm. Those who know Azrahn know that he is a gentle giant and completely harmless under normal conditions. But he does have a wee bit of an ornery streak in him and on this night he was taking delight in "freaking out" the itinerant preachers on the street corners.

"I was just having fun," he said, "knowing how harmless I am on the whole. The irony of it was that the preachers' messages included that we should not judge others, yet I terrified them by my presence."

After wearying of such mischief, Azrahn and Annie, along with a couple of friends, decided to go to the "Castle." "The Castle in Ybor, was a gothic tenement structure amid all sorts of modern buildings," Azrahn explained. "I am sure by now it has been judged a thorn in the side of the corporate takeover of Ybor City and has been torn down. But when this experience happened to Annie and me, everything was run down everywhere. The main strip, a block away, was blocked to traffic, and party-goers and bar-hoppers could get ripped without worrying about getting mowed down in traffic."

First, we will hear Azrahn's memory of that evening's strange encounter.

As Annie and I entered the Castle, this eerie feeling came over me. Something bizarre had entered the place, and as I scanned for the source of the disruption I came across a strange man of medium build. As I eyed him, I began to follow him at a distance around the Castle's immense dance floor and social areas. I got a very dreadful feeling about this individual.

Within a few minutes, he stopped and looked around. He knew someone was stalking him. He turned around and dead locked me and gave an imposing grin. With a strategic nod, he turned around and vanished before my eyes. I took a step back. The energy in the room hadn't changed, so I looked around to see if I could find him.

I did. He was standing on the side of a huge screen that displayed videos projected from across the room. To move instantly from one side of the dance floor to the other was an impossible maneuver under the best of circumstances, let alone amid crowded, partying drunkards in a dancing frenzy.

I picked up the pursuit. He looked my way, annoyed, and dashed away. I found him again at the other side of the bar at a table some ten seconds later. Now I was obsessed with what I was seeing. I wanted to meet this *thing* and find out what I was dealing with. As I approached him, I felt an inner heat that I never felt before, and an intense anger came over me. I stopped, and we made eye contact again.

Annie was onto him as well. She was terrified, but I was curious. I lost him once again, but the energy had changed and had calmed down. I instantly looked towards the door and headed for the stairs down to the lobby and out onto the streets of Ybor City. There was this lined walkway with trees, very legend of Sleepy Hollow looking— and once again it was here that I picked up his trail.

As I approached, I saw his black clothes wavering, and he disappeared once again. As I got half way down the tree lined trail, I heard deep within me a voice that spoke in a sinister tone: "Isn't it wonderful how the hunter becomes the hunted out here in the streets?"

I broke out in a sweat. It was the first time that I had actually thought about what I was doing. But my curiosity got the best of me once again. The sound—although from within—came from above me. I looked and saw the figure I had been pursuing.

"Be advised, not to see my face."

We had deadlocked eye-to-eye twice at least by this point, yet I had no clear image of this creature's face. That struck me as odd, but it didn't stick out beyond the other oddities that were mounting as the minutes passed. I turned around. Again it was gone. The energy moved towards the street preachers. A voice, deep inside me, felt more as a vibration than of an interpreted sound, said, "You should be grateful that your blood is tainted, friend. Do not pursue this further. This will be your only warning. Perhaps we will meet again. I will always be able to find what has found me. Now leave me be!"

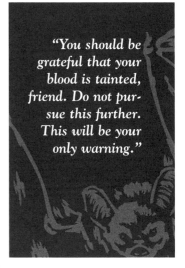

"You should be grateful that your blood is tainted, friend. Do not pursue this further. This will be your only warning."

With that my brain felt like someone squeezed it like a sponge. I collapsed in the street. A preacher named Shane picked me up and tried to get me to come to the river. Annie came to my aid as the preachers helped me to a bench on the street curb.

The next day the papers reported that there were two girls murdered in Ybor City. I am pretty confident that thing I was trailing was the culprit. The events of that evening was one of the few times that I was terrified by an encounter with the unknown.

About eight months after this incident, I was diagnosed with Hodgkin's Lymphoma. Then I understood what the being had meant about my blood being tainted.

Here is what Annie remembers from that strange night's encounter with a vampire.

The guy in the Castle was watching us for quite some time before Azrahn noticed him. I saw him sitting by the window in the corner of the small room with the bar. I was at the bar ordering an Amaretto and Darcy was with me. I am not sure why the man was so intrigued with us, but it was strange the way he looked at us.

After Darcy and I got our shots, I glanced up and he was gone. I wasn't sure how he got by us without me noticing because the bar was right next to the exit. Not long after, I remember Azrahn coming up to me and pointing him out in the other room. That's when I told him that I already knew about him. It seemed like he was always there. One minute on the dance floor, the next minute at a window, the next minute on a couch, a corner, and so on.

Yeah, to say I was shook up by him was an understatement. I know that there are a lot of interesting people who go to the Castle and I am far from judgmental, but that guy really got to me. His stare was piercing. You could almost feel it in the depth of your soul.

The next thing I knew, Azrahn was practically running out of the Castle, down the stairs. I grabbed Darcy and went after him. I found Azrahn appearing dumbfounded on one of the sidewalks, looking around frantically. It had only been a couple of minutes since he ran down the stairs. Darcy and I saw the weird guy again, out near the street, but then, like in the Castle, he was gone. Darcy said we shouldn't follow him because he was creepy.

Azrahn didn't listen to Darcy and continued after the guy. I followed Azrahn and the mysterious guy. I remember briefly seeing the man we followed, because his dark clothes stood out in the street crowd. The energy he let off was enough to floor someone, and it didn't seem good.

He seemed to mix into the rest of crowd, and I didn't see him again. The feelings were still there, though. It was extremely creepy and almost surreal. I felt like we were in a movie or something. When I looked back at Azrahn, I saw him with the preacher and it looked like he was helping him. I wasn't sure what happened to Azrahn at that point, because the man in the dark clothes had me so enthralled. He was all that was on my mind at that time.

I felt bad when Azrahn collapsed. I'm sorry I wasn't there to lift him up. But we had an interesting conversation on the way home. I'm just glad I only had one drink that night. I couldn't imagine having had more to drink and seeing all that we saw.

Clinical Vampirism

J ust before Christmas 2004, a man accosted a family on the streets of Birmingham, England, and bit all three members on their necks, hands, or arms before he fled the scene. The bizarre incident fueled fears of a crazed vampire stalking the streets of the city, and there were numerous reports of random vampiric attacks before the police arrested a man whom they believed was responsible for the attacks.

***

In March 2005, Diana Semenuha, 29, lured street children into her home in Odessa with promises of a clean place to sleep and hot meals. In return, Diana drank their blood. Olga Buravceva, a spokesperson for the Odessa police, received a tip that a vampire was taking blood from street urchins, then dumping them back out in the cold when she had finished with them. Diana Semenuha believed that ingesting human blood could cure her of a muscle-wasting medical condition. The blood that she did not use for her own purposes, she sold to Black Magic practitioners.

When the police raided Semenuha's apartment, they found seven children strapped to beds and benches. The windows were covered with thick black drapes and the only light came from black candles. The air in the rooms was heavy with the odor of incense. Satanic symbols were found throughout the apartment, and a large, black knife rested beside the silver goblet from which the vampire had drunk the blood of the street children.

***

In September 2001, 17-year-old Matthew Hardman spent several hours discussing vampires, life-after-death, and the paranormal with a German foreign exchange student, also 17. Hardman had noticed the girl, who lived in the same boarding house in northern Wales as some of his friends, and he found himself attracted to her for a very important reason. He could tell that she was a vampire. There was no mistaking the signs.

Those who believe that they must have human blood on which to subsist see themselves as true vampires. Psychiatrists have named this clinical vampirism "Renfield's Syndrome," after Dracula's toady follower (illustration by Dan Allen).

"I know that you are one of *them*," he said. "Please bite me on the neck so that I may become one of you." The girl was startled. The conversation had moved from Goth fashions, to ghosts, to vampires. And suddenly this strange young man who worked as a waiter and a kitchen porter at the restaurant of a nearby hotel wanted her to bite him on the neck.

Matthew begged the girl to "blood" him, to make him a vampire. He grabbed her by the shoulders, pressed his neck against her mouth, and cried out for the bite that would grant him immortality. The girl managed to scream and to bring others from the lodgings to investigate.

Matthew was by now in such a psychological state that everyone appeared to him to be a vampire. Since the girl would not oblige him, Matthew beseeched the young men to bite him and allow him to join their ancient cult. He knew that they all lived in the building because it was a home for vampires. Even as a police officer was handcuffing him, Matthew requested that the man bite his neck.

It was unfortunate at the time of that disturbance in the lodgings of his friends that the extent of Matthew Hardman's obsession with vampires was not fully noted for the psychological illness that it truly was. He was just written off as an impressionable teenager who loved to talk about vampires and spooky subjects and who had probably had too much to drink when he began to see imaginary fangs on all of his friends.

Two months later, in November, Matthew murdered 90-year-old Mabel Leyshon at her home in Llanfairpwll, Anglesey, Wales. Mrs. Leyshon had befriended Matthew since he was a boy of 13, but his thirst for blood compelled him to stab his elderly friend to death, cut out her heart, and drink her blood from a saucepan. Such a ritual, Matthew believed, would surely initiate him into the coveted ranks of the undead.

Convicted on August 2, 2002, the vampire wept as the jury found him guilty after less than two days' deliberation. Justice Richards pronounced the murder of Mrs. Leyshon an "act of great wickedness," one for which Matthew Hardman had shown no remorse. The teenaged would-be vampire may have hoped for immortality, the judge said, "But all you have achieved is the brutal ending of another person's life and the bringing of a life sentence upon yourself."

Although Justice Richards said that the defendant was declared to be of sound mind in planning the murder, he speculated that he believed that Hardman was "possibly disguising an undiagnosed psychiatric illness."

Renfield's Syndrome

That "undiagnosed psychiatric illness" to which Justice Richards made reference is known to psychiatrists as "clinical vampirism," a syndrome involving the delusion that one is actually a vampire and feels a need to ingest blood. Psychiatrists separate clinical vampirism from those individuals who romanticize vampire films and those who engage in role-playing vampire games.

Psychologist Richard Noll, author of *Bizarre Disease of the Mind*, has pointed out that many cases of clinical vampirism have much in common with the character of Renfield in Bram Stoker's *Dracula*, hence Noll's labeling of the mental illness, Renfield's Syndrome.

In the original telling of the story of Dracula, Renfield is a patient in a mental asylum who likes to eat bugs. In Tod Browning's classic film version, however, there is the suggestion that Renfield preceded Jonathan Harker as the first attorney to visit Dracula's castle and acquaint the Count with London real estate. The visit to the vampire's castle drove him mad and made him scurry after spiders and flies until Dracula, his Master, might enable him to seek larger game. Dwight Frye's maniacal laughter as he grabs for flies remain some of the film's more unforgettable scenes. (In spite of the undeniable imagery conjured by the term Renfield's Syndrome, it is not currently categorized in the *Diagnostic and Statistical Manual of Mental Disorders, 4th Edition*.)

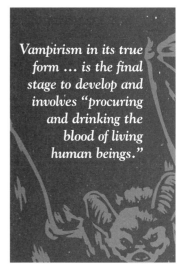

Vampirism in its true form ... is the final stage to develop and involves "procuring and drinking the blood of living human beings."

Noll theorizes that the majority of those suffering from Renfield's Syndrome are men who have come to believe that the drinking of blood will convey life-enhancing powers. The condition, he says, usually begins in childhood with an incident that somehow causes blood to be ingested. Later, in puberty, blood drinking is associated with sexual arousal.

In his book *Vampires, Werewolves & Demons: Twentieth Century Reports in the Psychiatric Literature*, Noll states that "Autovampirism," in which one ingests blood from one's own open wounds, may lead to "Zoophagia," the eating and/or the drinking of living creatures. Those afflicted with Renfield's Syndrome may often catch insects, birds, and small animals, such as dogs and cats. Slaughterhouses would offer a steady supply of fresh blood to vampires.

Vampirism in its true form, Noll states, is the final stage to develop and involves "procuring and drinking the blood of living human beings." Noll notes that this may be accomplished by "stealing the blood from hospitals, laboratories ... or by attempting to drink the blood directly from others. Usually this involves some sort of consensual sexual activity, but in lust-murder type cases and in other non-lethal violent crimes, the sexual activity and vampirism may not be consensual. The compulsion to drink blood almost always has a strong sexual component associated with it."

Vampireboy and Other Cases of Vampirism

Bobbi Jo O'Neal, RN, BSN, F-ABMDI, a deputy coroner for the Charleston County Coroner's Office in Charleston, South Carolina, discussed "Living Vampires" in an article for *Forensic Nurse* magazine (October 15, 2005) in which she advised forensic nurses that vampirism was a form of deviant behavior that many people considered rare or even non-existent.

Ms. O'Neal told of a 17-year-old white male who was found unresponsive in his bedroom. The teenager was on his knees, his head resting on the bed. Pronounced dead in the emergency room, the deceased was noted as having been prescribed Prozac and Adderral. Although he had been very popular and engaged in many high school activities, he had recently become more withdrawn and devoted increasing amounts of time to the Internet, where he was known as "Vampireboy."

According to Ms. O'Neal, during the scene investigation, a journal was found in which the teenager had described himself as a "Vampiresis." In great detail, the boy described how he became a vampire and how he had instructed others to do the same. "At autopsy it was noted that the canine teeth appeared to have been filed," she continued. "Sixteen ounces of blood was found in the stomach and four ounces of mucoid bloody fluid was found in the duodenum. There were no signs of ulceration or other cause for bleeding."

Ms. O'Neal cites a case involving a woman who was four months pregnant who enjoyed the sight of vomiting large amounts of blood which she had ingested. When blood transfusions were ordered, the patient unhooked the tubes, insisting that she would rather drink the blood. When the woman was later found dead, an autopsy revealed that her stomach was bloated with blood.

Porphyria—The Vampire Disease

An actual physical illness that might well be labeled "the vampire disease" is the rare disorder in the synthesis of the blood known as porphyria. Experts say that there may be as many as eight varieties of this genetic anomaly. Those afflicted often suffer abdominal pain, eruptions of the skin, sensitivity to light, difficulty in breathing, and unattractive transformations in personal appearance. Some researchers have estimated that there may be more than 50,000 individuals in the United States who suffer from one of the varieties of porphyria.

In her book *True Vampires*, Sondra London quotes the work of David Dolphin, Ph.D., a chemistry professor at the University of British Columbia, who made the controversial suggestion at a meeting of the American Association for the Advancement of Modern Science that blood-drinking vampires were victims of porphyria attempting to alleviate the symptoms of their dreadful disease. While these individuals may not actually grow fangs, Dr. Dolphin said, the lips and gums may be drawn back, thereby creating an illusion of the elongation of the teeth.

Dr. Dolphin's imaginative presentation was not well-received, and numerous scientists argued that there was no scientific basis for the claim that the ingestion of blood might relieve the pain of porphyria attacks.

Lycanthropy

Just as there are humans who envision themselves to be real vampires, there are those individuals who believe themselves capable of shape-shifting into wolves. Psychologists recognize a werewolf psychosis (lycanthropy or lupinomanis) in which persons so afflicted may believe that they change into a wolf at the full moon. Those who are so afflicted may actually "feel" their fur growing, their fingernails becoming claws, their jaw lengthening, their canine teeth elongating.

In their paper, "A Case of Lycanthropy," published in the *American Journal of Psychiatry* in 1977, psychiatrist Harvey Rosenstock and psychologist Kenneth Vincent discussed the case history of a 49-year-old woman who received daily psychotherapy

Those who believe that they change into werewolves at the time of the full Moon suffer from a werewolf psychosis known as lycanthropy, or lupinomanis (illustration by Ricardo Pustanio).

and antipsychotic drugs and who still perceived herself as a wolf-woman with claws, teeth, and fangs. Medical personnel would manage to get the woman under control until the next full moon—when she would snarl, howl, and resume her wolf-like behavior. Rosenstock and Vincent stated that the woman was eventually discharged and provided with antipsychotic medication, but she declared that she would haunt graveyards until she had found the male werewolf of her dreams.

The Vampire Community

When Kahlil was a teenager in the Philippines, new neighbors moved in from the southern provinces. Kahlil remembers that the adults seemed never to be around, but he recalls that their children were really popular. Emily was one of the kids, and she became Kahlil's best friend. Kahlil admits that he was an awkward teenager, but Emily was very approachable and kind. Kahlil tells his story below.

One evening on the way home from the Christmas gathering at church, Emily and I stayed a little longer and walked home by ourselves. We had actually never walked together before in the evening. It was an enjoyable walk, but there is something that I will never forget. For the first time, I saw her eyes in the evening, and for a moment I thought I saw them reflect light, much like the way an animal's eyes would. I shrugged it off as my imagination.

Another evening, I came to join their family for dinner. Emily invited me, saying that she wanted her family to accept me as one of their own. I thought it was peculiar at the time, because hardly anyone says anything this formal. Anyway, during dinner, I noticed that the family drank what I assumed to be red wine from one particular bottle. I didn't drink because I was underage. Neither did Emily drink any of the wine, because she was also underage.

Later, though, I caught her drinking the red wine in the kitchen. I followed her there when she had been sent to get a new bottle. She asked me not to tell anyone. When I asked to have a sip myself, Emily gave it some thought and then refused. I remember distinctly that the red wine looked a bit too thick.

In time, I became close to Emily, and she started confiding in me. At the time, I just thought she was strange, for her stories were very weird. Their family, she said, traveled a lot and would move between places within a couple of years, sometimes even months. She mentioned living in different countries. I did think their family looked a bit "foreign," but many in my country are children from mixed races. Emily's family had pale skin (perhaps with some tinge of brown), but they didn't look particularly European to me. Perhaps a bit more Indian, but without the accent. Her family spoke English but not "American-sounding" like most Filipinos. At times Emily's stories seemed a bit inconsistent—or so I thought—because it seemed that there were too many places in which their family could have lived.

One night I stayed overnight in their house for the first time. It was a bit unusual, but their family had become close friends. From the outside, their house appeared like any other, but on the inside, it was as if you were in a kind of museum. There were furniture pieces and a collection of things from all over the world. All these objects seemed to have a strange atmosphere to them.

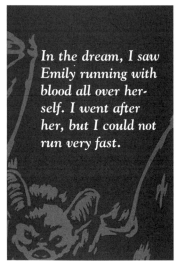

In the dream, I saw Emily running with blood all over herself. I went after her, but I could not run very fast.

I went to bed late, but I woke up in the middle of the night because of a bad dream. In the dream, I saw Emily running with blood all over herself. I went after her, but I could not run very fast. Slowly I inched toward her, and when she turned I saw that her eyes reflected the moonlight. She had blood all over her mouth with her fangs showing. That was when I woke up.

I went out of the room to get a glass of water and saw that Emily was there. I told her about the dream and I remember that she looked at me seriously all the time I was talking. I went back to bed and slept better. In the morning, we had breakfast as if nothing had happened.

During the summer, Emily and I became really good friends. I was not attracted to her for some reason, but we could really talk to each other and she confided more and more about her family's history. One day she started talking about her family's ancestors and how they were badly treated a long time ago. Emily talked about it as if it had happened in the recent past. I was amazed at her knowledge of different countries and of history.

A few months afterwards, the family left, and I never heard from Emily again. There were rumors that her father's business took them abroad. Were they a family of vampires? Perhaps I imagined everything, but I have never forgotten those incidents—the shining eyes, the blood wine, the strange dream, the tales of a persecuted ancestry, the constant moving from place to place, from country to country. Perhaps there are immortals who feed on blood and who appear just like normal people. They are not consumed by fire during the light of day or by the church. That's how they could slip through centuries unnoticed.

Sometimes I still dream of Emily, but they're not nightmares anymore. It's more like she is keeping me updated with their travels.

Could Kahlil have found himself living next to a very discreet family of vampires? A family that kept on the move from place to place, country to country, for generations, perhaps for centuries, having learned to supplement their diet for immortality with bottles of "thick red wine." Kahlil added as a kind of post script that there were no unsolved murders in his community that he recalled. Perhaps Emily's family had made the transition to animal blood.

The Modern-Day Subculture of Real Vampires

The late parapsychologist Dr. Steven Kaplan began keeping tabs on real vampires in 1972. He estimated that there were approximately 21 "real" vampires living secretly in the United States and Canada. He spoke to many of these individuals, some of whom claimed to be 300 years old, and he established the demographics of vampires, placing Massachusetts in the lead with three, followed by Arizona, California, and New Jersey, with two each, and the remaining 15 vampires were scattered throughout the other states and provinces.

By 1982, after Dr. Kaplan had established the Vampire Research Center in Elmhurst, New York, he had discovered a much more extensive vampire subculture living among the general population. According to the Vampire Research Center's 1989 census, the average male vampire appeared to be about 26 years old, had brown eyes and hair, stood five-foot-ten, and weighed 170 pounds. The average female vampire appeared to be about 23 years old, had brown eyes and black hair, was five-foot-six, and weighed 120 pounds.

Dr. Kaplan divided the creatures of the night into three basic categories:

1. Fetishists erotically attracted to blood

2. Vampire Imitators who adopt the traditional trappings of cape, coffin, and Carpathian mannerisms in search of powers of domination, immortality, sensuality, and charisma

3. Real vampires—men and women who have a physical addiction to blood, drink it, believe it will prolong their lives, and experience sexual satisfaction through the blood-drinking ritual.

Some true vampires murder their victims, Dr. Kaplan stated, but the vast majority find more socially acceptable ways to satisfy their hunger for human blood. One vampire worked as a technician in a hospital. He simply took blood from the hospital storage unit whenever he needed it. Although this man was supposedly well over 60, he passed for a man in his early twenties.

A 40-year-old vampire in Arizona still looked like a teenager and hung out around universities. He lured college girls into the desert and mesmerized them while he sipped their blood.

Michelle Belanger, author of the bestselling *Vampires in Their Own Words* (2007), *Sacred Hunger* (2005), and many other books, and who is herself a "psychic vampire," defined the contemporary vampire community for me in these words: "In recent years, there has been a growing community of individuals who identify as real vampires. In contrast to their fictional counterparts, modern vampires are not undead, nor are they repelled by garlic or crosses. These otherwise ordinary human beings identify with the vampire because they feel that they have a need to take the vital life force from others. Some, called psychic vampires, take this vital force in the form of psychic energy. Others, often called sanguinarians, take small amounts of blood from willing

According to recent statistics gathered by the vampire community itself, the great majority of their number consider themselves "Psychic Vampires," feeding off the energy, rather than the blood, of other humans (illustration by Ricardo Pustanio).

human donors. Psychic vampires who are active members of the modern vampire community stand in contrast with the unaware psychic vampires that sometimes prey upon unwilling victims. Psychic vampires who embrace their natures take energy only from willing donors, often seeking out individuals who suffer from an overabundance of energy and finding a healthy balance point through a mutual exchange. In addition to their professed need for energy, the vast majority of psychic vampires are also gifted psychics, with an inborn talent for sensing and working with the energy they are drawn to take from others."

Michelle also recommended that those who may be sincerely interested in learning some fascinating facts and figures on the modern vampire community carefully review the Vampire and Energy Workers Research Survey (reprinted below with permission.)

"Merticus and his team have collected extensive demographics on the community—from widely diagnosed medical conditions to age, level of education, and religious affiliation," she said. "From his survey, I can say that less than 1% of people who identify as real vampires have ever been convicted of a felony. The mean average age within the community currently stands in the middle thirties, with individuals in their fifties, sixties, and seventies who identify as real vampires. Individuals who identify as real vampires come from every possible religious background, from atheist to Buddhist, plus every flavor of Christian[ity] in between, and the vast majority of members of the vampire community have at least some college under their belts—with many possessing graduate level degrees."

An Updated Survey of Real Vampires
Conducted by Real Vampires Themselves

"When a serious member of the vampire community describes themselves as a "vampire," they are not trying to tell you that they think they're a fictional character with supernatural powers, that they have trouble distinguishing between a role-playing game and reality, or that they hope you're gullible enough to believe that they're hundreds of years old and live in a castle," Merticus, a spokesperson for the community, said. "They're not even claiming kinship with the folkloric monster that frightened the people of Central Europe, and has them performing vampire-banishing rituals to this day."

Merticus is the administrator for Voices of the Vampire Community (VVC), basically the current leadership network for the modern vampire community with Michelle Belanger, Sanguinarius, SphynxCatVP, Lady CG, and others. As a vampire, Merticus explains that there is most certainly "a visible and vibrant community of people who are using the label to describe themselves, but to this day there is no functioning definition of a real vampire. This is primarily because no one knows what the cause of the phenomenon actually is, and the community has coalesced around a set of loosely shared perceptions and symptoms rather than a central organizing principle. Therefore, we can describe some common experiences involved in being a vampire, but these shouldn't be taken as a definitive vampire checklist. There are no known necessary and sufficient conditions to be met before you can be a vampire. Likewise, there's no single definitive sign that someone is not a real vampire."

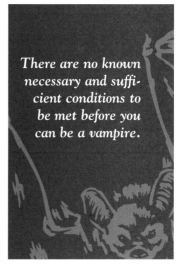

There are no known necessary and sufficient conditions to be met before you can be a vampire.

Merticus went on to add that the most common experience that vampires share is the need to take in life energy or blood, from sources outside themselves, to maintain spiritual, psychic, and physical health.

"Blood-drinking, or sanguinarian, vampires have to consume small, polite amounts of human blood from willing donors," Merticus said. "The majority of sanguinarians report taking only an ounce or less at a time; usually no more than once a week.

"Feeding is absolutely a health necessity; vampires have reported many negative physical symptoms when trying to ignore this need to feed. Psychic vampires, or psivamps, feed on psychic energy. Some psivamps enter into relationships with donors in the same way that sanguinarian vampires do, while others consciously train themselves away from human energy altogether, either for convenience or as a result of personal ethics. Some psivamps report a natural affinity for feeding on natural sources such as elemental or ambient natural energy. Others cultivate techniques for absorbing ambient energy from crowds and public places, so as not to take from any one source."

The Vampirism and Energy Work Research Study

The Vampirism and Energy Work Research Study is a detailed sociological and phenomenological study of the real vampire community conducted by Suscitatio Enterprises, LLC. Two surveys were released in 2006 that were answered by nearly 950 individuals from all paths within the vampire community and throughout the world. The first was the Vampire and Energy Work Research Survey (VEWRS), with 379 Questions, in March 2006; and the second was the Advanced Vampirism and Energy Work Research Survey (AVEWRS), with 688 Questions, in August 2006. From 2006 to 2009 a combined response (VEWRS and AVEWRS) reached over 1,450 surveys, or over 670,000 individually answered questions, making it the largest and most in-depth research study ever conducted on the real vampire/vampyre community or subculture.

There is also Twilight—the official meetup.com at http://www.meetup.com/twilight. Twilight is an independent, formal gathering of individuals involved in vampirism and the vampiric communities. It is not associated with the novels or the motion pictures. Their goal is to bring together the community's dedicated and serious members for discussion, practical and academic knowledge exchange, networking, and social engagement in a neutral environment.

Some of these statistics on VEWRS are universally applicable to the vampire community independent of one's personal identification with either of the primary feeding methods; psychic (psi) or sanguinarian (sang) vampirism. Lists are given in order or frequency where percentages are not applicable for the set.

Identity Type Response:

17% Sang/Sanguine Only
31% Psi/Psychic Only
52% Hybrid (Psychic and Sanguine +)

Those who are able to feed from psychic, psi, pranic, etc. energy constitute approximately 83 percent of the respondents based on question #285. Once adjusted for the specific feeding method currently employed this adjusts to approximately 65 percent identifying as Psychic Vampires and 35 percent identifying as Sanguinarian Vampires. It's important to note that there does exist a sizeable crossover of individuals who claim to be able to feed from both blood (sang) and pranic (psi) energy.

Location (In Order of Highest Vampire Population)

United States: California, Georgia, Texas, New York, Ohio, Illinois, and Florida

Internationally: Canada, United Kingdom, Australia, Netherlands, France, Ireland, Brazil, and Russia

Gender

62.0% Female / 38.0% Male (the female to male ratio within the vampire community is best approximated at 60/40)

Age

Median 28 (the highest concentration of self-identified vampires are between 25 to 35 years of age, with many well into their 50s and 60s)

Personality Type

INTJ [Introverted iNtuitive Thinking Judging; "the scientist" type], INFJ [Introverted iNtuitive Feeling Judging; "the protector" type], and INFP [Introverted iNtuitive Feeling Perceiving; "the idealist" type]: These personality types represent some of the lowest percentages among the general population (1.5 to 4.3%) but are the highest percentages (double and even triple all others) among self-identified vampires.

Intelligence Quotient

Nearly 75 percent of self-identified vampires have a tested IQ above 125

Physical Conditions

These reported physical conditions are significantly greater than the average prevalence rates of the general population.

Asthma: 19.9%
Anemia: 16%
Chronic Fatigue Syndrome: 8%
Fibromyalgia: 3.5%
Migraines/Severe Headaches: 24.6%

Do You Consider Yourself Goth?

Yes: 34%
No: 66%

Have You Ever Been Convicted of a Violent Crime?

Yes: 2.5%
No: 97.5%

Spirituality and Religion in Order of Number of Followers

Vampirism is not considered a religion by the majority of self-identified vampires—vampires share many diverse religious and spiritual beliefs. Vampires often have a pluralistic view of religion and spirituality. Furthermore, the classification of vampirism as a "New Religious Movement" or "cult" is not accurate nor representative of the often mainstream religious beliefs held by members of the modern vampire community. The following are listed in order of frequency among vampires.

- Magick
- Wicca
- Neo-Paganism
- Occultism
- Christianity
- Shamanism
- Agnostic

Member of a House (i.e., member of a group like the Blood Dragons, Vampire Church, or Sekhemu)

No: 75%
Yes: 25%

Some Relevant Comments Regarding the Survey

Merticus says that there is no way to tell how many vampires there are in the world, partly because individuals are solely responsible for their own self-identification. "The standard wisdom from the community is that only you can decide whether or not you are a vampire, after serious self-aware introspection," Merticus said. "The Vampire Community online and in the real world has definitely been growing in membership, but that's due to many factors.

"First, not everyone who participates in the Vampire Community, whether online or offline, is actually a vampire. Some just like the community atmosphere, and the Vampire Community rarely turns away anyone who wants to engage in healthy socialization.

"Second, the increase in widespread communication means that more interested individuals can find the community today, whereas we can only assume that in the past, real vampires may have gone their entire lives without discovering that there were others like themselves.

"Today, after receiving completed VEWRS/AVEWRS surveys from dozens of countries, and having received requests to translate the text of the survey into multiple languages, we know for certain that there are self-identifying vampires all over the world, that this is not just an American, or an English-speaking, or even a Western-Hemisphere phenomenon. We have heard from vampires in Asia, Europe, South America, and North America. However, we have nothing like a vampire head-count, and no foolproof vampire test to tell whether everyone claiming to be a vampire actually is one. We can say the Vampire Community has been growing in participation and visibility, but there's no way to tell what percentage of the population might be vampiric."

Pop Culture Loves Vampires

In the twenty-first century, with the ever-growing popularity of the Goth movements, the various vampire role-playing games, the continuing bestselling status of vampire novels, the popularity of vampire films, the high-ratings of television series based on vampires and the occult, it becomes an increasingly difficult task to estimate the current population of those who define themselves as some facet of the term, "vampire."

The vast majority of those enchanted by the vampire lifestyle are those young people who find dressing the part of an attractive and seductive member of the undead to appeal to their romantic sensibilities. For them it is like being able to dress up for Halloween 52 nights of the year.

While role-playing as vampires and victims may be considered quite harmless as long as the participants know when to draw the line between fantasy and reality, those who cross the boundaries of mental aberration into blood fetishism and obsessive blood-drinking may gradually develop a psychosis that can force them to mutilate or even kill others. On February 1, 2002, a 23-year-old woman who said that she became

A wide-spread contemporary vampire community has adjusted to the twenty-first century (illustration by Bill Oliver).

a vampire in London, then murdered a man in Germany and drank his blood, was jailed for the crime.

In the November 24, 2000, issue of the *New York Times*, Margaret Mittelbach and Michael Crewdson reported on the city's vampire scene that has been going strong since the mid-1990s and the many nightclubs that cater to the "daylight-challenged" in their article, "Vampires: Painting the Town Red." The journalists describe the activities in "dens" where as many as 300 "undead heads" dance, drink, and make merry late into the night. The dress code in such establishments is "gothic," "dark-fetish," "faerie," "Wiccan," or "Celtic" and the overwhelmingly predominant color of the clothing is black. On the "rare occasion" when a patron of these vampire havens smiles, Mittelbach and Crewdson note, one can make out "the glint of white fangs."

Other researchers have discovered that these "Human Living Vampires" believe that they require blood in order to function at their highest level of proficiency. They realize that they are not really immortal beings, but they may feel that they have extrasensory abilities that border on the supernatural that are accelerated with the ingestion of human blood. Most often the vital fluid is obtained from willing donors who permit the vampires to make small cuts or punctures in their flesh and lick or suck the blood.

A Paranormal Researcher Interviews a Real Vampire

My colleague Chris Holly, who lives on Long Island, New York, presently publishes and writes the website "Chris Holly's Paranormal World." Chris is published on many paranormal sites on the Internet and is presently working on a book of her true life-based articles. Chris has written about many aspects of the paranormal from UFO sightings to ghosts, from pagan witches to reincarnation. Her observations are available at http://endlessjrny.blogspot.com/ and http:// www.fttoufo.com/chrishollysparanormalworld.htm. Recently, Chris set out to explore the Vampire Community from the viewpoint of a paranormal researcher.

I recalled a truly bizarre experience from my past. Many years ago when I was attending college, a friend of mine told me of an extremely interesting experience that he had while attending his Ivy League university. He told me that a family line of so-called European royalty had a few family members attending his University at the same time that he was in school. He told me that there were many rumors circulating at the time that this family of royal bloods were a real and true line of immortal vampires. He told me that they were very strange people both in appearance and behavior.

It has always stuck with me how my friend told me that one thing and one thing alone drove the royal bloodline vampires wild; it was mortal people who portrayed themselves as vampires. This insult would move this family into instant rage to the point where they would stalk and hunt down imposters. He told me they searched for these people and had little mercy once they found them.

I always found this to be a extreme myth, yet a terrifying one, and I often wondered if those who are merely mortal humans living a modern day style of vampirism ever fear they may be walking a thin and dangerous line? If there were even a slight chance that I was making immortal beings wildly angry, I would be careful not to make claims that might bring them down on me.

I knew little about the subject of real vampires, so I set about attempting to make communication with someone in the vampire community. Eventually, I met a woman named "Vampypup" and her very knowledgeable companion, Redforce. Redforce is a man in his mid-40s. Looking at his photo he appears to be an average man of his age with the exception of his fangs! They are not obvious, and I am sure he needs to open his mouth in a certain way to display his teeth in a manner to view them—but, yes, he does have teeth that have been shaped into fangs. Besides that I found nothing unusual about him, of course one does need to get past the sharpened fangs.

I found him to be polite, articulate, and well-versed on the subject of vampirism. I sat and listened in fascination while he taught me the basics of those who consider and live the life of a modern-day vampire. The first thing he explained to me was that there are three categories into which most vampires fall.

First you have sanguine vampires, who are those who need to drink blood in order to feel that they can live normal healthy lives. They feel that the blood gives them a certain energy that they do not get otherwise. This type of vampire will drink blood from other humans, or some may use animal blood, while others have been known to drink their own blood.

The second type of vampire is the succubus vampire. This vampire is a sexually draining vampire who receives its needs from "feeding" on others via sexual activity. The more sexual activity they engage in, the more alive and connected they feel.

The most common type of vampire is known as the psychic vampire. The psychic vampire drains people of their energy and feeds on their emotions to fill themselves with certain needs missing in their own makeup. I think we all have come across such

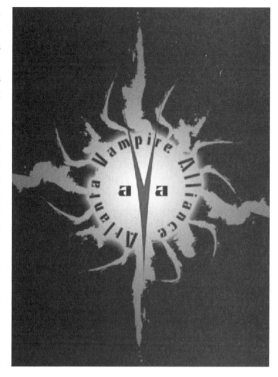

Logo of the Atlanta Vampire Alliance.

a person, be it in one's family or at work or among groups of friends that simply leave you exhausted and drained when you are around them. Most of us can peg people like this and do all we can to avoid them. Many do not realize they are practicing these energy-draining events and just walk around the world sucking the life out of the people around them as the only way they know how to interact, cope, and survive.

The truly dangerous vampires in my view are those who intentionally—and with skill—go about finding victims to drain spiritually in order to fill their own lifeless souls with the energy of others. Those who behave in this fashion are often in some shape or form part of the Psychic Vampire family. It is wise to distance yourself from them as soon as you realize that you are in their company, as they seem to feed endlessly without satisfaction.

I found out while talking to Redforce, my knowledge-filled Vampire, that with the invention of the Internet, web cams, and the various voice options, unscrupulous psychic vampires are now able to feed on unsuspecting people who populate the Internet chat rooms. No member of good standing in the vampire community would take advantage of the unsuspecting in such a manner.

Redforce told me that meditation or concentration should be done before entering public areas in order to defend against such energy vampires. One method of "shielding" is to visualize yourself in a protective globe or a heavy suit. I wear crystals and quartz and always pray to my guardian angels before advancing into the unknown. I feel the Internet is always a place of unknown danger, and I protect myself constantly. If an IPV enters a chat area that I am visiting, I place them on mute or ignore them from my screen. In real life I pray and rebuff those who wish to drain me of my energy by simply refusing to give them my time or attention. I just leave the room or area. It is as easy as just walking away.

I asked Redforce what would happen to the different types of vampires if they are not able to drink blood when they need to, or engage in sexual activity, or drain the energy from someone else. He told me that most can control their vampire lifestyle, but it has been known now and then for a vampire to do what is called "vamping out," which is a nice way to say "has a hissy fit" when in need for their vampire fix! He said they might do outlandish things until they can refuel the needs of their vampire lifestyle. I thought that would be a good time to keep distance between the vampires and me!

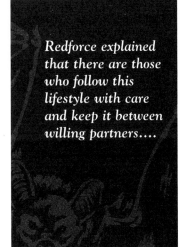

Redforce explained that there are those who follow this lifestyle with care and keep it between willing partners....

Redforce explained that there are those who follow this lifestyle with care and keep it between willing partners and that there are those who are not as kind and who can be dangerous. He stressed, however, that most who practice this lifestyle tend to stay to themselves and do not try to cause harm to those not in their circles. Of course, you have exceptions, and that is why we all need to be aware of those around us.

Redforce also told me that groups of people exist who are on missions to kill vampires. They try to locate those who live these lifestyles so they can drive a stake through their hearts. I thought he was kidding when he told me this, but sadly he was completely serious. I found the idea of people hunting other people who engage in a lifestyle different from theirs in order to drive a stake into their hearts rather terrifying. I hope anyone considering such actions understands that to do so is to commit cold-blooded murder.

I know that I was fortunate to come upon this young man. I am fully aware that there are many involved in this area who have taken it over the line and beyond unhealthy and dangerous limits. I also now know there are people like this man and his lady friend Vampypup who are just into something different from the norm, but harmless to those not interested in what they practice.

I also realize that the psychic vampires that prowl through the chat rooms and our lives now have a name and that we can reject them from attaching to our energy.

How Does a Real Vampire Define a Vampire?

"The fact is," Merticus, the administrator for Voices of the Vampire Community (VVC), said, "we tend not to. Vampires have an emerging identity that's built from the experience of being as they are. Vampires use introspection, self-awareness,

Logo of the Voices of the Vampire Community.

and the sharing of their experiences with others to create a collectively-discovered picture of what it means to be a vampire. This is entirely a process of self-discovery, so rather than there being some central vampiric ideal that we're aspiring to, we think of what a vampire is by thinking of what we know to be true of ourselves, and of the similarities in experience that others like us share.

"Many vampires are nocturnal and have difficulty with school and day shift work. Many are visually photosensitive and get physically ill from sun exposure. Others will mention having unusual sensory perceptions from the basic five senses, like light and smell sensitivity, to more esoteric extrasensory experiences. Many vampires reported seeing ghosts, having psychic dreams, or perceiving spirits, but some vampires have never had any ESP [extrasensory perception] or paranormal experiences. There are other experiences that may go along with being a vampire, but they aren't well-understood or universal enough to provide us with a definition of vampirism."

Merticus said that many misconceptions about the modern-day vampire community arise because so many of its members use the word "vampire" in a metaphorical sense and outsiders tend to ignore the context of its use. "The press and pop media gleefully ignore the metaphoric use of the word 'vampire' and leap to cinematic conclusions about those who identify themselves as vampires. Of course, they never really firmly establish what a 'vampire' is, much less the details of the vampire delusion. This is because members of the vampire community don't really think they are vampires. The label has been taken as a statement of identification, not with myth or fiction, but with one another, and the experiences that real vampires seem to share. This leads to the misconception that modern vampires identify with fictional vampires, and also to the misconception that members of this community are an extreme manifestation of another subculture—role-playing gamers, vampire fiction enthusiasts, Goths, or even body modification or blood fetishists. These diverse subcultures have all been erroneously referenced as recruiting grounds for the modern vampire subculture.

"The only common ground that vampires generally agree upon is that vampires share a need to feed on either blood or psychic energy in order to sustain their well-being. The need to feed, and the associated blood hunger or energy deficit are the only things that the Vampire Community can agree on that we know set us apart from other people. At this time, there is no scientific theory explaining why vampires need to feed, or why they tend to do so in very particular ways. It's at the center of the vampiric identity, intensely experienced, and yet to this day unexplainable. We hope that one day this need will be better understood and that our study will serve as a catalyst for increasing scientific and medical interest in future research into this phenomenon.

"One of the things we hope to accomplish by distributing data from the Vampirism and Energy Work Research Study is to put some of that old prejudice to rest by allowing vampires to speak for themselves about their own personal ethics, beliefs, and practices. Contrary to a common misconception, vampires are highly concerned with the effect their actions have on the people around them. The community has collectively put a lot of effort into the discussion of how to be a balanced and positive presence rather than parasitic."

Paranormal Researchers Meet the Vampires of San Francisco

On September 29, 2007, Paul Dale Roberts, General Manager and Ghost-writer of Haunted and Paranormal Investigations of Northern California, and Shannon McCabe, President of H.P.I. learned about The Vampire Tour of San Francisco from Ricardo Pustanio of Haunted America Tours (Ricardo is responsible for many of the brilliant illustrations in this book). Paul and Shannon added paranormal investigator Chris Grissom to the psychic safari and the three of them headed to San Francisco in Shannon's Ectoplasmamobile (also known as Ecto 1), with Shannon driving. Paul Dale Roberts related the following

We headed over to the elegant Hamilton Hotel to meet with a number of vampires. I glimpsed a lady in black approaching us. It was our first vampire of the evening. She calls herself Mina Harker (a character from Bram Stoker's *Dracula*). Her real name is Kitty Burns. Kitty had hosted a vampire tour in Transylvania on two occasions and once spent the night in Dracula's Castle. She hosted one tour with Eddie Munster, also known as Butch Patrick of the great old television series *The Munsters*.

Kitty explained that she got the idea for a vampire tour of San Francisco after she had booked a vampire tour in New Orleans during a business trip. She is a published playwright, so she thought, why not start her own tour? She immediately started writing a script for the tour, and she has now been giving the tour for six years. She says the tour is more lighthearted and that it doesn't really dwell on the dark side of vampirism.

We discussed various vampire clubs in existence around San Francisco, and how some people embrace the vampire culture. Kitty mentioned the role-playing vampire game called Masquerade.

I mention to Kitty that role-playing games like Masquerade can sometimes get out of hand. For a couple examples: A group of three teenagers were charged with the bludgeoning death of a Florida couple, the parents of a fourth girl in their group. These teenagers were involved in the fantasy role-playing game Vampire. Police said the teenagers "tortured puppies" and even "drank one another's blood." Police said [the teens] were attracted to vampires by a best-selling role-playing game.

A Virginia Beach man was sentenced to 26 years in prison for sexually molesting and biting eight teenage girls he had recruited for his vampire family through the playing of a game in which players assumed the roles of ancient vampires.

Kitty said that this is the dark side of vampirism that she shuns. Kitty explained that she dresses for the tour and wears a vampire costume of all black. Many Goths have taken her tour. One time Kitty said that she was approached by a real vampiress during the tour. The vampiress placed her hand on her shoulder and said, "Some of us really exist, darling."

A Virginia Beach man was sentenced to 26 years in prison for sexually molesting and biting eight teenage girls....

After I interviewed Kitty, I went over to the park across the street to interview two more vampires, Cole and Rhiannon. Rhiannon, a lovely, red-haired vampiress, tells me that she met Cole at a vampire oriented club called The Glass Cat when it was having a vampire ball. They have been friends ever since. Cole is a handsome young man, who wears a black trench coat, black shirt, black pants, black tie, and has long black hair. He definitely looks the part of a vampire. The reason why vampires wear black, Rhiannon and Cole explain, is because black is an absorbent color.

Cole states that when he was 17 years old, he had misconceptions of vampirism based on the vampires in Hollywood movies. When he met a woman who explained to him what vampirism is really about, he knew that true vampirism applied to his own persona.

Rhiannon said she didn't realize what it was at first, but she knew something was different about her, starting from what she had begun to sense in the third grade. She felt other people's energy; she felt empathy for others; she could feel people's energy signatures left behind on objects, sort of like psychometrics (object reading). She would walk past a school desk and feel the energy signature of the person who had sat on that desk.

Cole says that the scientific community needs to catch-up and discover what vampirism really is. It could be referred to as bio-deficiency syndrome, as he likes to call it. Cole elaborates and says that certain people that people call vampires, don't create enough energy within their beings and must acquire energy from others. Blood is a source of energy. Cole said that at times he takes in two or three teaspoons of blood. Other vampires may take their energy from ambient energy sources, such as from a Black Sabbath concert, where there is a high abundance of energy.

Rhiannon says perhaps vampires should be called energy absorbers. She does better from one person, a willing host to her energy feeding. She and Cole can absorb energy from a touch and do not attempt to take energy from an unwilling host. The touch can last from 30 seconds to a minute. I asked Rhiannon and Cole how they acquired their canines. Both have fangs that stand out, but they told me that their fangs are actually natural.

A number of vampire clubs thrive in San Francisco.

What about vampires that get their boost from the physical exertion of others? Or sexual vampires, a person who goes from one partner to another, acquiring energy from their conquests?

Cole tells me that in all cases, it's energy they are acquiring. To have sex is to exert energy. To be physical, such as when you are being pushed to do a lot of exercises, is exerting energy.

I can only wonder if Army drill sergeants who push soldiers over the limits are energy vampires. I can only wonder if playboys who go from one conquest to another, are also energy vampires.

When I brought up the darker side of vampirism, such as the serial killer Richard Trenton Chase (also known as The Vampire of Sacramento), Cole tells me that psychos are psychos, and they don't have to be vampires to be serial killers. Cole says that he is aware of 10 true vampires in San Francisco.

Now it is time for the Vampire Tour to commence. Kitty takes on the character of Mina Harker, and she tells of falling victim to Dracula. She discusses Bram Stoker's *Dracula*, and she elaborates in detail her transformation from a living human being to a vampiress. She has placed black lining around her eyes. Her skin is pale white. She wears a black cape, and her outfit is all black. Mina carries a candle holder with lighted candles as she starts her tour. She discusses everything about an underground vampire culture that originates at Nob Hill.

She blurs fiction with history as she talks about the following.

The Grace Church

Mina tells about the battleship *General Harrison* and the many ships that are part of the landfill that San Francisco is built upon. Beneath San Francisco are buried opium dens and brothels. Mina begins with a few vampire myths that Hollywood has perpetuated, such as that vampires cannot walk into churches.

While Mina is talking about the graveyard of ships that San Francisco is built upon, towering behind us is the majestic Grace Church where once Charles Crocker, the 1860s railroad tycoon, lived before the church was built. Crocker was also the founder of the Crocker Bank. Mina discusses the Wall of Spite that Crocker built around his neighbor's house in an effort to get him to move. She also described the presence of skull and crossbones near the wall. Mina reports that a series of fires at the church had been blamed on the vampire community.

She says one of old San Francisco's most colorful characters, Joshua Norton, the self-proclaimed Emperor of the United States and Protector of Mexico, couldn't have been a mere mortal, that he must have been a vampire to excel with the number of accomplishments achieved during his reign. Mina connects Dracula to Emperor Norton and goes on to discuss a Masonic cemetery. She tells how the Bay Bridge may be renamed the Norton Bridge.

Nob Spring Cleaners/Nob Hill Café

Nob Spring Cleaners is next to Nob Hill Café, and Mina explains that Jack the Ripper (who she claims is a vampire) came to San Francisco and changed his name to Choker Barnes. She claims that at the cafe the greatest vampire versus mortal battle happened, in which 20 people were killed. It was because a vampire den was discovered at the café, and since vampires are very secretive, they fought the mortals to retain that secrecy.

Mina elaborates on another Hollywood myth and talks about Buffy the Vampire Slayer. She says that Buffy's claim to be able to kill vampires with any type of wood is an untruth. Vampires can only be killed with ash wood, the wood from the cross on which Jesus Christ was crucified. Mina says that San Francisco City Hall is the second most haunted building in San Francisco and that Alcatraz takes the Number One spot.

James Flood's Home, Which Is Now Pacific Union Club

Mina explains how the vampire community gave James Flood protection and security, because they respected his knowledge on business affairs. Flood was one of four men who controlled the bonanza silver mines of Nevada's Comstock lode, the richest in history. The vampires wanted to make Flood one of them, but James stood up to the vampires and proclaimed that he came into the world as a mortal and he was leaving this world as a mortal. James Flood had an underground tunnel from his mansion to his mistress's house across the street. Some underground tunnels in San Francisco lead to brothels, Mina explains.

When Mina entered James Flood's home one night, she heard an unearthly voice tell her "It's true!" regarding an earlier comment that Mina had made in the house.

The Fairmont Hotel

Many movies have been made at this hotel from *Vertigo* to *The Rock*. The seventh floor is reputed to be very haunted. It could be haunted by World War II soldiers who once stayed on that floor.

A lady of the evening was murdered in the tower area of the hotel, and a guest once saw the phantom of this murder victim as she lay on a four poster bed that no longer exists in the hotel. The ghost was dressed in a red teddy, and she actually talked to the guest. When the guest told hotel management, they explained to him that they no longer had four poster beds in the room. When they accompanied the guest back to the room, there was no woman lying on a four- poster bed in a red teddy. The guest was startled and realized that he encountered the phantom of the murdered woman that night.

The penthouse of this hotel is reputed to be haunted, and Mae West's ghost is sometimes seen near the Penthouse. Chris Grissom pointed out to Shannon McCabe that there was a figure in one of the darkened windows that peeked out at the crowd. Shannon saw the figure, too. It was a head moving swiftly to the window, then moving back to hide. Chris and Shannon both thought this was quite odd. If it was a normal person, why wouldn't he or she just look normally from their window upon the crowd. Why go back and hide behind the wall? Could this have been a phantom? The tour was fun and informative and Mina presented the information with enthusiasm and delight.

As I was leaving the tour, I got a tap on the right shoulder. I turned around, and a man dressed all in black asked me how I enjoyed the tour. I told him it was a blast and wished it didn't have to end. He smiled and said that I have a lot more to learn about vampires.

I asked him what his name was. With a hypnotic stare, he said "Lee Stat" and walked backwards into the shadows. I tried to follow him, but he was nowhere around. As I rejoined Shannon and Chris, I thought about the name. Did he say "Lee Stat" or "Lestat" (the name of a vampire in the popular Anne Rice novels)? Hmmmm.

The Vampire Ghost of Guadalajara

This chapter was contributed by Pastor Robin Swope, who is known as the Paranormal Pastor. Swope has been a Christian minister for more than 15 years in both Mainline and Evangelical denominations. He has served as a missionary to Burkina Faso, West Africa, and ministered to the homeless in New York City's Hell's Kitchen. He is the founder and chief officiate of Open Gate Ministerial Services and a member of St. Paul's United Church of Christ in Erie, Pennsylvania. As Pastor Swope tells the story....

Maria had always been an inquisitive child. Her family had lived on Nardo Street in Guadalajara, Mexico, all of her young life. Like most of the children in her neighborhood the streets were their playground, and she had explored every nook and cranny that surrounded her home.

One spot that truly fascinated her was the cemetery that was only a few blocks away, El Panteon de Belen. It is an ancient cemetery with many supernatural legends surrounding its deceased occupants.

Maria was only two years old when she first went there on November 2, during a festival for the Day of the Dead. The cemetery had been turned into a museum long ago, and the Day of the Dead celebrations would go on into the night with puppet shows and plays performed throughout the graveyard's property. She didn't know when she first heard the story of the vampire's grave. It seemed as though it had been a part of her experience of El Panteon de Belen for as long as she could remember.

The story is told that long ago there was a vampire who stalked the countryside of Guadalajara in the early nineteenth century. Livestock and newborn babies were attacked in the middle of the night, and all of their blood was drained from their lifeless bodies. The local citizens were on alert, and during the dark hours of early morning a man was seen skulking back into his house after another reported attack of El Vampiro.

One should exercise great caution when exploring an alleged vampire's grave (illustration by Ricardo Pustanio).

A mob was formed, and they burst into his house and killed him while he lay in his bed. A crude wooden stake was driven through his heart and he was buried unceremoniously in El Panteon de Belen. According to the folklore of the region, the stake was fed by his preternatural blood, and soon it grew into a massive tree that burst open the tomb of El Vampiro. Legend has it that if you cut a limb from the tree, you will see blood mingled with the sap ooze from the stump. An old prophecy claims that once the tree completely overgrows the grave and pushes the coffin up to the ground, El Vampiro will be free to rise again and take his revenge upon the citizens of Guadalajara.

This story fascinated and frightened Maria, and she would often stare at the opened hole of the crypt of El Vampiro whenever she visited the cemetery. Sometimes she was sure she thought something moved in the shadows, but her mother told her that her imagination was overactive from watching too many movies on television. But as she grew, the fascination with the crypt and the certainty that something was moving in its stygian darkness motivated her to visit the grave more frequently.

When she was 11, her curiosity about the site was piqued, and she decided to investigate the grave up close without anyone to bother her. After her parents had gone to bed she sneaked out of the house after midnight and stealthily walked the busy streets of Guadalajara. Then she climbed over the walls of El Panteon de Belen. The caretaker was usually guarding the grounds with his dog, but luckily for her they had retreated to some location or another, and she was not harassed as she made her way through the moldy and decaying crypts to the great tree.

When she arrived at the grave of El Vampiro, she stood undecided for a few moments as fear gripped her heart, but she then cast these feelings aside and boldly skirted the makeshift fence that was erected to keep out the curious and the vandals during normal visiting hours. The cracked top of the crypt seemed like a bottomless pit as she carefully crawled toward it. She saw no movement now, only a gaping black pit where nothing was discernable.

Fear seized her heart, but she once again pushed these emotions aside and moved on with sheer determination. She let her legs drop down into the hole and took out the small candle and lighter that she had tucked away in her dress pockets. With a quick flick she lit the wick, and the small illumination gave her just enough light to find a footing in the crypt.

She lowered herself down only to find herself in a cramped oblong tomb not much larger than the metal casket she stood upon. There was just enough head room for her to slouch while on her knees as she beheld the old iron casket in the dim light. The metal was thin and very rusty, and it seemed to give a little as she distributed her weight on its lid. There was some writing on the lid at the head, and she scooted herself to get a closer look.

When she did so, the metal began to buckle and flake as the corroded metal gave way, and a small hole began to form at her knee no bigger than a baseball. She shifted her weight away and leaned to read the writing, but it was too rusted and the lighting too dim for her to distinguish what the old lettering actually said.

It was then she felt something touch her leg.

It was something that was coming out of the coffin.

She screamed and bumped her head on the inner lid of the crypt, but the daze that overcame her did not prevent her from quickly making her way out of the crypt's hole with remarkable speed. She ran all the way home, and it was not until she opened the door did she see the blood. It was trickling down her arm from a cut on the top of her head, and she had bled so much that the top half of her dress was a crimson stain.

When she arrived at the grave of El Vampiro, she stood undecided for a few moments as fear gripped her heart....

She managed to sneak in her house undetected and quickly disrobed and washed the cut on her head. Luckily it did not seem that bad and the blood had stopped flowing. Her hair would hide it as it healed, and she washed her dress in the sink to hide all evidence of her nightly excursion.

She did not sleep at all that night though, for with every slight sound outside of her window she was brought back to the terror she experienced in the crypt. She was sure El Vampiro was after her. After all, not only did something come out of the coffin and touch her, she had bled in the vampire's crypt. Surely, once he tasted her blood he would want more.

She felt sick the following day, partially because of the lack of sleep and partially because of the throbbing headache she felt from the wound on her head. But she did her household chores without complaining or without telling her parents what had transpired the night before. Even though exhausted from the previous night without sleep and a full day of work, that evening she could not rest, but instead, lay rocking in her bed for hours, fearful of the thing in the crypt. Finally she succumbed to exhaustion and fitfully fell into a half wakeful slumber.

She awoke to see a dark figure standing over her bed. It was a tall man with no discernable features who just stood there watching. Maria screamed and her parents ran to her bedside. As soon as the lights were turned on the figure vanished, but the young girl was hysterical. In tears she confessed to her parents of the previous night's adventure and the thing that she had seen at her bed. Her parents were terrified—not because of the dark figure, but because their daughter had been roaming the streets in the middle of the night and had hurt herself. They calmed her down and assured her that it was just a figure of her imagination.

The next day they brought her to a doctor who tended to her wound and found that there was a slight infection. He, too, assured little Maria that the specter at the end of her bed was just an illusion from her wound and lack of sleep.

But the dark figure returned the next night.

Maria awoke to pain on her head, and the dark figure was leaning over her. The girl's screams alerted her parents, and this time when they came into her room they found that her pillow had a spot of blood on it. Maria's wound had seemed to open once again. The girl was certain that it was El Vampiro, taking another drink of her blood.

After they had once again dressed her wound, the girl refused to sleep alone in the bed, so her mother sat by, resting in a chair. For two nights the mother slept in the room, and even though Maria slept soundly, she seemed to weaken. The wound also

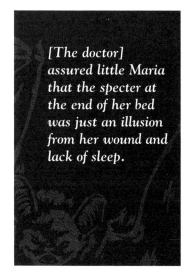

[The doctor] assured little Maria that the specter at the end of her bed was just an illusion from her wound and lack of sleep.

refused to heal. The doctor had no idea why the wound would seem to heal during the day, but reopen during the night. Maria was adamant that it was the work of the vampire ghost that attacked her, but her parents just regarded this as foolishness.

That all changed on the third night after Maria's fateful excursion. The mother sat with Maria for a while, until she fell off to sleep. Then she made herself ready to retire into her own bedroom, but first she stopped in the bathroom to freshen up before bed. On her way to her bedroom she quickly checked on Maria. Peering through the half-opened door she saw her daughter lying asleep in bed and what appeared to be a man standing over her in the darkness.

She screamed for her husband and burst the door open. In the half second before the specter disappeared, she swore she saw an entity look up at her with glowing eyes of fire. And once again the wound on Maria's head was bleeding.

The family was now convinced that they were dealing with no normal wound, but they had no idea what to do. While Maria's family was not religious, Maria's grandmother was a stout Pentecostal and she asked Rev. Guivez, her minister, for help. Although he had no formal training in such matters, he did believe in the supernatural powers of darkness and he decided to help anyway he could.

Reverend Guivez visited with the family one night and talked at length with Maria. He anointed the wound with oil and prayed over her and the family in her bedroom. Immediately a porcelain doll flew off a nearby shelf and crashed into the wall just above the Reverend's head. The minister was shaken up, but he kept his wits about him. He immediately demanded that the supernatural activity cease and that the entity who was appearing and causing harm to the girl leave the room at once.

Within seconds the room became cold and a mist began to swirl next to Maria. Every person there swore it looked like it was taking the shape of a man. Reverend Guivez immediately invoked the name of Christ and demanded that it cease and desist, and to his surprise the mist began to fade. With newfound authority he demanded again that the entity leave the house immediately.

Suddenly they heard the house cat in the next room screech in terror. The father turned to see it run frantically around the house as if insane. It then jumped out an open window and ran into the heavy traffic of Nardo Street. It was run over and killed instantly. The apparitions stopped, and within a few days Maria's wound began to heal for good. She never again went to El Panteon de Belen, not even to celebrate the Day of the Dead. Maria grew up to be a well-adjusted young woman with a fantastic story to tell.

After people in the church and the neighborhood heard of Maria's tale, Reverend Guivez was called to many individuals' homes and places where spiritual deliverance was needed. He quickly found himself doing more exorcisms than marriages in his ministry at the Pentecostal church.

According to Pastor Robin Swope's subsequent research, the tree over El Vampiro's crypt was cut down. Only a stump remains. There was no blood as the woodcutters took the saw to the old wood. But that has not stopped the stories of El Vampiro's hauntings. To this day his crypt has a vast hole on the top, beckoning visitors to El Panteon de Belen to come in for a closer look.

Ghosts that Bite

Janice said that she had gone to a movie with some girlfriends. She said good-bye to them in the small hamburger place where they had stopped for a snack afterward. When she got home, she went right to bed. She had promised her boss that she would come in early the next morning to help with inventory.

She had only lain there for a few minutes when Janice was certain that she heard something bumping into things in her bedroom. She sat up and looked around. She didn't turn on her bedside lamp, because there is a streetlight outside her apartment that lights things up inside. She saw no one or anything. She was just settling back down when she felt a pressure on the side of her bed, as if someone were lying down beside her.

She seemed to see something blacker than the dim light in the rest of the room, but she knew that she felt a heavy pressure cover the entire length of her body. She struggled against the weight of the invisible thing, but it seemed as though it had a dozen hands, all pinning her down against the mattress. And then it began to bite her.

"At first," Janice said, "it began making little nips and nibbles on my neck. I was terrified. I could not see anything that could be making these little kind of 'love bites' on me."

Janice tried to scream, but she could not make any sound come out. And the effort seemed to make the invisible thing bite her even harder on her shoulders and arms.

"I was struck dumb with terror," she said. "There seemed to be a deep cold that seeped through my blankets from whatever it was on top of me. Finally, in desperation, I managed to scream, 'For the love of God, leave me alone.' And, honest to God, it left me. It was gone."

Janice said that she wouldn't blame anyone if they thought she was crazy, but that is what happened to her. An invisible something—a ghost, a demon, whatever, manifested one night to start biting her. Janice said that she had no previous paranor-

Sometimes even the sweetest appearing of entities can have very sharp teeth! (illustration by Ricardo Pustanio)

mal experiences. She is not a witch or a Satanist who believes in such things as demon lovers, and she has no idea what she might have done to provoke such an attack.

"Do these kinds of things just happen to people for no reason at all?" Janice asked.

Of course the only honest answer is that they do happen to unsuspecting men and women all the time, but there is undoubtedly some reason behind such occurrences—or at least a reason that makes sense to some entity on some multidimensional level of reality.

A Ghost with Teeth Came Out of the Ouija Board

Linda said that she got into the habit of working the Ouija board with her roommates in college. They didn't work it every night, but almost always on weekends. If they didn't have dates on Saturday nights, they would work the board for kicks. If they had dates, they would work the Ouija when they got back to the room and ask it questions about the guys they had been with that night.

When she was home on holiday break, she decided to pass the time by working the board by herself. Both her parents were downstairs watching television. Her younger brother and sister were out on dates. What the heck, Linda decided, she would see what the spirits of Christmas Past, Present, and Future had to tell her. What she got that night was some activity from a nasty entity who went way past Scrooge for meanness.

"Some really foul things came through," she said. "Some really obscene nasties. The board had just started doing that a couple of weeks ago, and I decided I didn't want to expose myself to any more of such garbage when I was alone by myself."

After about 20 minutes of trying to get interested in a novel, Linda's attention was directed toward a strange scratching sound in a corner of the room. At first it sounded like a rat—which seemed improbable, but certainly not impossible.

"Then I swear that I saw a book pull itself out about three inches from a shelf," Linda said. "I started feeling really eerie, like when you watch a spooky movie all alone."

"Then it was like someone pushed me down on the bed and started to bite me on my arms and legs," Linda said. "I couldn't see anything. Whatever it was was completely invisible. Then it felt like two hands squeezing my breasts, and I thought, 'Oh, no, whatever the hell you are, you ain't biting the twins.'"

Linda got up and left her room. There was no way that she was going to sleep in her bed that night, and she knew that she couldn't tell her folks about it or they would probably accuse her of doing drugs.

"I came down to the family room where my parents were and made like I was going to watch the late movie with them. Then, when they went to bed, I just slept on the couch that night. The next morning, the whole thing seemed silly, but I did get rid of that Ouija board."

And, Linda added, when she returned to college, she suggested that she and her roommates put the board away and start playing Scrabble or something. After she told them of her negative experience, one of her roomies wanted to try the board and see if it would happen again. Thankfully, her other roommate agreed that they had probably been skating on thin psychic ice with the board and relying too much on its guidance. The Ouija board got placed under their shoes in the closet.

They never suspected that a fanged spirit would actually emerge from the Ouija board.

He Tried to Attack Her in Life and He Returned to Torment Her after His Death

Vanessa Hughes had never been a happy girl. Her mother had died while giving birth to her; her father had resented Vanessa for the seven years following her birth until he, too, died. The orphaned girl went to live with her older sister, Claire, who was married to Evan Cooper and occupied with rearing her own family. Vanessa felt unloved, unwanted, and unhappy.

As she grew up, Vanessa became increasingly moody and was often depressed. This attitude did not endear her to her sister's family, and by the time Vanessa was 17 years old, she was a bitter young lady. Despite her bouts with depression, Vanessa was a very lovely girl. Her figure had filled out more than adequately, and her long thick brown hair shone as it tumbled down her back. Her eyes lacked luster, but nature had endowed her with the beautiful bone structure of a classic beauty. Regretfully, the beauty of her face was cold, chiseled, for no inner light glowed from within.

There were many young men in the small town in Maine who were eager to date Vanessa, and she presented a considerable challenge to the young men of the early 1950s. By the teenaged standards of the twenty-first century, the 1950s were a time of innocence. Kids of that time would probably faint if they were to sit through an average motion picture of today with its nudity, open signs of affection between the sexes, scenes of love-making that do not cut away to waves crashing on the shore, or liberal use of profanity and the "F-word." Most teenagers of the 1950s were convinced that fire from Heaven would consume them if they uttered the "F-word." This time of social conservatism and sexual repression was the setting for Vanessa's experience with both sex and the supernatural.

Vanessa seldom went out, preferring to sit by herself and read. She was a withdrawn, introspective girl, and she seldom socialized. George Peterson had made no secret of the fact that he liked Vanessa. He would come to the Cooper household, where Vanessa lived, and try to persuade her to take a drive with him. Evan Cooper, Vanessa's brother-in-law, took an instant disliking to young Peterson.

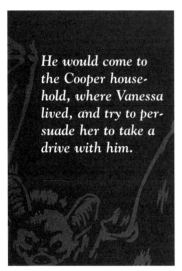

He would come to the Cooper household, where Vanessa lived, and try to persuade her to take a drive with him.

"Claire," Evan told his wife, "you be sure and talk to your sister and tell her we don't want that Peterson fellow coming around here. He comes over with his fancy foreign car, bragging about his daddy's business, and ogling Vanessa. I won't have it, Claire. You tell her I said so." Vanessa sullenly heard the news from her sister.

Whereas before Vanessa had been indifferent to George Peterson, she now became interested. So she was not supposed to see him, was that it? Well, she would show them. As soon as Vanessa was alone, she phoned George. She explained to him that he had been asked to stay away from the Cooper house. She requested his compliance.

"But George," she said coolly into the receiver. "My brother-in-law said nothing about *me* coming over to see *you*. He just said you weren't supposed to come *over here*."

George chuckled on the other end of the phone. "Okay, baby, I catch your drift. You want to meet me tonight? I'll pick you up in front of the drugstore a couple of blocks from your house."

"I'll be there," Vanessa answered.

George Peterson knew he was being used by Vanessa to spite her family, but it didn't bother him. He was confident that he could use that rebellious attitude to his own advantage. George picked up Vanessa at the appointed corner and suggested they go for a drive.

"Sure, why not," Vanessa replied, nervously, already tiring of her game.

The car took off for the outskirts of the city. Several minutes later, George parked the car in a secluded, wooded area.

"All right, Vanessa Hughes, let's see what you got," George said with a wide grin as he reached out for her.

Vanessa's eyes widened with fear, and she drew back as George tried to close in on her.

"Just a little kiss," he promised her. "That's all. Otherwise, I won't touch you."

Feeling extremely nervous, Vanessa leaned toward George, her lips slightly parted. George placed his mouth on hers, waited for her to relax and grow accustomed to the sensation. Then he clamped an arm over both of her arms and moved his free hand toward her breast.

"Just a little kiss," he muttered, mocking her. His hand closed roughly over her breast.

Vanessa struggled violently to free herself. Her stomach clenched with nausea at the brutal young man's touch, and she feared she would vomit.

"Stop it!" she cried, repulsed and horrified. "Stop it!"

A thought suddenly came to her, something that her sister had told her to do years before should she ever be attacked by a man. Vanessa did not know if she would be able to do it or not, for George was much stronger than she and would probably guess her meaning before she could land a well-placed punch in his groin. Thinking furiously, Vanessa decided that her only hope lay in deceiving him. She stopped struggling and threw her arms around his neck. George was startled, but quickly returned the kiss.

The kiss was a long one, and Vanessa had to swallow several times to keep from being ill. Then she gasped and held up her hand. "Air," she explained, leaning back against the car seat. "I've got to breathe."

George leaned back against the seat, too, confident now that he would not have to fight her to get what he wanted. He sighed, prepared to turn to her again.

"Jeez!" he shrieked loudly, as Vanessa's fist, with surprising strength, thudded into his groin.

"Now take me home, George," she ordered coldly, "and don't you ever touch me again."

"Why, you little bitch," George snapped at her, his eyes livid with rage. He reached in his pocket, drew out a switchblade. Vanessa's eyes widened with terror, as the knife slowly inched toward her. Vanessa was frozen with fear. She could neither move nor cry out. George, too, seemed mesmerized. Somewhere inside of himself he recognized that he was discovering a degree of violence he had not known he possessed. With trembling hands he brought the blade to Vanessa's throat. Steel contacted flesh, and two tiny drops of blood started to gleam in the moonlight.

All at once two headlights illuminated the car.

Someone else was approaching. George hastily closed the blade, shoved it back into his pocket. He stepped on the gas and gunned out of the area. Vanessa sat hunched on her side of the car, clutching her throat and crying softly. The vehicle proceeded at a dangerous speed into town, until Vanes-

He took out a blade, ready to kill....

sa could see the lights of her own house. George screeched to a halt. He refused to look at her.

Vanessa fumbled with the car door, slammed it behind her and ran to the house. Scarcely had the car door shut when George took off into the night. It was later discovered that he left town that evening. He was neither seen nor heard from again.

Vanessa let herself into the house with her key. Gratefully, she noted that everyone else was in bed. No one would trouble her. Inside her own room, Vanessa clutched her sides and rocked back and forth on her bed. Try as she would, she could think of nothing but George's hands all over her body and the cold steel blade as it had pressed against her throat. She got up and checked herself in a mirror. Only a slight mark showed.

"Thank God that other car came," Vanessa thought to herself. For the briefest moment, she allowed herself to think of what would have happened had the other car not arrived. In her mind's eye she saw the blade cut raggedly through her neck until with a small yelp she ran for the bathroom and vomited.

Vague forms and shadows drifted through her mind, accompanied by strange thoughts.

It took several minutes for the fear reaction to leave Vanessa. When she had finally calmed herself, she returned to her bedroom. Now that her initial fright had passed, Vanessa had an opportunity to regard the incident in a different light. She thought of her sister's talk, explaining that George was no longer welcome at the house. She remembered the resentment she had felt, and her subsequent call to George. It was true, she thought dismally, she had asked for the treatment she had received in the car. Was that what she had wanted all along, she wondered? Had she wanted a risqué petting session in the car just to prove to Claire and Evan that she was old enough to choose her own friends and do what she wanted?

Vanessa was overcome with guilt. Over and over again she dredged up the mental image of George rubbing his hands over her breasts, slipping his hand up her skirt. She wanted to disgust herself, to prove to herself that she wasn't as wicked as she now imagined herself to be. She wallowed repeatedly in the scene until her eyes filled with tears and she could take no more.

"I'm dirty," she told herself. "Dirty, filthy, unclean."

At last she was able to close her eyes and sleep, but her rest was fitful, uneasy. Vague forms and shadows drifted through her mind, accompanied by strange thoughts. She dreamed she saw the faces of Claire's family, smiling lovingly upon her. There was Claire, Evan, and the children, Rose and Sammy. Then, as she was beginning to return their smiles, their faces became ghastly caricatures of themselves, and Vanessa found herself staring into the eyes of a horde of angry demons.

The following morning Vanessa determined to tell no one what had befallen her the night before, or of the strange dream she had. In the ensuing days, she became increasingly nervous and almost completely withdrawn. Evan Cooper began to complain to his wife about her sister's attitude.

"At least we won't have to worry about that Peterson creep coming around anymore," Evan announced at dinner one night. "I heard at work today that he got killed in a car accident. He left town fast for some reason and got himself killed somewhere in Vermont. Good riddance to bad rubbish, I say."

Vanessa felt a wave of nausea flood over her and she excused herself from the table. Had George got out of town because he was afraid that she would report the threat that he had made on her life, how he had nearly cut her throat? Was it her fault that he got killed in an accident?

Vanessa went to bed early. She was tired, she explained, and felt a headache coming on. Vanessa got into bed, slid her feet to the bottom. All at once she felt something moving, under the mattress, against her thigh.

Then something bit her. "A rat!" she thought immediately, as she jumped out of bed. "There's a rat in the mattress eating its way to the top." Vanessa called to her sister, asking Claire to come to the room. "There's a rat in the mattress," she insisted. "I felt it. It bit me."

Claire was convinced there was no rat in the mattress. Vanessa's ankle was bleeding. She must have cut herself on something, but Claire knew they had no rats in the house. Finally, Claire had to strip down the bed and prove to the increasingly distraught Vanessa that no rat had invaded her bed. Claire remade the bed and urged Vanessa to go to sleep.

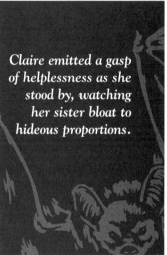

Claire emitted a gasp of helplessness as she stood by, watching her sister bloat to hideous proportions.

Vanessa had just lain back down when the two women saw a book rise off Vanessa's dresser, float across the room, and settle on a nearby chair, all of its own volition. They were astounded. There was no further phenomena that night.

Two nights later, however, Vanessa again complained of feeling ill and excused herself early. It was shortly before ten that evening, and Claire followed her sister a few moments later with a glass of water and two aspirins. When she saw Vanessa, she uttered a shout of horror, dropped the glass, and rushed to her sister's side.

Vanessa's hair stood completely on end, like the erect quills of a porcupine. Before Claire could reach her side, Vanessa had hopped out of bed, screaming that something was biting her. Claire managed to help her sister back into bed, but Vanessa had barely sunk her head onto the pillow when bloody scratches appeared on her arms and her body began to swell.

Claire emitted a gasp of helplessness as she stood by, watching her sister bloat to hideous proportions. Vanessa looked dreadful and she was moaning with pain. And now scratches appeared on her forehead. All the noise in the bedroom caused Evan and his brother Jim who was visiting the Coopers to come running into the bedroom. Just as the two crossed the threshold, a tremendous explosion sounded. Evan rushed to the window and looked outside for the source, but there was nothing to be seen.

Claire asked Evan to check on Rose and Sam and to be certain that they were asleep and not being disturbed by the incredible occurrences in Vanessa's room. Jim stood at the foot of Vanessa's bed and gaped at her distorted body. Three sharp raps, seemingly produced from somewhere within the room, sounded and Vanessa's body started slowly to return to normal size. With her family gathered around her, Vanessa slipped into an exhausted slumber, unable to give the astounded Coopers any clues as to the cause of her affliction.

Vanessa awakened the next morning, apparently none the worse for the physical ordeal that she had undergone. Claire had bandaged her scratches as she slept. Claire questioned her sister carefully, but Vanessa was able to give no explanation of what had happened.

Four days passed without incident, and the Cooper household was beginning to settle down once more. Vanessa seemed to be suffering no ill effects, though her nerves were noticeably shaken.

On the fifth night, once more at ten o'clock, things began happening again. This time Vanessa's body began to bloat much more violently and rapidly than before. Soon she was painfully swelled beyond recognition, and once again the family stood helplessly around her, not knowing what to do. The afflicted girl writhed and screamed with pain as bloody scratches appeared on her arms and legs.

While Claire tried to soothe Vanessa, the two men once more came running to the room and tried to hold her down. The sheets flew off the bed and hurled themselves into a corner of the room. Claire tried to pick them up, but they twisted like living beings, trying to elude her grasp. The only way the sheets could be induced to stay on the bed was if Evan, Jim, and Claire sat on different corners of the bed.

As the three were seated in this manner, the pillow upon which Vanessa's head fitfully rested shot out from under her and smacked Evan in the face. Then, as if controlled by some invisible force, it returned to its position under Vanessa's head. For some time the three grappled with this unseen intelligence attacking Vanessa, then, abruptly, the phenomena ended with the same three explosive sounds they had heard at the conclusion of the session five nights earlier. Once again, Vanessa fell into a deep sleep.

The Coopers knew they were dealing with something totally bizarre and beyond their capabilities. They were unsure as to whether anyone else in the community would be able to handle the situation, but they determined not to struggle through another episode unassisted. On that previous night, Rose and Sam had awakened and had begun screaming, wondering fearfully what was happening to Aunt Vanessa in her room.

Evan made up his mind to visit a prominent physician in the county, Dr. Myron Mitchell. Evan managed to take off a few hours from work the next day and called upon the doctor, explaining the bizarre circumstances as best as possible. Dr. Mitchell was intrigued, though he suspected his leg was being pulled by a clever hoax. Evan told him that they were not pulling any kind of prank and that the last thing that the family wanted was any kind of attention or publicity about the events occurring in their home. Finally, after much protesting, Dr. Mitchell promised to visit the Cooper home that evening.

Dr. Mitchell arrived shortly after 10 o'clock, ready to laugh along with the joke. Vanessa seemed to have broken the timetable of seizures spaced every five nights. Whatever was troubling her had settled down to serious, nightly attacks, and Dr. Mitchell was able to see with his own eyes that this was no prank. The girl before him was hideously distorted and very obviously in severe pain.

When he had the opportunity to examine her wounds, Dr. Mitchell stated that among the scratches there appeared to be a number of bite marks. It was as if something invisible was biting the teenager.

More violent phenomena began to manifest on that night. The furniture jumped around, the house rattled, and a series of loud explosions rocked the modest home. The manifestation was especially violent as Dr. Mitchell leaned over his patient and attempted to give her an examination. The pillow, which had flown into Evan's face the night before, again became airborne. The pillow flew around the room in dizzying circles until Evan angrily made a grab for it. The instant the man's fingers touched the pillow his hair stood up on end, as Vanessa's had done on one of the first nights of the disturbance. A look of shock flashed over his features. The pillow, seemingly having received the reaction it had been seeking, dutifully returned to Vanessa's bed and slid under her head. Dr. Mitchell completed his examination and turned to Claire, who was anxiously awaiting his diagnosis.

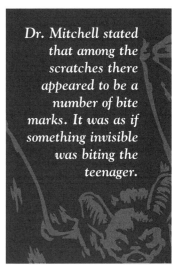

Dr. Mitchell stated that among the scratches there appeared to be a number of bite marks. It was as if something invisible was biting the teenager.

"I don't know what it is, Mrs. Cooper," Dr. Mitchell told her, shaking his head. "I've never seen anything like it. She appears to be in good health. I don't know how to explain the swelling or the marks that look like bites and scratches."

"But isn't there anything you can do, doctor? Look how she suffers!" The doctor could only shake his head once more. "I'm afraid there's nothing I can do. I think you need to take her to a specialist … or a priest … or an exorcist … not a small town doctor."

While Claire and the doctor stood conversing, the three loud knocks sounded once more, indicating that the phenomena would cease. "Watch her, Dr. Mitchell," Claire whispered. "That's the sign."

Dr. Mitchell watched with amazement as the swelling slowly went down, returning Vanessa's body to normal. As always, the stricken girl fell immediately into a deep slumber. These nightly episodes began to take their toll on young Vanessa. Each morning when she awakened, her body was progressively weaker. Claire feared that her sister's resistance would become so low that the girl would be susceptible to serious, more conventional diseases.

Claire was also distressed that there was no more hiding the truth from the children. Something terrible was happening to Aunt Vanessa. The next evening Dr. Mitchell arrived earlier, hoping to delay the trouble by giving Vanessa a heavy dosage of morphine. His plan did not work.

At precisely ten o'clock, a malicious laughter filled the room. Some entity seemed greatly amused at Dr. Mitchell's puny efforts to silence it. Vanessa went berserk, running around the bedroom and screaming hysterically. A methodical pounding noise sounded on the roof.

"Help me with her," Dr. Mitchell shouted to Jim and Evan. The two men sprang forward, and together the three of them managed to bring Vanessa under control. No sooner was Vanessa in bed, however, when a scratching noise sounded above the headboard.

Claire and the three men fixed their attention on the wall above the bed, as an invisible hand scratched out an ominous message: *Vanessa Hughes, I will kill you!*

"It's George's ghost," Vanessa said. "That's who has been biting me. Now he has come to kill me!"

Claire clapped a hand to her mouth and turned her frightened eyes to her husband. "I've had enough of this," Evan shouted to the room at large. "Leave us alone!" Evan hung his head. "I just feel so helpless!" he said as he drove an angry fist into the palm of his right hand. The entity that had entered the Cooper household seemed to have summoned enough energy to operate day and night.

As word of Vanessa's affliction spread, newsmen and psychic investigators converged on the Cooper home from around the country. Several managed to get interviews with members of the beleaguered household. It was Dr. Allen Clark, a parapsychologist, who finally persuaded Vanessa to unburden herself and speak of her terrible experience with George Peterson. It was clear to the researcher that the two events were related.

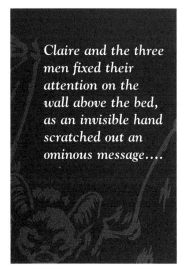

Claire and the three men fixed their attention on the wall above the bed, as an invisible hand scratched out an ominous message....

Three months after the disturbances had first begun, Vanessa finally collapsed from the constant physical strain. She contracted a severe case of hepatitis, with other complications. During the course of this illness, Vanessa lived with another sister, Mrs. Kelly Brooks of Tampa, Florida. While in the Brooks' home for a period of four months, Vanessa suffered no visitation from the terrible force that had attacked so viciously in Maine.

Two days after Vanessa returned to the Coopers, the phenomena resumed, stronger than ever. Vanessa was sitting in the living room, watching television, when she suddenly jumped up and started pointing to a corner of the room.

"Look at him there!" she cried, miserably. "It is George, and he says I cannot stay here. God, I wish I were dead!"

Claire calmed Vanessa and asked her what she had seen. Vanessa insisted that she had seen George Peterson standing in the corner. He had said that if she stayed overnight in the Cooper house he would set fire to it and burn it to the ground.

"Where shall I go," Vanessa moaned softly. "What shall I do? Who will take me in?"

Claire started to assure Vanessa that she always had a home with them when a sudden shower of lighted matches fell from nowhere. Vanessa collapsed, sobbing, on the floor. It was arranged for friends of the family to take Vanessa in for the night. The next morning Vanessa decided to stay with friends living on a small farm in northern Florida. She was determined to bring no more harm to the Coopers or to do anything to endanger her niece and nephew. From that point on, the manifestations ceased.

Psychic investigator Clark wrote a detailed report of his own assessment of the case. In his opinion, Vanessa Hughes was possessed by a fragmented portion of her own psyche, which had been severed due to the severe shock she had experienced the night George Peterson first tried to rape, then murder her. This shock was so severe that Vanessa could not tolerate thinking about it. It broke away from her, acting like an independent entity.

Vanessa had been convinced that she was in some way responsible for Peterson's actions, and her continued guilt had been the energy source that kept the "entity" alive for nearly 10 months. This guilt Vanessa felt most strongly in the presence of her brother-in-law, Evan Cooper, whose strict sense of morality constantly stalked Vanessa while she was living under his roof. Unconscious resentment of Evan's restrictive moral code became the second source of energy for the fragmented psyche; and on one level, the manifestations were designed specifically to irritate Evan Cooper, such as the incidents with the pillow.

Once out of the restrictive atmosphere of the Cooper home, Vanessa was able to relax and quite literally "pull herself together." With the cessation of the seizures, she was able to slowly regain her strength and once more think about living a normal life.

Her nightmarish experience had taught her several things, many of which she would not pinpoint in words, but words were unnecessary. The hardened lines of her features were replaced with a softer look, and Vanessa determined that no matter what her past had been, loved or unloved, she would start out afresh. Never again would she allow her mind to experience the same torment, nor would she subject those she cared for to a violent rampage, such as the one she had unleashed in the Coopers' home in Maine.

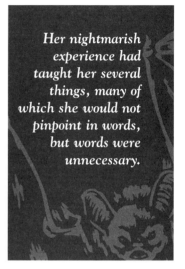

Her nightmarish experience had taught her several things, many of which she would not pinpoint in words, but words were unnecessary.

The Biting Bug-Eyed Invisible Monster

One of the most documented encounters with a ghost that bites occurred in Manila, Philippines in 1951. Eighteen-year-old Clarita Villanueva was found by the police running through the streets of the city, sobbing that a bug-eyed monster with a black cape was after her, biting her and attempting to eat her.

Confused as to what to do with the young woman, the police put her in a jail cell so that they might observe her for a period of time before they made a decision if she were insane and should be committed to a mental asylum. Clarita writhed on the floor of the jail cell and moaned as if in terrible pain. She sat upright, her eyes wide, her arms flailing at an invisible foe, screaming that the monster was coming to bite her again.

The policeman who had been posted to observe the girl in the cell was astonished to see vivid teeth marks appear on Clarita's upper arms and shoulders. He quickly opened the cell door, knelt beside the girl and helped her to her feet. Again the girl screamed and more red bites appeared on her arm. The startled officer was at a loss when he tried to think of a way to protect the teenager. It was as if an invisible monster would wrap its entire mouth around her slim arm and sink its teeth deep into her flesh. The officer helped Clarita into the hall and together they fled the cell to seek out his captain. The captain took one look at the two of them and phoned the Mayor Arsenio Lacson as well as the chief of police and the medical examiner.

The mayor and the police official had already completed their inconclusive examination of Clarita when Dr. Mariana Lara, the medical examiner, arrived, muttering about being dragged out of bed in the middle of the night to observe a young woman who was obviously suffering from epileptic seizures and was inflicting wounds upon herself.

The chief wondered how the girl could bite herself on the back of her neck. Mayor Lacson questioned Clarita while Dr. Lara examined her. What, he wanted to know, was attacking her?

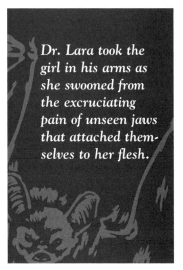

Dr. Lara took the girl in his arms as she swooned from the excruciating pain of unseen jaws that attached themselves to her flesh.

The girl sobbed that she did not know what to call it. It resembled a man with a long, flowing black cape. It was very ugly and came at her with its fangs bared, ready to sink into her flesh. The medical examiner admitted that the indentations in the girl's skin certainly appeared to be the prints of teeth. The girl was not drunk, nor was she under the influence of any drug.

The Police Chief noted the date—May 10, 1951—on the calendar. A man with a strong religious background, he briefly entertained the theory that they may be witnessing the onset of a manifestation of stigmata, but there were no special holy days in the Philippines during the month of May. Clarita spent the rest of the night closely attended by an officer, who had been assigned the eerie task of keeping watch for the monster.

The next morning, the girl was brought to court to face a charge of vagrancy that had been brought against her. There, before the incredulous eyes of the entire court, Clarita endured another attack by her invisible monster. Reporters rushed to stand beside her for a closer look. Dr. Lara took the girl in his arms as she swooned from the excruciating pain of unseen jaws that attached themselves to her flesh.

"This girl is definitely not having an epileptic fit," Dr. Lara told the reporters. "These teeth prints are real, but they are most certainly not self-inflicted." There was no need for medical expertise to attest to the reality of the teeth marks to the reporters. They were serving as startled witnesses to the cruel indentations that were appearing on the girl's arms, shoulders, palms, and neck.

Dr. Lara told a police officer to send at once for the Mayor and the Archbishop, declaring that this case was outside his realm of physiology and medicine. By the time Mayor Lacson arrived, the unfortunate girl had become a veritable mass of deeply embedded teeth prints and swollen and bruised flesh. Even as he held one of Clarita's hands in one of his own, deep teeth marks appeared on opposite sides of her index finger, as if a hungry fiend were trying to chew the digit off.

The mayor declared that the girl must be taken to a hospital. Dr. Lara agreed, and the two men helped Clarita into the Mayor's car. The driver thought that Clarita was a victim of some horrible beating until the teeth of the invisible monster began to attack her in the automobile.

The driver wheeled the mayor's car through the Manila traffic, one eye on the signals and the other on the tortured girl who sat between him and the doctor. For some reason, the attacks ceased when the girl entered the hospital, and she began to recover the health that had been deteriorated by the monster's merciless jaws. Clarita Villanueva never again suffered from the terrible invisible teeth that tore at her flesh.

"This whole phenomena simply defies rational explanation," Dr. Lara once commented. "I don't mind saying that I was scared out of my wits."

Vampire Gangs

There's not much remaining of the Vampire Hotel that used to sit in the hills of the Land Between the Lakes National Recreation Area located in southwestern Kentucky and northwestern Tennessee. Rod Ferrell and his Vampire Clan used to hang out there in the late 1990s, but after Ferrell and his vampires set out across four states to commit a double-murder, the structure, which was already in an advanced state of ruin, was demolished.

Some vampire wannabes still trek up the hills to soak up some of the energy left there by Ferrell, also known as Vesago. All that remains of the building is its foundation, but evidence of its popularity as a site for vampire pilgrimages can be found in the charred bits of wood that was used for bonfires and the graffiti scrawled on some of the 10-foot-high portions of the foundation walls. Vampires, pagans, and disciples of the macabre have drawn skulls, "power" numbers, pentagrams, and numerous references to the antichrist. In addition, there are invitations to those who would make such pilgrimages to "follow Ferrell to death" and "those who venture here need not fear evil."

By the time that he was 16, Roderick Justin Ferrell had joined his mother, Sondra Gibson, a sometimes waitress/dancer/hooker, and about 30 other vampires playing *Vampire: The Masquerade* in rural southwestern Kentucky. Gibson was later quoted that she saw nothing wrong in playing the game with her son. After all, she commiserated, it was hard in these times to find some activity that parents could do together with their kids. The vampire mom eventually earned a felony conviction for writing a very explicit letter to a 14-year-old boy inviting him to join her in a vampire ceremony that involved sexual intercourse.

Rod Ferrell began the school year in September 1995 by being expelled. This suited him just fine. Now he could play the vampire lifestyle to the fullest, sleeping all day and carousing all night with his vampire clan. Rod and his "children of the night" went up into the Kentucky hills and hung out at an old building that they renamed The Vampire Hotel. In October, one of their night terrors drove Rod and a group of

Some biker vampire wannabes still hike up the southwestern Kentucky hill country and visit the Vampire Hotel, which was once the hangout of Rod Ferrell and his Vampire Clan (illustration by Ricardo Pustanio).

teenagers to break into an animal shelter and set about beating, mutilating, and stomping 40 dogs, viciously killing one of them. Later, Ferrell would tell psychiatrists that he had tortured and mutilated small animals since the age of nine.

It was about this time that Ferrell decided that he was Vesago, a 500-year-old vampire that had returned to Earth with a special mission. He had been assigned to open the Gates to Hell. In order to accomplish this, Ferrell's inner guidance told him that he would need to kill a lot of people and drink a great deal of blood.

On Friday, November 22, 1996, Rod told Che (Charity Keesee), his 17-year-old girlfriend whom he had impregnated, that she was going to accompany him and his best friend, Scott Anderson, on a trip, because he was tired of the Kentucky cops bugging him. Che's best friend, Dana Cooper, 19, came along out of concern for her friend's pregnancy.

Ferrell told the group that they were traveling to New Orleans, where there were many vampires who were able to drink blood freely and live in grand style. First, though, they would stop in Eustis, Florida, and pick up a girl that Ferrell had met while staying with his maternal grandparents the summer before. She also wanted to be a vampire and live the night stalker lifestyle.

Even though 15-year-old Heather "Zoey" Wendorf's grandfather had been Evangelist Billy Graham's attorney, none of the preacher's teachings had rubbed off on her. Zoey went so far as to declare that she had been demons in several past lives. She frightened her "straight" friends by proclaiming that she drank blood and called up spirits of the dead. Zoey Wendorf was definitely Rod Ferrell's kind of girl, and he was especially taken with her when she told him that she looked up to him as if he were a father to her and she would live for the day when he would return to Eustis and take her away to join his vampire family.

When the Kentucky vampires arrived in Eustis, they got pulled over by a Florida Highway Patrol officer who checked their identities, then let them go. Ferrell once again felt that the cops were conspiring against him, and he told the others that they were just going to pick up Heather and her friend Jeanine and get out of town. Heather was thrilled to see her vampire dream lover arrive, but Jeanine, who had also been one of Ferrell's girlfriends, changed her mind about leaving with the vampire clan and told them to come back for her in a couple of years. Ferrell took Heather to a cemetery where they conducted a blood-drinking ritual and she officially became a vampire.

Their confessions would differ appreciably, but it was at the cemetery that Rod later told police investigators, that Heather begged him to kill her father and stepmother, who were making her life a living hell. Heather's story was that Ferrell only said that he was going to rob her parents and take her father's Ford Explorer for the trip to New Orleans.

The reality is that on November 25, 1996, Ferrell entered the Wendorf home and fractured the skull and ribs of 42-year-old Richard Wendorf with a crowbar while he lay sleeping on a couch. Although Ferrell later claimed that he had not intended to kill Heather's stepmother, he said that she lunged at him and threw a steaming cup of coffee at him. This attack angered him, so he killed her as well.

According to some accounts, all the members of the vampire clan drank some of the victims' blood before they got into Wendorf's Explorer and headed for New Orleans. The vampire family drove straight through to New Orleans, but they soon became disenchanted with the city. It was not the mystical city of their vampiric dreams. The Big Easy was very intimidating to four teenagers from rural Kentucky and one from a small Florida town—even if they were vampires and murderers. Che "freaked out," Ferrell later said in disgust, putting the blame on the pregnant girl for their decision to leave New Orleans.

They took the back roads, seeking a nice forested area where they might found a new bucolic retreat for vampires. Nothing seemed as sound and as inviting as the Vampire Hotel back in Kentucky. The vampire clan ended up in Baton Rouge on Thanksgiving Day. They were broke, but Che thought that she could telephone her mother in South Dakota for help.

Che's mother was horrified by the stories of the vampire lifestyle and murders that she heard from her teenaged daughter. She immediately called the police and told them of the clan's whereabouts, then she contacted Che and told her to go to a motel room and charge it to her credit card. The police were waiting for Ferrell and his clan at Howard Johnson's.

The group was held in a Baton Rouge jail for a week before being extradited to Florida. They were initially booked at Lake County jail, then, later moved to a juvenile facility in Ocala. After his conviction on February 12, 1998, Rod Ferrell held the record as the youngest inmate on Death Row in the United States. In September 1999, the Florida Supreme Court reduced his sentence to life without parole.

Ferrell had absolved all the other members of the vampire clan of any participation in the murders, with the exception of Scott Anderson, who he said was an accessory. On March 30, Anderson agreed to plead guilty in exchange for two life sen-

Biker jacket referencing the vampire Nosferatu (illustration by Ricardo Pustanio).

tences. Heather Wendorf had all charges against her dropped when she assumed the role of State's witness against her vampire master. Charity Keesee and Dana Cooper were convicted of murder in the third degree. On August 13, 1998, Charity was sentenced to 10-and-a-half years in prison, but she won an early release in March 2006. On July 15, Dana was sentenced to 15 years in prison and is expected to be released in 2013.

On March 2, 1998, Rod Ferrell wrote to crime author Sondra London when he was the youngest man on Death Row in the United States. Ferrell told London (*True Vampires*, 2004) that he was working on "art" (apparently a book) entitled "Lost Enigma," which he admitted had no plot as yet. Ferrell said that he had so many thoughts and ideas that scattered just as quickly as they gathered.

Then, in a surprisingly metaphysical close to the letter, Ferrell writes: "Do you know what the most beautiful word in the world is? It is ONE! To reach the essence of One is to find true sanctification."

It is to be hoped that the majority of us cannot envision reaching the essence of oneness by torturing and killing small animals and by murdering two innocent and helpless human beings.

Many members of the modern vampire community have spoken out that Rod Ferrell should by no means serve as a typical portrait of what it is to be a vampire. At the time of his approaching trial in 1998, the vampire community was quite vocal in expressing a collective opinion that Ferrell should be tried as a murderer, not as a vampire.

Heavy Metal, Grass, and Human Sacrifice

In the early morning hours of January 26, 1988, a patrol officer in Gonzales, Louisiana, stopped a van with Georgia license plates because it had been driving in a suspicious manner. A plate check showed that the van had been reported stolen and the three teenagers inside the vehicle—all from Douglasville, Georgia—were booked into the Gonzales jail.

Terry Belcher and Robert McIntyre, both 16, and Malisa Earnest, 17, claimed that they had just borrowed the McIntyres' family van for a little vacation time in New Orleans, Graceland for vampires. They were not criminals, just teenagers looking for some fun. While it was true that the van did belong to Robert's parents, it had been reported stolen. The police were inclined to be tolerant toward the kids, but the McIntyres' complaint implied that the teenagers had taken the van without parental permission. The authorities felt they had no choice other than to detain the teenagers until they heard from Robert's parents.

Later that day, Sergeant Bill Landry was contacted by a female inmate at the county jail who insisted that she speak with him. Landry recognized the woman as an informant who had helped the police solve a number of cases. The informant had been picked up for loitering, and she had shared a jail cell with Malisa Earnest, the teenager from Georgia.

Heavy metal rock is part of the subculture for some satanic cult members.

"She told me how she and another girl were picked up by two guys who took them to a deserted farmhouse," the 23-year-old informant told Landry. "They got high on grass, listened to heavy metal, drank blood, worshipped Satan, and murdered the other girl."

The street-smart informant said that she was accustomed to meeting plenty of tough and violent people on the streets, but the sweet teenager from Georgia with the pretty smile had scared her silly.

"I believe her," she told Landry. "I believe those kids did a human sacrifice." Sergeant Landry did his best to calm the woman. Later, he told Major Phil Miller the incredible story. "I know this informant and I trust her. She was so scared, I know she wasn't making it up."

A crime check revealed only that Terry Belcher had been arrested on a few misdemeanor charges. Robert McIntyre and Malisa Earnest both had clean records, but the police did learn that Malisa had recently been sent to a juvenile home and that she and three other girls were listed as runaways. Two of the girls had returned, but Malisa and a 17-year-old named Theresa Simmons were on the records as still missing.

The police in Gonzales saw no reason to charge Malisa with auto theft. According to everyone's testimony, she had merely been a hitchhiker picked up by the boys, so she was released on her own recognizance. It was after McIntyre and Belcher had been flown back to Georgia that Sheriff Earl Lee of Douglas County played a hunch that eventually broke the case and revealed a terrible crime of satanic human sacrifice. Sheriff Lee simply started speaking about Satanism as a general topic, and Terry Belcher, who had previously been close-mouthed during his incarceration, suddenly became animated and talkative.

The teenager explained that he had been a member of a satanic cult for a year. All nine of the members of the coven accepted Satan as their savior. Belcher told the sheriff that he had just been an average high school kid until he met a woman in Douglasville who claimed to be a satanic witch. The woman had enticed him with promises of power and sex, then asked him if he liked such heavy metal artists as Ozzy Osbourne and Judas Priest. When Belcher replied that they were his idols, the Satanist told him that many of their songs were about satanic rituals and that the lyrics were filled with satanic messages.

He went on to tell the lawman how he had begun to meet regularly with the Satanist. They would listen to heavy metal music and read from *The Satanic Bible*. Soon, he had become a Satanist and was participating in the sacrifice of animals and the drinking of their blood. Proudly, the teenager traced his evolution from follower to the high priest of his own coven. "I had followers. I had power. It was neat," he boasted.

Eventually, the whole sordid story was revealed to the persistent Sheriff Lee. Belcher stated that Robert was a member of his coven. When they picked up the two runaway girls, he was delighted to discover that Malisa had already dabbled in Satanism and was more than willing to accept him as her high priest. Belcher and McIntyre had performed numerous animal sacrifices and blood rituals, and they had discussed a human sacrifice for quite some time. Malisa was completely in favor of the idea, and the three of them decided that Theresa Simmons would make a perfect offering to Satan.

After working themselves into a frenzy on grass and heavy metal music in the upstairs bedroom of the abandoned farmhouse, they looped a leather shoelace around Theresa's neck and took turns tightening it. When they knew that she was dead, they read from *The Satanic Bible* and chanted over the body, hoping that their sacrifice would enable Satan to materialize before them.

Much was made of Belcher's jailhouse conversion to Christianity and his renouncing of the teachings of Satan, but during his trial in May 1988, he seemed to recount his career as a satanic cultist with great relish and enthusiasm. He told of slaughtering large numbers of dogs, cats, and chickens to Satan and drinking their blood and eating their eyeballs and intestines.

"I got power for doing these rituals," he testified. "I got money, sex, drugs—anything I wanted. It was easy. Satan helped me to get them."

Ostentatiously wearing a cross around his neck, Belcher pleaded guilty to murder and received an automatic life sentence. He also agreed to testify against his former satanic follower, Robert McIntyre.

On June 10, 1988, McIntyre was also sentenced to life imprisonment. Malisa Earnest was found guilty of being an accessory to murder and was sentenced to a three-year prison term.

The Reign of Terror of the Chicago Rippers

On May 23, 1981, Linda Sutton, 28, was abducted. Her mutilated body was found 10 days later in a field near the Rip Van Winkle Motel in Villa Park, Illinois. The body of Rose Davis, 30, from Broadview, about three miles southeast of Elmhurst, was found in an alley in Chicago at about the same time. She'd been strangled, stabbed, and mutilated. In both cases, the left breasts of the victims had been cut off.

On May 15, 1982, Lorraine A. Borowski, 21, left her home in the Elmhurst Terrace Apartments in Elmhurst, one of Chicago's western suburbs, about 7:30 A.M. to have the office open at 8:00 when the rest of the Saturday office staff was due to arrive. Witnesses had seen Lorraine getting out of her car in the parking lot, but she never opened the office and had apparently not even entered the building. After only a few hours, she was reported missing.

Generally, in the case of a missing person, police wait 24 hours before beginning an investigation, but because of the number of missing women during that period, a squad was dispatched immediately to take a look. The lawmen closely examined Lorry Borowski's car. There was nothing about it that was suspicious.

On Saturday, May 29, 1982, Shui Mak, who lived in Lombard, was abducted while she was walking along a road in Hanover Park in northwest Cook County, in which the city of Chicago is located.

Sandra Delaware, 18, of Chicago, who had a prostitution record, was found stabbed and strangled on August 27, 1982. Her left breast had been cut off.

On Saturday, September 11, 1982 on her forty-second birthday, Carole Pappas, wife of Chicago Cubs pitcher Milt Pappas, drove her burgundy and white 1980 Buick to a shopping center in Wheaton, Illinois. No trace of her had been found since her disappearance.

Beverly Washington, age 20, of Chicago, whose body had been discovered on October 6, 1982, had her left breast amputated with a single smooth cut. In none of the cases was there any indication of hacking or even multiple cuts.

It seemed the murders were no longer confined to the western suburbs of Chicago. Media began calling them the Jack The Ripper Murders. Some of the victims had been from impeccable backgrounds; others were known hookers. Generally, the bodies and disappearances were centered in the Du Page County area. One victim had been a resident of Chicago's elegant Gold Coast. Another had been a streetwalker whose body had been found under a bridge in a lower-class Chicago area. There was no mistaking, however, the mutilations and missing left breasts, and sometimes both breasts. Police investigators had come to believe that they were looking for a person or persons who kidnapped, sexually abused, mutilated, and killed women of procreative age. This indicated young men at the peak of their sexual vigor. As closely as the investigators could catalog the crimes, 15 women had been killed.

Linda Sutton's body was found in a field in Illinois in 1982 after she had been abducted 10 days earlier.

On October 10, 1982, a body was found that had been exposed to the abrasions of nature. A dental check confirmed that the body was that of Lorraine Borowski. After the discovery of Lorraine Borowski's body, the killings ended. But the heat was on the police to find who had committed these atrocities on their murder victims.

The remains of the body of Linda Sutton, the first victim, had been found in a field near the Rip Van Winkle Motel on North Avenue in Villa Park. Investigators went to talk to the management. After many hours spent going through the registrations at the motel for the past several months, the manager recalled a group of young men that he thought must be cultists or Satanists. He'd heard that they had secret rites in their rooms. They'd had girls in, prostitutes he was pretty sure. The strange thing was, though, the manager said, he didn't recall ever seeing any of the girls walk out with any of the four men. He did have an old forwarding address for one of them.

Investigators went to an address in the 900 block of West North Avenue to have a talk with Andrew Kokoraleis, 20, and his brother, Thomas C. Kokoraleis, 23. Only Tom Kokoraleis was home. The detectives introduced themselves and asked if they could come in. When the investigators began to ask a few questions about Linda Sutton, Tom seemed to be evasive and nervous. The investigators advised Tom Kokoraleis of his rights and told him that there were inconsistencies in his responses. They suggested that it might be easier to talk at headquarters. Since Andrew Kokoraleis hadn't shown up, the investigators made arrangements for someone to meet him when he arrived home.

In the interrogation room, the detectives told Tom Kokoraleis that they thought he was lying to them. He maintained he was telling them the truth. The polygraph, or lie detector, test, to which Kokoraleis voluntarily consented, led the polygraph operator to believe Kokoraleis was not being entirely candid with the police.

For the next two days, Tom Kokoraleis took investigators to the motel, to fields in Du Page County, to Chicago, to various streets, and to alleys to point out details of his story. Later, in the interrogation room with a tape recorder running, Kokoraleis admitted he knew about the death of a girl in Chicago.

Gecht, acting as high priest, then stepped behind the altar and read passages from The Satanic Bible *by Anton LaVey.*

He had watched as his friend Robin Gecht, 27, killed her. The ceremony was held in a chapel on the second floor of Gecht's Chicago home. Gecht was an unemployed carpenter, who had once worked for John Wayne Gacy, the infamous killer of 33 young men in the Chicago area. These ritual ceremonies had been held there for 9 or 10 women that Kokoraleis knew about. He thought there had been more, but he wasn't certain. Gecht was the one who conducted the "services."

The services all began by the Kokoraleis brothers, Gecht, and Edward Spreitzer, 23, a self-employed electrician, raping the victim. The rituals continued by cutting the victim with knives or stabbing her with an ice pick. When she was screaming steadily, they would then join in raping her over and over. They would continue until the victim's mind could no longer stand the assault, and she lay helpless.

At that time, Gecht, acting as high priest, then stepped behind the altar and read passages from *The Satanic Bible* by Anton LaVey. Next, he would read verses from the Bible to mock and deride Satan's arch-enemy, Christ. In order to desecrate God's most beloved creation, man, Gecht insisted that the most important thing in the ceremony was to leave Satan's mark on the victim. He then took a thin, strong wire, looped it around the victim's left breast, and with a firm, strong stroke, he pulled the wire straight, cutting off the breast in one smooth move. Sometimes the procedure was repeated on a victim's right breast. Kokoraleis said at that time Gecht had 9 or 10 breasts in a box. Later, Kokoraleis thought, he had about 15.

Continuing with the ceremony, Gecht would cut the breast into pieces, then in Satanic communion, each communicant ate his piece of breast. The gory information was relayed to Chicago investigators who were working on cases believed to be the work of the Rippers. Gecht and Spreitzer were picked up.

Armed with a search warrant, the Chicago police found evidence in the second floor chapel of Satan in Gecht's home to corroborate some of Thomas Kokoraleis's statement. In Du Page County, sheriffs police picked up Andrew Kokoraleis.

The case was immediately forwarded to the state's attorney's office. First Assistant State's Attorney Michael Higgins speculated that a number of other murders might be tied to the group. Largely because the evidence found on the second floor of his home was incontrovertible, Robin Gecht was the first of the cannibal gang member to be convicted. At the end of September 1983, in Cook County Court in Chicago, he was found guilty of the attempted murder, rape, and aggravated battery in the mutilation-murder of Sandra Delaware, whose body was left under the bridge in the 1800 block of West Fullerton Avenue in Chicago. Gecht was sentenced to 120 years in the Menard Correctional Center.

On April 2, 1984, Edward Spreitzer was described by prosecutors as a sadist. Spreitzer pleaded guilty to murdering four people: Rose Davis, 30, whose body had been found in an alley in the Gold Coast district; Sandra Delaware, who he'd killed in the company of Robin Gecht; and Shui Mak, whom he held down while she was raped and mutilated. Spreitzer was also convicted of killing Raphael Torado in a drive-by shooting as Torado stood by a telephone booth. Spreitzer was sentenced to natural life on each of the four counts of murder plus additional sentences on charges of rape, deviant sexual assault, kidnapping, and attempted murder.

On May 15, 1984, the jury of 10 women and 2 men listened to the tape in which Thomas Kokoraleis described the method of the cult's killing of its victims. One courtroom spectator fainted; another dashed out of the courtroom gagging and holding her hand over her mouth.

On May 18, the jury found Thomas C. Kokoraleis, now 24, guilty of the abduction, rape, and murder of Lorraine Borowski. While awaiting sentencing for life imprisonment, Kokoraleis said he'd take police to the field where Carole Pappas was buried. With Kokoraleis leading, the detectives went to the field Kokoraleis designated. No body or evidence was found there. (On August 7, 1987, police pulled Carole Pappas' automobile from a shallow pond in Wheaton. Her body was found inside. It was unlikely that the Chicago Rippers had anything to do with her death.)

Andrew Kokoraleis was executed by lethal injection on March 16, 1999. Edward Spreitzer's sentence was commuted to life imprisonment.

Be Cautious
If You Boast You Are a Vampire

The man who had found the pools of blood in the corridor and in the parking lot of the Ocean Breeze Apartments on April 20, 1986, was waiting at the front entrance of the apartments for the two patrol officers from the Virginia Beach Police Department. The trail of blood led up the stairs to Apartment 348. A volunteered pass key from the manager turned the lock, and the opened door released the sickening odor of decaying flesh. Fighting back their nausea and fearing the worst, the officers found a grisly assortment of body parts heaped in a pool of blood in the middle of the apartment floor.

Later, after the proper search warrant had been obtained, investigating officers Sgt. Brian Kroft and Det. Tom Parks carefully examined the apartment with lab technicians. The place had been trashed, and there were unmistakable signs of a desperate struggle in the living room. Chunks of flesh and viscera, quite likely human, were dispatched to the state crime lab for the definitive analysis.

The investigators learned that the apartment had been rented by Marty Hughes, a husky middle-aged carpenter with a receding hairline and a thick mustache. The manager described Hughes as a model tenant. On-site at the construction company where Hughes had worked, the foreman depicted the carpenter as one of his best men. He had known something was wrong when Marty did not show up on the job without calling.

Although the man worked as a laborer in construction, the police investigators soon discovered that Marty Hughes had highbrow tastes that seemed to be in marked contrast to his blue-collar background. The man was not only an expert on the Civil War, but he also taught Gaelic, the ancient Celtic language of Ireland and certain Highland Scottish regions. In addition, Hughes took great delight in playing the bagpipes and the bluegrass mandolin.

Lt. Donald Hagen was finding it increasingly difficult to ascertain why anyone would kill a man that everyone seemed to like. What could the motive possibly be for such a bloody murder? Learning that Hughes had lived in Boston, Massachusetts,

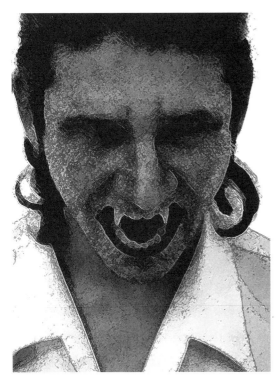

Porphyria is an illness that affects the blood and causes people to believe they are vampires.

Hagen assigned Sgt. Kroft to check out the murder victim's connections in that area. Once again it was determined that Hughes left nothing but friends behind wherever he traveled. But later telephone calls provided the sergeant with an astonishing bit of information. According to certain of Hughes' relatives, the husky Celtic scholar, musician, historian, and contemporary Renaissance Man, also believed himself to be a vampire.

Lt. Hagen was not in the mood for jokes about Dracula and Barnabas Collins. "You don't mean like those vampires in the horror movies, do you, Sergeant?"

Kroft explained that Hughes was diagnosed as suffering from a rare and very peculiar kind of blood disease that made him develop vampire-like symptoms. "It's called 'porphyria,' Lieutenant. Its victims are overly sensitive to sunlight and have an aversion to garlic, just like the vampires in the movies. In addition, the disease causes the person's gums to recede, making it look like he or she has fangs."

The lieutenant wondered aloud if those bloody hunks of human flesh and organs that were left in the apartment could be the grisly remains of one of Hughes' victims. Had the man slipped over the edge and convinced himself that he truly was a creature of the night who must sustain himself on human blood? On the other hand, the gory remains could be those of Hughes himself. Sgt. Kroft noted that Hughes had been receiving injections from a medical doctor to "pep up his blood" against the rare disease.

"Then let's have the medical examiner contact Hughes' doctor and find out what the exact medication was," Lt. Hagen suggested. "If Hughes is our chopped-up victim, there might be some traces of the drug in the body parts we took from the apartment."

By the next day, the investigators had received their answer: Traces of the drug heme-arginate used to relieve those afflicted with porphyria were detected in the human organs left in Hughes' apartment. The police now had an identity for their gruesome pile of body parts. The next steps were to determine a motive and a murder suspect. The only meager clues that the investigators had were a few unidentified fingerprints on a beer bottle and the smudged impressions of bloody tennis shoes that led away from Hughes' apartment. Lab technicians stated that the small size of the shoes indicated that they had been worn by someone weighing around 130 pounds.

"It's a small shoe size, like a kid would wear," they theorized. "It would be hard to imagine such a little guy demolishing a husky, 200-pound carpenter."

Police investigators were nearly out of leads when a 16-year-old girl and her 17-year-old boyfriend came forward with a startling story. They knew the murderer of

Marty Hughes to be Dean Bolan, because he had told them so. The police got lucky. Bolan had talked about the murder to other friends.

"I thought Dean was kidding," another witness, who insisted upon anonymity, admitted to the police. "He called me on the night of April 23, yelling about how he had killed someone. He said his clothes were all bloody and everything. He asked if he could bring the body over and burn it up in my stove!"

"I thought he was nuts, completely insane," the witness continued. "I did set some clothes out for him, though. I mean, he kept screaming that he was covered from head to toe with blood."

Providing a change of clothes for Bolan could make the witness an accessory to murder, but the police let it go. They wanted to know what Bolan looked like.

"He's a quiet little guy," the witness said. "He's only about five-foot-four. Can't weigh over 130 pounds or so."

Police investigators later determined that Dean Bolan tipped the scales at only 120 pounds, but fear of the "Evil Undead" had granted him superhuman strength on that terrible night of April 23.

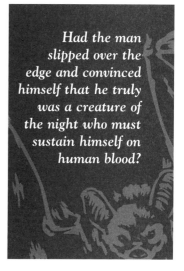

Had the man slipped over the edge and convinced himself that he truly was a creature of the night who must sustain himself on human blood?

The remarkable details of Marty Hughes' death were learned during the sensational "Vampire Murder Trial" that began at the Circuit Courthouse in January 1987. According to defense attorney Peter Gaines, Bolan had killed Hughes in self-defense. Hughes, according to the defense, appeared affable and agreeable only to those who did not know him well. The big carpenter had a Jekyll-and-Hyde twist to his personality. What is more, he regularly performed occult rituals to summon spirits from the dead.

Bolan and Hughes had met on a construction job two years earlier, and they had kept in touch. They were, the small man insisted, friends. Bolan testified that the fateful evening in April had begun innocently enough in Hughes' apartment. After they had shared a pizza and a few beers, Hughes had stood up and began dancing in a circle. "I am a vampire. I am evil. I am a vampire," he chanted over and over.

Bolan stated that he knew about the porphyria, the "vampire's disease," and he assumed that his friend was just joking around, making light of his affliction.

But then Hughes presented his guest with a most intriguing offer. "You can have your pick of any one of three evil spirits." Marty said to Dean. "I will allow you to make contact with the spirit of Billy the Kid … Adolf Hitler … or Jack the Ripper. Choose one. Tell me quick! Which one do you want?"

Still believing his friend to be joking, Bolan chose the spirit of Jack the Ripper. Hughes pulled a book off his cluttered shelves. He began reading aloud in eerie-sounding Gaelic phrases. He made a few peculiar movements, then began to shout that he had become possessed by an evil spirit. "I am evil. I am evil. I am evil," he chanted.

Bolan testified that he now became very uneasy. Hughes no longer sounded as though he might be teasing or joking around. Everything took on a sharp and jagged edge when Hughes told Bolan that the evil spirit was communicating with him, giving him orders.

"The evil spirit commands that I must kill you," Marty told Dean.

Bolan's eyes bulged in horror when he saw his friend moving toward him with a maniacal gleam in his eyes and a knife in his hand. The two men fought; Hughes tripped and fell on the blade. Although his defense attorney maintained the storyline of self-defense, neither Bolan nor his lawyer offered a really sound explanation to satisfy the question of why he had not simply called the police and told them the facts of his friend's death. Instead, they confessed to the jury, Dean panicked and decided that he must somehow get rid of Hughes' body.

Since the victim weighed well over 200 pounds, he was too heavy for Bolan to lift. He couldn't just leave the corpse there in the apartment. It would be impossible to drag it down the stairs without being detected.

Frightened. Confused. What was there left for him to do?

"Because there was no way to dispose of the body as it was," defense attorney Gaines told a stunned and disgusted jury, "he did the unimaginable. He cut the body in half."

Bolan and his attorney admitted that the concept of dismemberment may sound loathsome and insane to the rational mind, but it seemed the best idea at the time. Setting to work on his friend's body with a hacksaw, stuffing body parts into foot lockers and garbage bags, all the gore seemed logical in the context of the madness of the evening.

After six hours in deliberation, the jury reached a verdict that found Dean Bolan guilty of second-degree murder. The fearful vampire killer who swore that Marty Hughes became truly possessed by an evil spirit after the chanting of ancient Celtic ritual has served his 20-year term in prison.

Although the above story is true and really happened, legal advisors requested that all names, dates, and places be changed to protect innocent parties.

The Countess Alucard

Elizabeth Page, 41, of Worchester, England, loved stories and motion pictures about vampires so much that she legally changed her name to Elizabeth Page-Alucard (Alucard is Dracula spelled backwards). On October 7, 1989, she was battered with a stainless steel milk jug and then strangled to death.

Ms. Page-Alucard was an administrator-counselor at a drug rehabilitation center. She had once been an addict, but in the three years that she had worked at the center, she had been clean. Although apparently drug free, it seemed that in nature she was closer in spirit to Dr. Jekyll and Mr. Hyde, with two completely different sides, than she was to Dracula. She was very moody, so her fellow counselors at the drug center said, and she would often fly into tantrums or fits of rage. Then, hours later, she would be laughing and cheerful.

As it turned out, she may have been testy because she found out that her boyfriend David Bingham was taking money from the center's safe and forging her name to make it appear that she had been withdrawing funds. Finally, when it appeared that Bingham was setting her up to take the blame for the stolen funds, Elizabeth, who was known to have a tongue as cruel as any vampire's, not only blew up at her lover, but dredged up personal things from his past to hurt him more than any outburst of temper could hope to do.

Page-Alucard went berserk with full Dracula-like force until her torrent of cruelty reached the point where Bingham picked up the milk jug and smashed her over the head with it. As she lay unconscious, but still breathing, he strangled her. The woman who had joked with her friends that she was really a vampire lay dead by her lover's hands, not a stake through the heart.

The Vampire with Political Ambitions and the Teenaged Vampire Hunter

Jonathan "The Impaler" Sharkey, the self-proclaimed King of the Vampyre Nation, the founder of The Vampyres, Witches, and Pagans Party, who ran for the office of Governor of Minnesota in 2008, was jailed in Rochester, Minnesota, on February 4, 2009, on charges for threatening a teenaged girl. Sharkey, 44, of Toms River, New Jersey, lived in Princeton, Minnesota, when he ran for governor of the state. When his bid for governor failed, he declared himself the Vampyres, Witches, and Pagans Party candidate for president of the United States.

It was during his candidacy for president that he received a message of support from a 15-year-old girl on his MySpace page. According to the teenager, who was at that time in tenth grade, she and The Impaler began dating online. When she wished to break off the relationship, she issued a criminal complaint that he threatened her. According to the alleged charges against him, the girl tried to scare the Impaler into leaving her alone by emailing him that she was a member of an elite vampire hunting society and that he could be put in great danger if he attempted to continue their relationship. Undaunted, the King of the Vampyre Nation told the girl that she was his wife and his Princess.

The girl's father stated that he tried speaking directly to Sharkey, but the vampire continued to bombard her with telephone calls and emails. After the father personally confronted him and spoke to him, the Impaler allegedly threatened to behead the girl's parents if she didn't email him at least three times a day and call him at least once a day.

In the summer of 2008, Sharkey was charged with felony harassment and two misdemeanors: coercion with intent to inflict bodily harm and coercion to expose a secret or disgrace. The Impaler was supposed to appear in August, but he said that he could not travel because he had been hurt in a professional wrestling match. He told

Jonathan "The Impaler" Sharkey claimed to be king of the vampires and even had ambitions of becoming governor of New Jersey.

a Rochester police sergeant that he was a vampire and must drink human blood for strength.

While he was recuperating from his injury in Tracy City, Tennessee, the capitol of the Vampyre Nation, Sharkey threatened to sue the Olmstead County attorney's office for wrongful and vindictive prosecution. He also wrote to the U.S. Justice Department demanding that his former "Princess" be prosecuted for belonging to a domestic terrorist group, the elite vampire hunting squad, that had threatened to assassinate him.

On June 1, 2009, Jonathan Albert Sharkey, 44, who ran for Minnesota gover-nor as "the Impaler" on the Vampyres, Witches, and Pagans party ticket, plead-ed guilty to two counts of harassment through use of mail. Charges of coercion to inflict bodily harm and coercion to expose a secret were dismissed. Sharkey was sentenced to 90 days in prison.

Killing a Vampire in the Twenty-first Century

In the early pages of this book we learned how people in ancient and medieval times dealt with those who had been cursed to become a vampire. If a village was under attack by a creature of the undead that was driven to leave his or her grave by a craving for human blood, the village priest and a few stalwart men would dig through the rot of the grave, drive a wooden stake through the predator's heart, and decapitate the vampire.

Today, as we move forward into the twenty-first century, a time of scientific thinking, remarkable technology, and a space program that charts the physical universe and dreams of moving us to other planets, the methods of killing a vampire are not very much different than they were a thousand years ago.

Protecting a Romanian Village from a Vampire

Just before midnight in July 2004, six dark figures stealthily entered the graveyard in the small Romanian village of Marotinul de Sus. They had discussed their plans many times for many weeks, and each of them knew well his particular assignment. Without a wasted movement, they moved toward the simple plot of Petre Toma, a man who had once led a respectable life as a teacher in the village. For whatever reason, they had discovered that Toma had chosen to become a member of the undead and rise from his grave at night to drink the blood of the living while they were sleeping. In point of terrible fact, Toma had chosen three members of their own family as victims.

When the men saw that they were unobserved by anyone out walking near the cemetery that night, Gheorghe Marinescu, Mitrica Mircea, Popa Stelica, Constantin Florea, Ionescu Ion, and Pascu Oprea—all related, all loyal to the work that must be done—began digging up the grave of the vampire. The corpse was dragged from its

In some Romanian villages, when there is evidence that a member of the undead has been leaving his coffin at night, the vampire slayers go into action (illustration by Ricardo Pustanio).

resting place in a simple grave, and at the precise stroke of midnight, Marinescu began the ritual that had been passed from generation to generation in their family.

After Gheorghe Marinescu had completed the recitation of the words that would hold the vampire fast, a pitchfork was driven through the chest of Petre Toma. Then, as they had discussed the process of killing a vampire so many times, Toma's chest was opened, his heart removed, and stakes were driven through the rest of his body. The vampire killers doused the body liberally with garlic, then carefully replaced it in the grave.

In order to ensure that the vampire would cease rising at night to seek blood from the villagers, the men had to observe one more important step in the ritual. Carrying Toma's heart impaled on the end of a pitchfork, the men walked to a crossroads where Marinescu's wife, son, and daughter-in-law were waiting beside a fire that they had built. Here, the family burned the heart of the vampire, dissolved the ashes in water, then each of them drank the mix until the last drop had been imbibed.

The vampire slayers knew that they had done a righteous act. Marinescu's wife, son, and daughter-in-law were very aware that Petre Toma had returned to haunt them and to drink their blood. They had no idea why Toma chose them as his victims, but shortly after Toma's burial on Christmas Day in 2003 he began to appear to them in dreams. After the dreams of Toma began, they began to feel sick and weak. For some unknown reason, the man who had been a highly respected teacher and who had passed away at the age of 76, had chosen to return as a vampire.

The members of Marinescu's family eagerly awaited the men that night as they sat at the crossroads. They had become very weak, but the moment they drank the ashes of the vampire's heart, they immediately began to feel better. There was no question in the minds of those who had unearthed Toma's body that they had located the vampire. In the illumination from their flashlights they had all seen traces of blood around his mouth. When they stabbed him to remove his heart, he had emitted a long sigh. There was no doubt at all that they had the right body.

When word traveled throughout the village of Marotinul de Sus the next day that a vampire had been laid to a more holy rest, the reaction of many was great relief. The consensus was that it was a good thing that Marinescu and his family had performed the ritual. Once a vampire began its nightly quests for blood, the entire village would be placed in jeopardy.

Local police brought charges against the six men only after Petre Toma's daughter, Floarea Cotoran, complained about the desecration of her father's grave. When the police came to arrest him, Marinescu was both surprised and defensive. He had acted in self-defense, he protested. If he and his relatives hadn't dealt with the vampire in the manner prescribed in the old rituals, his wife, son, and daughter-in-law would have died. Marinescu went on to declare that they had not committed a crime. They had, in fact, done a good thing and had acted to protect the community.

When word of the vampire killers spread throughout Romania and made headlines in the larger cities, journalists who arrived in Marotinul de Sus to cover the story found that a sizeable portion of the population supported Marinescu and his relatives. A number of interviewees expressed no reluctance in admitting that they had also drunk ashes from the hearts of vampires to combat a mysterious illness and were at once cured. Others said that they knew of dozens of such vampires who had been killed because they were haunting the living. No one had ever made a fuss about it before Toma's daughter went to the police.

A policeman told Bucharest journalist Monica Petrescu that they had been aware of such graveyard rituals being conducted in the area for years, but no one had ever before complained about the desecrations. Sensing the feelings of the community, Floarea Cotoran made plans to leave Marotinul de Sus.

After the holy water and the prayers, some Romanian villages still follow through with a stake through the heart (illustration by Ricardo Pustanio).

In May 2005, Gheorghe Marinescu, Mitrica Mircea, Popa Stelica, Constantin Florea, Ionescu Ion, and Pascu Oprea were sentenced to six months in jail for the unlawful exhumation of a body.

As Monica Petrescu continued to research belief in vampires in modern-day Romania she learned that many communities across the country take the threat of vampires very seriously. At first, she assumed that such ancient beliefs and rituals would be more prevalent in rural communities, but she spoke with Maria Tedescu, a law student in Bucharest, who told her, "We all have our little superstitions. But vampires are different. They are not something to be taken lightly. I know it may sound silly and I can't totally explain it, but I think they exist. I always wear a crucifix … just in case."

Suspected of Being a Vampire, She was Beaten to Death

On April 30, 2007, near Georgetown, Guyana, an elderly woman was suspected of being a Higues, a vampiric entity that can enter a home's smallest crack and drink the blood of human babies. Once satisfied with a meal of blood, the Higues leaves the home and assumes the shape of a harmless old woman.

Unfortunately for this particular elderly woman, whose behavior and certain personal traits were deemed unusual and suspicious, an angry crowd of Guyanese villagers accused her of being such an evil vampire spirit and beat her to death.

The village, about 15 miles east of Georgetown, Guyana, South America, contains many practitioners of Obeah, a religion that combines the beliefs brought to Guyana by slaves from Africa, folk magic, and Roman Catholicism. The belief in Higues remains very strong. Apparently, though, there appears to be no special ritual for dispatching a vampire as the ones that exist in Romania and elsewhere. The villagers seem to dispose of the Higues by the most expedient means at hand.

Iran's "Vampire of the Desert" Received Public Execution

Public executions are rare in Iran, but an exception was made on March 18, 2005, for Mohammed Bijeh, "the Tehran Desert Vampire." For the vampire's death, the authorities wanted maximum exposure. Early on the morning of the execution, two police cars drove through the streets of Pakdasht announcing the event and encouraging everyone to gather outside the court at 9:00 A.M. to be witnesses.

Mohammed Bijeh, a 30-year-old bricklayer, was convicted of killing at least 17 children and 3 adults. Authorities speculated that there could have been many victims whose remains had not been found. According to bits and pieces of overheard conversation between Bijeh and his victims, the young man would lure children to go with him into the desert on the pretext of hunting for small animals. Once they were far from any witnesses, he would sexually abuse them and kill them. Bijeh was the oldest of seven children, and he had left school at a very young age to labor in the brickworks, pressing mud into brick molds. Bijeh grew up in poverty, and he claimed that his mother beat him often without reason. At the same time, the sight of his blood flowing from his body made him feel euphoric.

Perhaps it was a desire to attain a more lasting sense of euphoria that caused Bijeh to become a heroin addict and to begin murdering children in 2002. He would watch small children playing in the mud near the brickworks and become aroused. Others who lived and worked in the slum area would occasionally see Bijeh carrying sacks, but they had no idea of their contents.

Ali Baghi, 24, a heroin addict, was accused of sometimes serving as Bijeh's accomplice. Baghi told the court how the two of them would often slaughter animals and leave their carcasses near the shallow graves where they buried many of the children. The smell of the rotting flesh would disguise the stench rising from the decomposing bodies of the children. Baghi was sentenced to 15 years in prison for his complicity in the murders and rapes.

Shortly after the murders began in 2002, the police began an investigation that did place Bijeh in jail for several months. He was released due to lack of evidence and soon murdered seven more children. One of the vampire's ploys was to tell children of the doves that he had taught to perform. If they wished to see the remarkable birds doing tricks, they must follow him to the small brick bird coop. Conveniently for Bijeh, there was a lime pit not far from the bird coop where the bodies of the trusting children could easily be tossed.

The killings by the vampire of the desert continued for another year after Bijeh's release. Many of the victims had come from poor Afghan refugee families, who hesitated to report their children missing for fear that they would be expelled from Iran for making trouble. The police, however, were outraged when they learned of the deaths of the children that had been perpetrated over so many years and several officers were dismissed or suspended for incompetence. When it was learned that the police had actually had the vampire in their custody two years before, the government and the judiciary opened inquiries into the handling of the case.

Once apprehended, Bijeh was defiantly unrepentant and raged that he had committed the murders as an act of revenge against society. He also added that his stepmother had abused him. Such arguments carried little weight with the Pakdasht court.

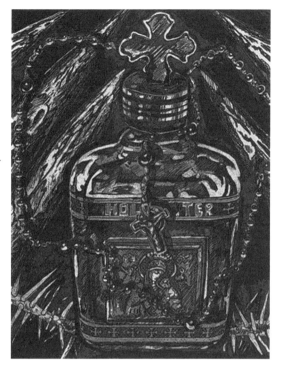

The basic weapons for helping to send a vampire to its eternal rest have remained the same in some countries for many centuries: a crucifix and some holy water (illustration by Ricardo Pustanio).

As is the custom, Bijeh's trial was held behind closed doors. In such cases of heinous crimes against children, it is the Iranian contention that a public trial with the murderer's description of how he performed his acts against their children would only bring pain to the families. On the other hand, it was their finding in this case that a public execution of the vampire of the desert would bring closure and peace to the violated families.

Public executions are never held in Iran when capital punishment has been decreed for political crimes or in sentences in which women were found guilty. But in the case of Bijeh, a senior court official said, defending their decision, a public execution would help the people's emotions to be calmed down.

As Mohammed Bijeh was brought out to Pakdasht's main square, the gathering of about 5,000 began chanting, "Allahu Akbar" (God is great). Relatives of the murdered and the missing screamed out the names of their loved ones. Court officials took turns administering 100 lashes to Bijeh's bare back. Three times, the convicted vampire of the desert collapsed to his knees under the violent force of the lashings.

As one of the mothers of a child that had been a victim of his savagery placed the noose around his neck, a relative of another of the children lured to the desert could no longer control his anger and grief and leaped to the platform to begin his own beating of Bijeh.

After the lashings had been administered, the noose placed around his neck, a crane hoisted Bijeh high into the air, hanging him. The crowd began chanting "Marg bar Bijeh" (Death to Bijeh) and demanded that the crane hoist him higher and higher above Pakdasht, then lower him, and lift him writhing above them once more as they shouted, "Again … again … again!"

Such an execution should most certainly discourage anyone from wishing to become a future "Tehran desert vampire."

Bizarre Strangers in the Night

Gladys Worthington was awakened at about 2:00 A.M. on June 21, 1975, by the unmistakable pressure of a hand on her throat. Her husband was at work on the night shift at the plant, but her four dogs were sleeping downstairs. Why hadn't they warned her? Understandably startled, Mrs. Worthington probed the darkness, desperately trying to see her assailant.

"I could see nothing," she said later. "But I felt a tingling sensation running up my body from my toes. I tried to scream, but I couldn't. As quickly as it came, the sensation went."

Mrs. Worthington lay back down. Perhaps she had been troubled by a nightmare so terrible that her conscious mind had already snuffed it from memory. After all, weird things had been happening in their house on Salvin Street, Croxdale, Durham, England. Both she and her husband had got the "shivers" witnessing objects moving about of their own accord. And then there was the time when they had caught sight of a ghostly white figure.

Uneasy, but more relaxed, Mrs. Worthington closed her eyes. Perhaps she could get back to sleep. Things would look better in the morning. Then, once again, with terrible pressure and terrifying purpose, the hand was at her throat! Mrs. Worthington struggled upright to face her attacker, but, as before, there was no visible molester. She lay awake for the rest of the night, not wanting another replay of the frightening scene.

When morning came, Mrs. Worthington told London reporters: "I got up thinking I had been dreaming. I went to the mirror to make up my face; and got a terrible shock. There were five bruises like pressure marks from a thumb and four fingers."

Mrs. Worthington's doctor agreed that the marks on her throat had been made by heavy pressure ("apparently a hand"), but he would not accept her story about being strangled by a ghost.

Individuals such as Gladys Worthington are not very receptive to skeptical researchers who assess such experiences as hers as "sleep paralysis" and a manifestation of the "Old Hag" phenomenon. While the boundaries between sleep and wakefulness may become blurry, the vast majority of people feel quite strongly that they can tell the difference between wakefulness and vivid dreams—especially those dreams that leave physical evidence.

He Resisted the "Bat Woman's" Lullaby

Martin Garcia said that he was just falling asleep one night in his home in Albuquerque when he heard a tapping on a pane of one the windows in his bedroom. "I had had a long day at work and I had grabbed a pizza on the way home from work to eat alone in the kitchen," he said. "My wife was visiting her mother in Texas, so I sat up watching television much later than usual. This was Delores's first night away from me in many years, and it didn't feel right to go to bed without her. I knew her mom was sick, so what could I say when she felt that she must go to be with her?"

At first Martin thought that it must be some weird night-flying bird tapping its beak against the window. He lay there wondering what kind of bird would be flying at night. He concluded that it must have been a big bat flying into the pane. Poor hungry bat had been swooping to catch a big bug for a midnight snack and had flown smack into the window.

"When I heard the voice at the window, I sat up straight in bed," Martin said. "I swear that I heard a voice outside of the second-floor bedroom window." Martin got out of bed and walked to the window. "I had to rub my eyes in disbelief, for there, hovering just outside the window, was some kind of dark form," he said. "The moon was very bright that night, and I could make out what seemed to be a female form. Her features were shadowed, but in the moonlight I could see that she was smiling."

As Martin stood in his bedroom, shocked by what he was seeing, he heard whatever it was, asking him to open the window so she could come in. "I started to shiver with fear," Martin admitted. "A guy at work who had served in Vietnam swore that one night he and two of his buddies had seen a naked woman with wings flying over the jungle. When they had shouted in surprise, the woman swung around and swooped down to hover just a few feet above them. My friend said that all three of them saw her and said that she glowed a kind of greenish color. She smiled at them, showed her fangs, then continued on her way into the night. My friend said that most guys didn't believe them, but a few others had claimed to have seen flying women. Other men just teased them about being horny and delusional, but my friend said that he was convinced that it was only because they had weapons that the Bat-Woman didn't attack them."

With thoughts of the Bat-Women of Vietnam and memories of all the vampire movies that he had seen since he was a kid, Martin felt his heart pounding so hard that he was afraid it would burst from his chest. And then he became even more frightened

Remember: If you hear a tapping on your window at night, don't invite your strange visitor into your bedroom (illustration by Bill Oliver).

when the thought came to him that if the night creature was a vampire, the sound of his heart beat would only make her appetite all the sharper.

"At least my Bat-Woman wasn't naked," Martin said. "She wore some kind of dark, swirling nightgown-type garment. It kind of reminded me of pictures of old burial shrouds." In his account, Martin said that he saw no wings on the entity. "She seemed to just bob up and down outside the window. One of the weirdest aspects of the whole episode—if I can single out just one—was the eerie song that she sang. It was as if the melody got inside my head. It was kind of like a lullaby. I can't remember any of the words. In fact, I don't remember if there really were any lyrics."

Martin was in the process of opening the window when a warning voice deep within his very essence warned him to close it fast. "I slammed the window shut and

I remembered all the vampire movies that I had seen as a kid where the professors warned everyone that a vampire has to be invited into a person's home," Martin said. The creature appeared to be momentarily startled by the loud noise the window made as Martin slammed it closed, so he took advantage of the distraction to run to the wall and remove the large crucifix that Delores had placed over their bed.

"When I held the crucifix before me and stood where the Bat Woman could see me clearly, she only laughed," Martin said. "And then the laughter became a hideous mocking cackle that I shall never forget. It was when she turned away from my bedroom window and flew into the night that I thought I saw that she had wings." Martin confided his story to the friend at work who had seen a similar being in Vietnam. "He believed me, told me to be careful, that the thing might come back," Martin said, "but a couple of guys who overheard me telling the story at lunch break only teased me about my missing my wife so bad that I was dreaming up women who came flying after me in the night."

Martin didn't tell Delores about the encounter until she had returned home. She listened quietly and respectfully. She did not laugh. She told him that on that very night she had dreamed that he was being threatened by an evil force. She had awakened, knelt at the bedside, and prayed for his protection.

A Vampire Followed Her since Childhood

Carol, 30, said that her first encounter with a vampire-like entity that sought to enter her bedroom window occurred when she was only about eight or nine years old. Her family lived on the third floor of an apartment building with both her parents and her three siblings.

"I remember it was night time," Carol said. "I went to the bedroom which I shared with my younger sister. As you entered the bedroom, the first thing you saw was the window. I looked at the window from where I was standing and saw a man with black hair floating outside. My sister saw him as well."

As Carol and her sister watched in fear and amazement, the being placed his hands on the outside of the window. "He had a strange smile, and he had fangs," Carol said. "I heard him say in my head, 'Let me in,' over and over again. My sister and I just stared. We can't remember what happened after that."

The second encounter that Carol had with this being was as an adult and occurred in a dream. In the dream, a creature that people mistook for a large bird suddenly flew into her window. "Now the bird looked human, but I knew he was a vampire," Carol said. "I noticed two strange holes on his neck. I knew he wanted me to come with him. It's as if he wanted me for himself, as if he were trying to seduce me. I woke up soon after that."

On Friday, September 9, 2007, at 4:45 in the morning, the dream seemed to become a kind of multidimensional reality. Carol recalls that she had awakened for "some unknown reason. I was trying to fall back asleep. All of a sudden I felt like I entered a trance of some sort. I saw myself going to my window. When I looked outside I saw a strange man walking in my driveway. He had black hair and wore black clothing. As soon as he saw me, he sort of flew towards my window and floated there."

Carol said that the being asked her to let him in. "I looked over to where my husband was sleeping and then I looked towards the being," she said. "I was curious. I opened the window just a tiny crack when he quickly grabbed my hand. I remembered how his hands had long finger nails. When he grabbed my hand, he told me how he had something for me and that he would place it outside in a small jewelry box. He said it was a pendant necklace that was round and orange. All of a sudden the being was in my room. He took his hand and reached down to grab my hand from where I was lying in bed and literally pulled me out of my body. I felt strange vibrations all over my body. I saw myself hovering over my body with him. We were both floating in the air. He was trying to caress me with kisses. Then we were dancing in this strange place. I knew that he was some kind of dark being. I felt like he was a vampire. I can't remember anything after that."

He was trying to caress me with kisses. Then we were dancing in this strange place. I knew that he was some kind of dark being.

Carol said that she does not know the being's identity and said that she had other encounters with him "but they are just too weird to even describe. Sometimes I feel that it's my mind playing tricks on me." Carol admitted that, in spite of her better judgment, she felt "so compelled towards him. In the other encounters that I've had with him in my dreams, he revealed some weird information. When I asked him what he does, he answered, 'I roam. It's both a blessing and a curse.' He also told me that he's not going to hurt me. If he wanted to harm me, he would have done it long ago."

Pondering her strange relationship with an entity that she first encountered when she was only a child, Carol said that she knew that he was some kind of vampire creature. "I don't know what he wants with me," she said. "I cannot shake his eyes. I'm not afraid of him. I'm just curious and strangely allured to him."

My advice to Carol was that she use our techniques of warding off negative entities and break off her fascination with this multidimensional being as quickly as possible. No matter how appealing and attractive these beings may appear, there is no possibility of having a relationship of mutual respect. These parasitic entities exist only to possess and exploit.

The Winged Being Hitch-Hiked on a Plane

Judging from the email that I receive, a good number of individuals are somehow psychically conditioned from childhood to see vampiric-like winged beings. Ian saw such an entity while he was flying in an airplane. When he was a boy of eight, Ian saw

The thing on the wing of the plane looked like some kind of prehistoric reptile.

what he believed to be Mothman. In his early twenties, he experienced missing time when he was driving. When he regained awareness of his environment, he found that he had driven 15 miles in the opposite direction from which he had been driving. Again, while in his mid-twenties, he had another strange experience which he attributed to some kind of interaction with Mothman.

Then, in September 2007, he was flying in a plane from Detroit to Las Vegas when he saw something so bizarre that he cannot begin to explain it. The flight was roughly over northern Nevada, Ian said, when he looked out of his window seat to see something standing on the wing next to the engine. It was very large, and when Ian looked again he convinced himself that it was somehow part of the engine.

He was flying in a half-empty plane and had an entire seating section to himself. His seat was next to a window overlooking the front end of the airplane's wing. Because he was rather bored with the flight, Ian continued to look out the window at the large, hulking object on the wing. After a few minutes of concentrated attention, Ian saw that the "airplane part" had a large pearl-like eye and a large mouth full of gleaming "pearls." The body was red and was surrounded by a swirling pale blue light.

Ian decided that whatever it was, it had to be a part of the airplane and that his eyes were playing tricks on him. The airplane began to drop in elevation, and Ian looked away from the window and began reading the book that he had brought with him. When he next looked out the window, the Thing was still there. He thought about taking its picture on his cell phone, but he decided that he was just being paranoid. There was nothing there on the wing that shouldn't be there.

"Then it struck me that I was seeing something strange, but very special," Ian said. "A feeling of evil came over me. I did not want to look at it any longer."

A few minutes later, Ian could no longer resist looking out the window. As he watched, the Thing detached itself from the wing of the airplane and began a slow descent. Ian continued to watch it until it disappeared from sight. Ian said that he had been questioning for months what it was that he had seen on the airplane's wing. The sketch that he attached to an email looked to me like a large-winged reptilian creature, suggestive of a pterosaur, supposedly extinct for over 60 million years. Could such a monster of the air still exist? Was it just hitching a ride on an airplane to conserve its energy?

Ian said "no way" was it some kind of alien spacecraft. The more he sketches his memory of the being, the more it looks to him like some kind of giant insect.

Whatever it may have been, it doesn't usually come as optional equipment for modern airplanes. It may, however, have been one of the reptilian-like creatures from the multidimensional spaces between Earth and the stars that seek to trouble the minds and souls of humans.

Any Emmy Award-winning TV Producer Meets a Ghostly Vampire

When I queried my friend and colleague Tim R. Swartz, an Emmy Award-winning television producer, if he had ever had any encounters with vampires, he sent me this fascinating case that he investigated in 1982. Swartz related the following story.

I was working for a television station in Dayton, Ohio at the time, and I worked with an engineer who had a girlfriend who was experiencing some sort of unusual phenomenon. The engineer was a Christian, and he told me that he wanted nothing to do with the situation, but he also wanted to help his girlfriend with her problem. Since he knew that I investigated things such as ghosts and UFOs, he thought that maybe I could somehow help. The girlfriend, Marilyn D., worked in Human Resources for a large company in Cincinnati. When I met her, I noticed right away that she looked thin, pale, and ill. She reassured me that she felt fine and went right into her story.

A few years earlier, Marilyn had been a senior in college and one night, along with her roommate and some other girlfriends, conducted a séance just for the fun of it. For a half-hour or so, nothing happened, and just as the young women were ready to call it an evening, Marilyn's roommate suddenly went into what seemed to be a trance and began to address Marilyn directly. "The voice that came out of the mouth of my roommate was totally different from her normal voice," Marilyn said. "The spirit was clearly a man as its voice was lower and gruff. It also spoke with an odd accent and occasionally used words no one could understand."

The entity identified itself as the spirit of Marilyn's lover from a past life. The spirit refused to give Marilyn his name, instead it told her that in her previous life, she had spurned him for someone with more money and social class and he killed himself as

The victim of this vampiric harassment drew a sketch of her night stalker. Here is a professional artist's interpretation of that sketch (illustration by Ricardo Pustanio).

a result of her betrayal. Marilyn was shocked to hear the strange voice tell her that it still loved her and that she would eventually succumb to its seduction. At that point the spirit withdrew, leaving the roommate in a very confused and disoriented state.

From that moment on, according to Marilyn, her spirit suitor never left her side. She could hear its voice in her ear, telling her how much it loved and needed her and that they were destined to be together. Her apartment at night took on a life all of its own with strange raps and unearthly voices that whispered half-heard words in the shadows. As well, household items began to move about on their own.

Marilyn's roommate finally moved out when she saw the door of a coat closet open and close on its own. Once Marilyn was by herself, she began to see her ghostly beau whom she described as tall, dark-skinned, and with eyes and a mouth that seemed much too large for its thin face. She would awaken in the middle of the night to see

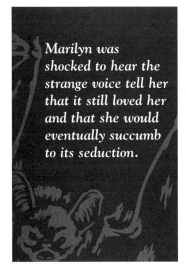

Marilyn was shocked to hear the strange voice tell her that it still loved her and that she would eventually succumb to its seduction.

it standing at the foot of her bed with a hungry grin on its face and its eyes seeming to radiate a light all their own. Marilyn explained to me that she tried moving several times, but the entity would follow her wherever she went.

Even more disturbing, she said, was that it had started getting into bed with her, lying on top of her and biting her at various places on her body. It explained that because it had killed itself in its previous life, it had to drink her blood in order to stay in the material world. She showed me several small bruises on her arms and legs that she said were the places that it had bit her last.

I convinced Marilyn to let me stay in her apartment overnight to see if I could experience any of the poltergeist phenomena for myself. Marilyn's boyfriend also joined me, confessing that this was the first time he had stayed at her place overnight as his religious beliefs prohibited him from taking their relationship to a physical level before marriage. I brought with me my trusty film camera as well as a television video camera from work. However, even though I brought with me a set of freshly charged batteries for the camera, batteries that normally would work for more than an hour, within 15 minutes in the apartment, the batteries were completely dead.

Marilyn stayed in her room, and we camped out in the living room of her small apartment. We kept a small light on over the oven so that we weren't in total darkness, and waited. We didn't have to wait very long as odd noises soon began to emanate from various locations around the place.

At times it would sound like a small animal scratching first in one corner, and then another. Then there would be strange knocks and raps on the walls and furniture. We tried to engage whatever was making the noises by asking questions and trying to get it to knock in response, but it ignored us and continued with its random noises. At one point the scratching and raps got so loud and persistent that I wondered how the neighbors could stand the mad cacophony. (I later discovered that none of Marilyn's neighbors had ever heard a thing from her apartment, a fact that amazed me considering how loud the noises were when I was there.)

At 3:00 A.M., I heard a strange whispering sound coming from Marilyn's room, so I peeked in (she had left her door open). I could see in the half-darkness that Marilyn was obviously asleep, but was writhing on her bed as if in the throes of passion. It may have been the lighting, but it looked to me as if there was someone with Marilyn that night, someone who was invisible to my eyes, but whose physical presence could clearly be seen as it made love to the young woman.

We left the next morning even more confused than when we had started. None of the photographs I had taken turned out, and my video camera had been useless. Marilyn called me a few days later and confessed that she had omitted telling me something about her relationship with the spirit. She said that starting several months earlier it had started coming to her at night, making love to her as it bit and drank her blood.

Marilyn said that her "Dracula," as she often referred to it, was the best lover she had ever had and that she was addicted to its nightly visitations—despite the fact that she usually felt exhausted and weak the next day.

> *We left the next morning even more confused than when we had started. None of the photographs I had taken turned out, and my video camera had been useless.*

This case had taken a strange turn that I had not expected. In the past, Marilyn had a healthy sex life and enjoyed the company of a number of men. However, after she started dating her current boyfriend, who did not believe in sex before marriage, she began to feel depressed and frustrated from their lack of physical contact. That is when her spirit friend began to push itself onto her sexually, something that she resisted at first, but soon relented when her resolve finally weakened.

I wish that I could say that this case had a satisfying resolution, but often with these sort of cases things do not turn out happily. Not too long after my investigation, Marilyn broke up with her boyfriend and moved to another apartment. I soon moved to another city and lost touch with her.

Several years later I found out that Marilyn had died of complications from anorexia, a condition that started with her shortly after she graduated from college. So I am left with a strange story of a girl who said that a spirit would make love to her and drink her blood, a girl that would later die of anorexia. I often wonder if her experiences were symptoms of her disease, or if her disease was a symptom of her experiences. I will never know for sure.

The Mysterious Lady in Black

K evin Stewart's friends didn't prove to be very much help when it came to reconstructing exactly what had happened to the young man the night that his spirit was ensnared by a vampiric entity. A number of his classmates at the Texas college that Kevin attended admitted that they like to tease him about his strict Southern Baptist beliefs and that they did their best to lure him into joining them in bars and in weekend drinking parties. On every previous occasion, Kevin had good-naturedly declined their offers and said that his father would "blow his stack" if he were to accept their invitation.

Something about that night was different.

On the night that Kevin met the mysterious lady in black, one of Kevin's friends, Charles, recalled that he and three other guys from the dormitory had taken a break from a late-night study session and had gone out for a bite to eat at a small café that was popular with students. They were surprised to see Kevin enter the café so late at night, but when they saw his bulging book bag, they surmised that he had been studying in the library.

Charles yelled out Kevin's name, and Kevin turned and smiled, recognizing his friends. "Say, Kevin," Charles said when he was seated at the table with them, "the fellows and I are going out drinking tonight. Why don't you join us?" Charles said later that he was only giving Kevin a hard time, for it was test week and a very unwise time to go drinking. In spite of knowing that there was no way that they would think of partying that night, Charles continued the playful banter by suggesting that maybe, like his father, Kevin was afraid that bad boys like them would drive the devils into him.

Charles let out a short laugh and punched Kevin playfully on the shoulder. "How about it, boys?" he said, including the circle of friends seated at the table with an expansive sweep of his arm. "Shall we drive the devils of drink into poor Kevin?"

The others laughed jovially, and Kevin joined them, a little nervously. Then in a loud voice he declared: "Well, then, we had better start now, because it will take a whole lot of drink and devils to shake my father's religion out of me."

For a moment Charles was completely stunned. With two major tests the next morning, there was no way that he had been serious about going out and tossing down some drinks. But Kevin had accepted his *faux* invitation to go out on a drinking party. Now, in spite of the big tests he and the others faced the next day, he would have to follow through with the booze or he would never hear the last of it. They were all 21 and they all had driver's licenses, so all they had to do now was to find a bar that was still serving drinks.

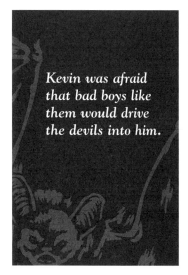

Kevin was afraid that bad boys like them would drive the devils into him.

"Well said, Kevin," the others cried, as they rose from their chairs and prepared to commence with the evening's drinking binge. Charles put his arm around Kevin and said that they all knew that under that stern Southern Baptist exterior there beat the heart of a true cool dude.

In the meantime, Kevin's parents waited anxiously for their son to return from school. The elder Stewart had managed to amass quite a fortune in his lifetime, but he had come by it slowly. He had begun as a clothing sales clerk and finally became prosperous as a clothing merchant in Dallas. All his life, though, John Stewart had been a devoted follower of Christianity, and he wished his son to be similarly devout. As a consequence, the rather strict elder man usually forbade Kevin to keep company with some of the other sons of other prominent businessmen in Dallas. These young men, the anxious father felt, were lazy playboys, who, because they had never had to work for money, did not understand its true value. The easy accessibility of spending cash seemed to encourage vice rather than religious fervor, and the "playboy" sons were often out drinking, gambling, and mixing with women of questionable morals. Such behavior Stewart scorned, yet he feared his son, Kevin, might find it only too attractive.

As the hours dragged by and Kevin did not return, Stewart felt his anxiety turn to anger. Where could the boy be? As John Stewart paced the room with mounting fury, his wife, Madeline, became increasingly nervous.

"John, please stop pacing so. Remember your blood pressure," she said. "Kevin will return."

"I know he will return," John replied grimly. "It is *how* he will return that concerns me. He'll be full of drink, no doubt."

The angry man slammed his fist against a wall. "I told him not to go out with those irresponsible boys. I tell him to read and study the Bible, to study the lives of successful Baptist businessmen, and always to walk with God in his heart, and what does he do? He goes out drinking. Drinking! How can he have the nerve to enter our home after such behavior?"

"John," his wife replied, eager to placate her furious husband. "Kevin is barely 21. He is at the age when it is hard to resist the temptation to rebel, hard to resist the pressures of his friends. Be easy on him, please. And you must be easy on yourself, too. Look, it is time for bed and your blood is so stirred you will not be able to sleep."

"Don't you worry," Stewart told his wife. "I'll sleep. But tomorrow, when I awaken, I will teach Kevin a lesson in obedience that he will never forget. He may be 21, but he still lives under my roof."

After that threatening declaration, John Stewart stalked grimly to his bedroom. An hour later, Madeline Stewart walked into their bedroom and looked down at her husband, who lay in fitful slumber. The house was still, yet she strained her ears for the slightest sound, the slightest indication that Kevin had returned home. The woman had found herself unable to sleep. She feared for her son's safety when he was out so late at night, and she feared for the expression of her husband's anger in the morning. What would he do to Kevin to teach him a "lesson he would never forget?" Madeline hoped that by intercepting Kevin that night, she could prepare him for his father's wrath in the morning.

It did not take long for the five college men to find a bar that was still serving drinks at one o'clock. Later, Charles told paranormal researchers that the others were quite amazed at how many beers and whiskey shots that Kevin put away.

The lady in black (illustration by Ricardo Pustanio).

"We all believed him to be a solid, non-drinking Southern Baptist Junior Saint, but Kevin surprised us by not only keeping up with us drink for drink, but in his ability to hold his booze," Charles said.

Charles and the others thought that it was around 2:30 that she entered the bar. "This lady, dressed completely in black with raven-black hair, sat alone at the table directly across from us," he said. "She wore a dark scarf that covered most of her face, but the portion that was visible was gorgeous. And her dark eyes were incredible. They seemed unusually large and they were extremely hypnotic."

The college men had just enough to drink to drown their inhibitions, and they soon began to make some very flirtatious and openly sexual remarks to the lady in black. "Suddenly, she got to her feet and stood directly in front of our table," Charles said. "She was quite tall, and her scarf fell away from her face so that I could see that she was dark-complexioned and a real knock-out—even though she was an older woman, maybe in her mid-forties. She grabbed Kevin's hand and pulled him into a standing position, and the rest of us starting hooting and laughing."

According to Charles, Kevin uttered not a sound. He just stared into the mysterious woman's eyes. And when she pulled him to the door, he meekly followed her outside. Charles said that was the last they saw of either of them that night. "Kevin walked out with the sexy lady, and we got stuck with paying his share of the bill," Charles grumbled.

Madeline Stewart had just shifted to a more comfortable position as she sat reading in bed when she thought she heard muffled footsteps in the next room. As noiselessly as possible, she slipped from her bed and made her way to the front of the house. A thin crack of light was visible from behind the bathroom door, and she indulged in a moment's righteous satisfaction at the thought of her son paying for his disobedience with an upset stomach and violent retching. Tactfully, she decided to leave him alone.

A half hour later, however, the bathroom door which had been locked from the inside still had not swung open. Perhaps Kevin was suffering from more than temporary nausea. "Kevin," Madeline said softly through the door, "is there anything the matter? You have been in there for a long time. Come out. I want to talk to you."

The stranger in the bathroom started to chuckle obscenely, then she burst into deep guffaws of devilish merriment.

Madeline listened carefully for a response, but there was none. "Kevin?" she called once more in a low voice. "You can come out. If you are drunk, I won't tell your father, but you must come to bed now." Again she listened carefully for a response. What she heard nearly caused the poor woman to faint.

"You idiotic bitch," shouted a coarse woman's voice from within the bathroom. "I don't give a damn what this boy's father thinks. It sure as hell doesn't concern me."

"Kevin," Madeline barely whispered.

"*Kevin,*" the voice on the other side of the door mimicked. "Woman, you haven't got a 'Kevin' anymore, so don't call me that again. And don't call me your 'son' either, because I am definitely not your baby boy.

The stranger in the bathroom started to chuckle obscenely, then she burst into deep guffaws of devilish merriment. "You might say I'm your daughter," the voice uttered, immensely amused at the idea. "After all, I am using your son's body. Oh, this is hilarious," she laughed. "A woman in a boy's body. I haven't tried that before." Whoever was in the bathroom went into peals of laughter, and each cadence acted as a stinging slap in Madeline Stewart's face. With a sob of horror, she tore herself away from the bathroom door and fled to her sleeping husband's side.

"John! John!" she cried, violently shaking him by the shoulders. "Someone has broken into our home."

John Stewart awakened with a start and stared with disbelieving eyes at his distraught wife. "Madeline, calm yourself! Tell me what has frightened you." Madeline's voice was trembling as she told her husband that somehow a coarse and vulgar woman had broken into their home and had barricaded herself in one of the bathrooms. As the two made their way to the bathroom, the malicious laughter again rang throughout the house. John Stewart glanced quickly down at his wife and hurried toward the bathroom door.

"Who is in there?" Stewart demanded to know. "Come out of there immediately or I shall have you arrested!" The only response was another roar of laughter. "Come out at once or I'll break down the door!" Stewart threatened. Still the laughter did not stop and the handle of the door did not turn.

Stewart threw the weight of his body against the bathroom door and crashed into the small room. He had expected to see some vulgar street woman who had trespassed into their home, but instead he found himself staring directly into the eyes of his only son.

"Oh, this is all really too funny," said a woman's voice. "Just get the hell away from me, and I'll go out the door and leave you alone."

"Kevin, what has happened to you?" Stewart demanded. "Why are you talking that way?"

The creature that had possessed Kevin stopped chuckling and stared coldly at Stewart. "Listen, you ignorant old bastard! I am not Kevin. I've got this body now, and I'm not going to give it up, so you just forget about ever having had a son. Just let go of my arm, or I'll bite it off." The thing cocked its head to one side and raised an eyebrow, waiting for a response to its challenge. When it saw the look of fear on Stewart's face, its expression changed to a hideous grin, and once again the evil laughter reverberated throughout the house.

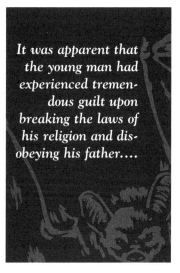

It was apparent that the young man had experienced tremendous guilt upon breaking the laws of his religion and disobeying his father....

Somehow, Madeline and John managed to drag their screaming son to his room and prop a door against the handle so he could not get out. The rest of the sleepless night they listened to roars of rage and howls of anger issuing from Kevin's room. The pounding on the door and the screams did not stop until sunrise.

The next morning the Stewarts took their son to Dr. Martinez, a prominent psychiatrist of Dallas. Dr. Martinez interviewed Kevin, Madeline, and John, separately. At the conclusion of these sessions, he called the anxious parents into his private office. Kevin had suffered a nervous breakdown, the doctor explained. It was apparent that the young man had experienced tremendous guilt upon breaking the laws of his religion and disobeying his father by going on a drinking binge with his college friends. Fearful of John's rage, Kevin had fled a confrontation altogether and created a substitute personality.

It was Dr. Martinez's belief that Kevin's breakdown was simple enough to diagnose and treat. He ordered the young man sent to a private mental rehabilitation center in Dallas, then assured the Stewarts that all would soon be well with their son. Kevin stayed at the rehabilitation facility for two months without responding to treatment. A good share of the time, he had to be kept sedated because of his violent behavior.

The Stewarts sadly decided that psychiatry was not the answer, and brought their son back home. John employed a male nurse to help Madeline control Kevin during the daylight hours. Teddy, a husky middle-aged man, fought off Kevin's occasional physical attacks, but he was extremely confused by the screeching woman's voice that came from the young man's body. He told Madeline that he didn't mind the profanity, the cursing, and the attempts to hit or to scratch him, but that shrieking voice certainly did bother him. Teddy stayed until early evening, joined the Stewarts for the evening meal, then left at Kevin's bedtime, when the young man was sedated.

Kevin had been home for about a week when a professor in anthropology from a local college telephoned the Stewarts and asked if he might visit the beleaguered family. He had been hearing some strange rumors from certain students and a friend of his who was a female nurse at the mental asylum where Kevin had been sequestered. The nurse had heard Kevin speaking in a number of unfamiliar languages in a very loud female voice.

When the professor arrived at the Stewart residence, he apologized for the intrusion and asked to speak with the "woman" inhabiting Kevin's body. Teddy brought Kevin into the study and stood by as the professor introduced himself to the "woman inside of Kevin."

The professor had not conversed with the entity very long before he joined John and Madeline in the living room and excitedly informed them that he had made an interesting discovery. While trying to persuade the uncooperative woman to talk with him, he had heard her mutter something in an Egyptian Arabic dialect. The language was well-known to the professor, and he immediately began asking her questions in her native tongue. At last she agreed to tell him her story while he tape recorded their conversation. Later, a paranormal researcher was able to obtain a transcript of the professor's later tape recording in which he translated his original recording into English:

> I lived on the earth in Cairo, hundreds of years ago, and I was happy to be alive. The sun felt good on my body, and my feet enjoyed the feel of damp earth beneath them. Then, at the age of 15, I joined a cult of vampires who kidnapped men and women and sacrificed them to the Old Gods. We would catch some of the blood from our victims and drink it from a ceremonial cup.

> Because I was still a virgin, I was betrayed by the other cultists, and during a full moon ritual, I was sacrificed by those whom I believed to be my friends. With my dying breath, I cursed them as they pierced my body and drained my blood into the ceremonial cup. I felt cruelly robbed, for before my death I had been eager to live a full life of experience and adventure. I refused to accept the verdict of the gods and sought immediately to enter another body.

> I did not want to occupy an old body, one that had already experienced much and was ready to die. I wanted a young body, so that I would have a long span of years ahead of me. I wanted to touch with hands, see with physical eyes, hear, smell, and feel again the things I had delighted in while still living. I had wandered as a restless spirit for a very long time when I came upon a lovely young woman. She was saddened because her lover had left her for another. She was drinking heavily to drown her disappointment, and her spirit was weak and vulnerable. I entered her mind and caused her to slash her wrists. As she lay dying in a pool of her blood, my spirit entered her body and I possessed her. I lapped up some of her blood to give me strength, and for

many hundreds of years, I continued my life as a seductress and a vampire, restoring myself with blood donated by willing lovers.

The woman told the professor that she would inhabit a woman's body until the individual aged, then she would seek another beautiful young woman to replace the one growing older. She traveled from Egypt to Persia, then to Europe and Scandinavia, and now to the United States. Then she described the events of the night that she encountered Kevin, drinking with his friends in the bar.

> I was attracted to the soul lodged in this boy's body. He was about the age that I had been when I died, and he was healthy. Also, I could see that his soul was not anchored firmly within its physical form, for it had been loosened with drink and fear of his father's wrath. I was greedy for young life again, so I entered, forcefully. The boy struggled only a short time, for I was the stronger. Once inside the body, I was almost wild with delirium. I had never in all those many centuries possessed the body of a young man.

> Kevin's parents were so foolish when they found me. They refused to believe what had happened and persisted in calling me their son. I, female, and a son, too! I could only laugh. But I so resented it when they locked me up. If they wouldn't have released me when they did, I would have taken the body of one of the nurses. There was one there who was very attractive.

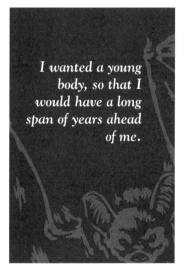

I wanted a young body, so that I would have a long span of years ahead of me.

The professor undertook to counsel the entity after hearing her story: "It is not right for you to have taken the body that rightfully belongs to another. It is time to quit your earthly existence. For your sake as much as for Kevin's, you must follow the will of God and return this body to its rightful owner."

"Never!" the spirit parasite cried, an ugly, defiant edge creeping into her voice. "I wrestled for this body. It is mine! I will never give it up!"

The Stewarts were at once baffled and encouraged by this successful attempt at communicating with the usurper of their son's body, but they became despondent upon learning of her stubborn refusal to vacate the body. They were also disappointed when Teddy told them that he would not be returning the next day. Witnessing the session with the professor in which a young college man spoke in a foreign tongue in a female voice had been too much for him. He, too, was a good Baptist, and he wasn't going to stay to work in any house that was sheltering a demon.

As a man of faith, John Stewart said that he understood. After both Teddy and the professor had left them, Stewart said that he had known from that first night that it had to be a demon that had possessed his son. He reached for the telephone and called his pastor to come to their home at once and conduct a spirit cleansing.

Although the pastor arrived that night and did his best to confront the spirit invader, the woman only laughed at him and mocked his words and his ritual. When the man of God persisted, the very room became alive with evil and explosive violence. Furniture overturned. Pictures flew off the wall. Several of Madeline's collector plates became airborne and smashed into the walls.

Worst of all, Kevin's features became distorted into a mask of malignant animosity, and he began to bellow a terrible, unearthly howl that caused one of their neighbors to pound on their door and ask what was going on in the Stewart household. Dr. Martinez had given them a prescription for tranquilizers, and with the help of the pastor, who was himself shaking from the ordeal, the Stewarts managed to calm their son and get him into his bed.

Kevin's features became distorted into a mask of malignant animosity, and he began to bellow a terrible, unearthly howl....

The next morning, John Stewart called the professor and asked for his advice. The Stewarts were at the end of their wits and their endurance. "Do not despair," the professor told them. "There is a spirit medium living 20 miles outside of Dallas. She is a very wise woman, and in my opinion, genuinely possesses many strange and wonderful abilities. What is even better for you and Kevin, she spent many years in the Middle East and fluently speaks several Arabic dialects. Call her, and see if she will help you."

The Stewarts were eager to do anything that would restore their son to his body, but John had severe reservations about contacting a spirit medium. According to church doctrine, such men and women were akin to Satanists. The Bible warned against such women, as the Witch of Endor, who communicated with spirits. The professor assured John that it was not so. He suggested that Stewart look upon the medium as a kind of spiritual counselor, a shaman, perhaps.

Madeline insisted that they not delay, and they contacted the woman and arranged for her to travel to their home in Dallas. The first thing the medium did when she arrived was to reassure the Stewarts that she was quite familiar with such entities as the one who afflicted their son. While she was studying in Egypt, she had been apprentice to a very wise elderly sage who had explained the best methods of expelling such demons, and she had learned special chants and rituals to expedite such an expulsion.

The medium drew a large circle around Kevin, who was seated in the center of the room. Though this circle was made only of chalk, she said that the invading spirit could not force Kevin's body to step outside it, no matter how hard she tried. Sensing that she was about to be ousted, the Egyptian girl began to curse everyone present in vile terms. The medium addressed the spirit parasite in the Egyptian Arabic dialect, ordering it to leave in the name of God. This brought on a torrent of rage from the possessing entity, but the medium continued, unperturbed.

Following this preliminary stage of the exorcism, the medium dipped into her arcane lore and began assaulting the demon in more esoteric ways. She chanted softly in an unknown tongue, gradually increasing her volume. The spirit medium's voice grew strong and authoritative. Her incantations filled the room, drowning out the hideous shrieks and hysterical sobs of the demon.

Suddenly the Egyptian woman's voice rang out from within Kevin's shaking form. "No! No! I shall never leave this body. Never!"

No sooner had she uttered those words than Kevin's body jerked upright and fell upon the floor. He flailed wildly, as though having a seizure, and shuddered and writhed upon the floor. Saliva foamed at the corners of his trembling lips, and the Stewarts were horrorstricken with the thought that their son would die.

John Stewart was ready to stride through the circle, but the medium restrained him. "It is horrible, I know," she whispered, "but it will soon be over." A single agonized scream pierced the air and the writhing body of Kevin Stewart lay still. "Your son has returned to his body," the medium stated simply.

No sound, no movement issued forth from the inert body on the floor. Madeline Stewart took a tentative step in the direction of her son, then stopped, afraid.

A single agonized scream pierced the air and the writhing body of Kevin Stewart lay still.

"Wait for just a few seconds more," the medium assured her, "then your son will awaken as if from a deep sleep." The medium scarcely had time to complete her sentence when the young man's body stirred. Stewart and his wife stared with disbelief, then joy, as their son sat up, rubbed his eyes dazedly, and spoke in his own natural voice: "What has happened? Why am I here on the floor?"

Then seeing his parents standing above him, Kevin said in an apologetic tone, "Oh, no, did I come home drunk last night? Father, Mother, forgive me, but after studying in the library, I stopped to chat with my friends in a café. I did not intend to go drinking. I don't know what made me do it."

John and Madeline knelt and embraced their son and told him that they forgave him. For Kevin, it was as if the past several months had only been one night of ill-advised drinking. As Madeline showed the medium to the door, she couldn't help asking what had become of the woman who had come from ancient times to possess their son.

The medium sighed and shook her head. "It is not given to us mortals to know these things for certain," she said. "We can only trust that the Great Harmony that rules the universe has taken her soul to find peace at last."

Interviewing a 3,000-Year-Old Vampire in Her "House of Pain"

I could not help seeing certain strange similarities between the case of Kevin Stewart's bizarre possession by a Beautiful Lady in Black with an interview that my friend and colleague Paul Dale Roberts conducted in February 2009. This interview was conducted in Carol Gillis' home, a home she calls "The House of Pain." Shannon McCabe observed the interview and did the artwork which accompanies the interview. With Roberts's permission, I have excerpted portions of the interview with Carol Gillis, Vampire, below.

Paranormal investigators Paul Roberts and Shannon McCabe interviewed Carol Gillis, a vampire who claims to be 3,000 years old (illustration by Shannon McCabe).

Q: *How old are you?*

A: Three millennia. 3,000 years old.

Q: *When did you become a vampire?*

A: I was kidnapped from my home on my nineteenth year of life as a human and sold in slavery to the fledging court of Tutankhamen of Egypt. I was used as a dancing girl. I was chosen in the twenty-fifth year of my life, by my maker who was a high ranking Egyptian and changed into a vampire.

Q: *When you became a vampire, did you have the craving?*

A: When I awoke from the change, the blood thirst was immediate and extremely powerful.

Q: *How did you quench your thirst?*

A: I grabbed a person and drank their blood. There are very many vessels on the human body. I usually drink from the victim's wrist.

Q: *Your appearance is of a woman in her early 40s. For how long have you looked that age?*

A: Approximately 400 years.

Q: *Do you get common head colds, and do you face other infectious diseases that humans get?*

A: I never catch colds or other infectious diseases that are common to humans.

Q: *Do you have any special powers? Can you fly or do anything else that would be considered superhuman?*

A: I am fast and strong, but I do not have superhuman powers.

Q: *As an immortal and being so wise, have you gathered a mass fortune of wealth?*

A: Yes. Swiss bank accounts are wonderful.

Q: *How do you feed now?*

A: I mainly feed on animals. I go up to Alaska and the Sierras to feed on various wildlife. The animals I feed off of will die after I finish my feeding.

Q: *As an immortal, can you feel pain if someone hits you?*

A: Yes, but not the way you feel pain. I can be killed and I can be damaged. I have a healing factor. The healing factor allows my body to heal any damages to my body quickly.

Q: *Is there any way of dying as a vampire?*

A: Beheading, dismemberment, and immolation.

The Mysterious Lady in Black of Baden-Baden

Apparently not all enigmatic female entities dressed in black are as bad as the one that invaded the body of Kevin Stewart. After listening to one of my radio interviews regarding various entities from the world of shadows, a man we'll call Timothy wrote to share a series of encounters with a mysterious lady in black that he had experienced while living in Germany from 1992 to 1995. Timothy related this tale.

My father was in the Canadian armed forces and was posted in Baden-Baden [Germany]. Instead of going to university right after I graduated from high school, I decided to move there for a few years and "find myself."

I'll see if I can paint a picture of how the shop section of CFB Baden-Baden looked like in September 1992. It was a very long cobblestone street with shops on both sides. Cars couldn't travel on it, pedestrians only. Near the entrance of the shopping area on one side was a movie theater and the Canex (shopping establishment). Beside the theater were some Black Forest trees and a number of empty buildings. The other side of the street housed a complex of fast food stores, and a small building with washers and dryers in which all of the restaurants washed their linens. As you moved up the street, there was a large gap with some tables that had probably been a parade area after the Second World War. Past that was a book store and Pizza Plus where I worked.

One Sunday I was working prep at the pizza place and was getting ready for the day. I was taking a load of things to be washed when I noticed that the street was devoid of anything moving but myself. It struck me as odd at the time, because there was always someone walking around there. It was overcast and no wind. It was one of those gray days.

On my way back to Pizza Plus, something caught my eye. I looked down to the entrance of the shopping area, and I noticed this female figure dressed all in black with what looked like black sunglasses. Her hair was black, as well, and I'll have to say that my impression was that she had very pale skin. I had a good 200 feet of clear view, and

The strange woman wore a black dress and sunglasses and had very pale skin.

the only thing standing there was this figure in black. She struck me as odd because there was no one else around but the two of us, so I took a second look. Keep in mind this second glance did not take long in happening after I turned away the first time.

She was gone.

I stopped and looked around, and there was nothing at the end of the street. I was alone again. It was kind of creepy. I knew that I saw something, and there was no way someone could disappear or move out of view in the time it took for me to turn my head and look back again.

As I was heading back to the pizza place, I turned and looked back because I felt like I needed to do so—and there she was again. I actually stopped and turned to face her fully. I almost felt that she was watching me and checking me out. I'll admit I was doing the same. She was far away, and yet I could see her clear as day. I didn't feel threatened, only curious. And I got the impression the feeling was mutual. I heard some noise behind me. It was a military vehicle driving by the end of that side of the street. When I looked back she was gone.

After that initial sighting in 1992, I saw her many times during the three years that I lived in Germany. It felt weird when I didn't see her or "feel" her nearby. It was a little unsettling at first, but I got used to it pretty quick. Sometimes, it would be weird. I would be driving down the highway, and I would see her standing on the side of the road, watching me as I drove by.

Day, night, it didn't matter. She always looked the same. I'd say she stood just under five-feet-nine inches. She had long black hair, and she always dressed in black clothing, nothing flashy nothing bland. When I went for walks at night, I would talk softly to her. Oddly enough, I never asked her questions. I felt like I didn't need to. And I won't lie. A small part of me was afraid that if I did ask her any questions, she would either leave or answer back in words for which I might not be prepared to hear.

In retrospect, I wish I had asked a few questions. I only know at the time that I simply didn't feel like I needed to communicate with her in that way. It just felt right that she would be close by. I never saw her up close, but I could feel whenever she was near. I could see her shadow in windows as I walked by them. I always felt like she was watching and waiting. I would talk to her when I went for walks. Never really out loud, but in my mind if that makes any sense.

I know it sounds like she was a stalker. I didn't see her every day. I just knew she was there. I never once felt threatened. She was my woman in black. I firmly believe that she wasn't a ghost. Not once did I ever get that feeling. She always seemed to be very solid to me. She could come and go at will, but she was always dressed in black.

As I said, it was my impression that she had very pale skin. She had long, dark hair, but I never saw her eyes. I remember telling my dad about her once, and he just looked at me and smiled. Germany was an old country, he said, and the Black Forest is like that. When I finally moved back to Canada, I knew she was not with me anymore. Looking back I am very surprised at how little I questioned of the situation.

Who was she? What was she? Why me? What did she want from me? Why did she not follow me to Canada when she followed me all over Germany?

There will be times when I will think about her and feel a little sad. In a small way I think I miss her, and I can't say why. I really feel like I left a part of me behind in Germany—and my mysterious lady in black still has that special part of me.

A Vampiric Demon Conjured by the Occult Stole His Wife

R yan Harris is a sober, intelligent man. He works quietly and diligently and rears his two children as best he can. He never stops hoping that someday the horrible vampiric demon that seized his wife Elena will release her, and she will be able to come home to him and the children. In 1998, he told the remarkable story of how a monster that seemed to come from another dimension of time and space had stolen his wife.

Ryan Harris met Elena Sanchez in 1981 while both were in college. In addition to her physical attractiveness, something about her immediately attracted him to her. Perhaps it was the elusiveness that lured him towards her, urging him to try and capture those qualities within her. Perhaps it was the hint of the exotic she displayed in her tastes and interests.

Elena was deeply involved in the occult and practiced many of its related disciplines. She was accomplished in Hatha Yoga, meditated often, and had studied a few texts on ceremonial magic. She frequently took solitary walks through the woods in back of the college, and when Ryan persuaded her to take him along, he was amazed at the empathy she seemed to share with the forest creatures. Her influence extended to the plant kingdom, for no one could persuade plants to grow as strongly and beautifully as she.

There were times that Ryan would come upon Elena while she was engaged in other practices, and though he never knew much about these rituals, they gave him a vaguely uneasy feeling. He could not be sure, but he felt at times that Elena's assiduous reading of the Bible did not necessarily restrict her to the beneficent side of occultism. Indeed, sometimes it seemed as though she flirted with the darker, malevolent forces. Aside from Elena's occult leanings, the girl was very musically minded, an extremely talented artist, and she had a jovial air about her that at once charmed and delighted her young suitor.

The two had been dating for some time; and, just before graduation, Ryan gathered his courage to ask Elena to marry him. Elena regarded Ryan gravely. "I will marry

What he thought was a product of his wife's dreams was suddenly there in the bedroom: A hideous creature with white fangs curling around a serpent-like mouth. Its eyes were bright red orbs, like openings into a world in which one would be lost forever (illustration by Bill Oliver).

you," she told the anxiously waiting Ryan, "but not because I love you. Don't get me wrong, though, because I am very fond of you. I'll marry you because I know I must: It is my karma and yours."

She looked at him, tears brimming in her eyes, then clutched his hand. "Oh, Ryan, I'm afraid it won't work out very well, not at all. Still, if it is to be, it will be, and there's nothing we can do about it. It has been ordained by powers greater than we." Elena broke off when she saw the strange expression in Ryan's eyes. She leaned over and hugged him impulsively. "Oh, forget all that nonsense I was babbling. Yes, dear, yes, I'll marry you!"

Ryan forgot Elena's sad prophecy in the years immediately following their marriage in June 1986. Both of them had come from small towns in the Pacific Northwest, and they were eager to try city life. They settled enthusiastically in Portland, where Ryan found work as an accountant for a large printing company. The two experienced no marital difficulties other than the usual adjustment of one person's habits to another's until Elena became pregnant with their first child in the late spring of 1987. It was then that something began to go very wrong, causing Ryan to remember her unhappy prediction that their marriage would "not work out very well, not at all."

Elena began having a series of terrifying nightmares, all with the same disturbing theme. She insisted that a demon was trying to possess her body. She became waspish and ill-tempered, resentful of Ryan. According to Elena, the demon appeared to her in two forms. One was as a frightening creature with a human face, the talons and legs of an eagle, the body and tail of a cat, and the leathery wings of a bat. The other form was in one sense far more insidious. It was of a man, who bore a strong resemblance to Ryan.

Elena said that she held the demon responsible for the wild ideas that she found herself entertaining. She was convinced that the monster was trying to persuade her that Ryan was the source of her problems; and after a time, it appeared as though the creature had succeeded in convincing her of it, for she began acting hostile whenever her husband was near her. Ryan felt certain that his wife was the victim of some delusion, and it hurt him deeply that in her fantasies she would cast him as the villain. He could not believe his wife was becoming insane, nor could he accept her own explanation of what was happening to her. He did not know what he should do.

One day, while working out in the garage, Ryan heard a tremendous crash in the kitchen. When he rushed to the area, he found Elena standing amidst thousands of shards of glass. She looked confused, horrified.

"It was the glass pitcher," she explained. "I don't know why I did it. I just felt an uncontrollable urge to smash it."

On another occasion, Ryan was rummaging about in the basement when he found a sheet, ripped to shreds.

"Elena," he asked, confronting her with the bits of cloth, "did you do this?"

"Yes," she answered helplessly. "I don't know what came over me. I felt this urge to destroy. To destroy whatever I could get my hands on the fastest."

Then, somewhere in the midst of several similar incidents, Elena began to get defensive about her actions. She lied, tried to hide any evidence of her destructive moods. Finally, Ryan came upon her while she was in the act of strangling a neighborhood cat with an electric cord. He rushed towards her and tried to pull her away from the unfortunate animal. Elena turned to him, her face flushed, a malevolent gleam in her eye. Ryan was shocked at the sight of her and backed away as she loosened the hold of the noose around the cat's throat.

It was not until after Elena began getting that dreadful gleam in her eye whenever she picked a fight with Ryan that he decided something would have to be done. He turned to the Harris's family doctor, explaining the situation as best he could. Then he arranged for Elena to see the doctor, leading her to believe it was for a minor physical ailment about which she had been complaining.

The Harris's doctor was not qualified as a psychiatrist, but after talking to Elena at great length he could only shake his head. "Sound mind, sound body," he told Ryan. "I find nothing wrong with her."

In the meantime, the nightmares had continued. Elena became quite wild in her bedtime thrashings, and Ryan feared that she would miscarry.

It was with great relief that Ryan held his firstborn son in his arms in February 1988. The delivery had been perfect and right on schedule. Perhaps now Elena's nightmares would cease and peace would return to their home.

The birth of Robert Daniel Harris apparently did not impress the demon. It continued to disturb the Harris's household with unabated vigor. Ryan tried to leave his family problems at home each day when he went to work, but Elena's erratic behavior and the continued nighttime manifestations of the monstrous demon became increasingly hard for him to ignore. It was difficult to get a restful night's sleep hearing from his wife that a monstrous entity may be lurking in the shadows. Ryan's work began to suffer and he feared losing his job.

Elena became quite wild in her bedtime thrashings, and Ryan feared that she would miscarry.

The situation continued on this shaky turf for another two years, when another child was born to them, and baby girl Emily entered a troubled home on the afternoon of January 22, 1990. Ryan wondered at the wisdom of bringing a child into such a confusing environment; and a year after Emily's birth, he began to think seriously of bringing both the children to stay with his mother until Elena was better.

Matters had become far bleaker in the Harris's household. Elena seemed to suffer a complete split in her personality, and Ryan feared that his wife had finally succumbed to paranoid schizophrenia. As "Elena," she was a good, if troubled, wife and mother, the affectionate, sensitive woman Ryan had married. As "Alyssa" she was quarrelsome, violent, and unkempt. "Alyssa" began insulting the neighbors, harassing service people, and picking fights with strangers. Ryan suffered much embarrassment from her public attacks in stores, restaurants, and social gatherings. Finally a sympathetic coworker persuaded Ryan to consider having have his wife committed to an institution for the insane.

Although he was extremely reluctant to begin such seemingly drastic proceedings, close friends convinced him that it might well be the best thing for Elena, as well for the safety of their children. Perhaps she would only be under professional care for a brief period of time.

At the sanity hearing in May 1992, Elena completely submerged, and "Alyssa" came out, showing her best side. She argued brilliantly in her own defense, and half succeeded in craftily convincing the judge that Ryan had manufactured the entire story to be rid of her. With true deviousness she managed to discredit the testimony of several of the witnesses. She even suggested that her neighbor's testimony was false because the woman had been having an affair with Ryan.

With a sinking feeling in his heart, Ryan listened to the judge dismiss the case. He could only hope that the judge had done the right thing, but he feared the decision could only turn to tragedy. Ryan was convinced that his wife was completely insane. Forced as he was to accept the court's ruling, Ryan did not feel that he had a right to so sentence his children. Regretfully, he brought Robert and Emily to his parents' home north of Portland for temporary care.

This decision proved wise for the children, but unfortunate for Elena. No longer faced with the constant strain of remaining normal in front of her children, Elena took a turn for the worse. The "Alyssa" personality became dominant, and Ryan found himself living in a nightmare. The neighbors on the Harris's block became so antagonistic that Ryan decided to quit his job and leave the city. He could think of nothing else to do, so Ryan took Elena to her mother's home.

Mrs. Sanchez still had younger children at home and could not care adequately for her ailing older daughter. She suggested that the two go to the small acreage that the Sanchez family owned outside of town. The house on the place was neither large nor elegant, but it would certainly suffice for the two of them. Perhaps there, away from other people, Elena would recover her health and cease to believe in the demon.

For a time this move to the country seemed to make life easier for the beleaguered couple. Ryan planted a small garden and tried to be as self-sufficient as possible. Elena's condition did not improve, but somehow the situation seemed more tolerable with no other people around. Elena insisted that the demon had followed them, and she reported frequently that it had appeared to her. Ryan could not bring himself to believe in the possibility of demons and possession, and he continued to believe that his wife was insane.

The demon pursued his wife and him, finally revealing its horrifying form.

Throughout this whole period, Ryan had never once seen the demon or heard him. He had always had to rely on Elena's word that the creature actually existed, and this he could not do. Then, on a frightening night in October 1992, he saw with his own eyes the loathsome thing that had plagued his wife for so many years and that had so tragically disrupted his family's life.

It was a cool, moonlit evening. The only sound in the room was the gentle rustle of cloth as a light breeze breathed in through the window. Ryan Harris lay in peaceful slumber, Elena beside him. He rolled over on his side, suddenly aware of a noise that had awakened him.

"Out, thou foul demon! Why dost thou torment me? Go, and leave me in peace."

Harris's eyes fluttered open, his body tensed, his mind snapped to immediate alertness.

"Wilt thou never leave me and my afflicted family? Go, I abjure thee, in the name of the light. Leave me be!"

Harris could not believe his ears. The strange words, the King James-sounding English, were issuing forth from the mouth of his wife. Harris turned slowly to his wife, his arm out-stretched to shake her into wakefulness. She had to be having one horrible and incredibly weird nightmare about the demon.

"Thou shalt never claim this body or this soul. Leave me, for though thou try me sorely, I shall never yield to thee."

Elena Harris was sitting upright in bed, her eyes staring into the darkness at the foot of the bed. With a sudden attack of fear, Ryan Harris realized that his wife was not dreaming. She was addressing the demon that she had claimed for years was trying to invade her body—the very vampiric demon which Ryan Harris was convinced was only a figment of her imagination.

"Elena, what's going on? There's nothing in this bedroom but us."

Harris's eyes had finally grown accustomed to the darkness. The force of Elena's stare led his eyes to the foot of the bed, and what he saw in the pale moonlight caused a sickening wave of nausea to shake both his body and his mind and cut off his words.

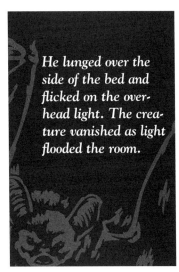

He lunged over the side of the bed and flicked on the overhead light. The creature vanished as light flooded the room.

"O, my God," he uttered slowly. "O, my God, my God."

The creature was loathsome, hideous looking. It was surrounded by a sickly luminescent cloud of green, and the face was a ghastly nightmare. White fangs curled around a thin, serpent-like mouth. Coarse, reddish-colored hair flowed around the perimeter of the skull, deathly gray in color. The eyes dominated the horrible visage. Bright red orbs, like endless tunnels through which one could be forever lost. Most hideous of all was the quite-human emotion gleaming incongruously in the primeval creature's eyes—the all too-human stare of savage lust.

"What in hell are you?" Harris screamed, his voice cracking. Neither the creature nor his wife responded to his cry.

Elena seemed hypnotized by the vile thing, unable to break eye contact.

"Thou loathsome denizen of Hell, thou shalt roast for all time for what thou has attempted with me, thou shalt...."

"Enough!" Harris cried."For God's sake, stop it!"

He lunged over the side of the bed and flicked on the overhead light. The creature vanished as light flooded the room. Ryan and Elena reached for each other, and Ryan held the sobbing body of his wife in his arms.

After witnessing the demon himself, Ryan no longer believed in the learned doctors or the detailed medical texts which called his wife's tormentor a delusion. He felt as though the medical and scientific professions had abandoned him, for who in the twentieth century would actually believe that a demon was stalking their house? Ryan felt there was no one for him to turn to, and the thought frightened him.

One evening, shortly after he had witnessed the demon, they were spending a quiet evening at home. Ryan was reading a few seed catalogues and Elena was busily sketching. After some minutes, Elena stood up and regarded her picture. Then she crossed over to Ryan and placed it in his lap without comment. The picture was a gross caricature of Ryan. Somehow Elena had pictured her husband as a man full of evil intent and hideous capabilities.

"Elena, what have you done?" he asked, stupefied. "This can't be me." "Of course it's not," she replied. "It's the demon."

"The demon? But it can't be!" Ryan protested. "I saw the demon myself. It didn't look like a man. And it didn't look like me!"

"But I told you, dear," Elena patiently explained, in the tone that she might take with a small child. "The demon comes to me in two forms. One is of the beast you saw that night; the other is of a man."

"But it can't be...."

"Of course it is, darling," Elena said, a strange smile beginning to play over her lips. "He was here all the time I was drawing him. He stood right in the middle of the floor and stared at me the whole time."

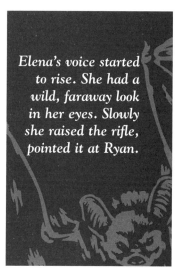

Elena's voice started to rise. She had a wild, faraway look in her eyes. Slowly she raised the rifle, pointed it at Ryan.

The horrifying gleam had returned to her eyes. Without taking her eyes off Ryan, Elena reached for the wall shelf where Ryan kept a fully loaded .22 caliber rifle.

"Don't you see, Ryan," she said, her face hardening, "the demon is you. That's why I have to kill you, dear. You see, I have to kill you, don't I? Because the demon left the center of the room and went straight into you."

Elena's voice started to rise. She had a wild, faraway look in her eyes. Slowly she raised the rifle, pointed it at Ryan. Ryan heard a click and knew that she had released the safety catch. Her finger tightened on the trigger.

"He couldn't get me, so he went into you. He's got you now, but I can free you. Don't worry," she soothed.

Ryan stared at Elena, speechless. He felt paralyzed. He seemed to be hearing her voice from a great distance. In a mindless daze he realized that his wife was going to murder him. Suddenly a noise on the roof diverted both of them, and Ryan regained his senses. Something was walking with measured tread across the roof of the house.

"Elena!" Ryan shouted. "Listen!"

The unmistakable hopping, scratching sound of what sounded like a large bird could be heard over their heads. The utter stillness in the room only served to amplify the noise of the footsteps on the roof.

"The demon is not in me," Ryan stated. "That there is a demon in our lives, I do not doubt, but Elena, the demon is not in me. Listen up there! He is hovering over our heads, waiting to see what you will do.

"Don't you see what he's doing?" Ryan continued. "If he appears in a form like mine, then it is to trick you into believing that I am he. He wants to turn you against me, because he knows that if I were out of the picture and you were alone, he would have a better chance at claiming you. If he were able to cause you to pull that trigger he would have you! He doesn't own your body yet, but he's trying, and killing me would be all the leverage he would need."

Elena faltered. "But when I finished the drawing he walked right to you and entered into you."

"He's trying to trick you," Ryan argued. "He's not interested in me; it's you he wants. He would never try for me unless he failed utterly with you, and you know he hasn't given up on you yet. Just listen, Elena. He's not in me—he's up there, on the roof!"

Elena swung the rifle toward the ceiling and wildly jerked the trigger.

"Away with you, thou foul and loathsome creature," she screamed. "You are destroying my life, miming my husband. You shall never find comfort here! Never! Never! Never!"

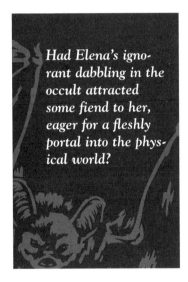

Had Elena's ignorant dabbling in the occult attracted some fiend to her, eager for a fleshly portal into the physical world?

The bullet tore through the roof as Elena shrieked hysterically. From up on the roof there was a mad scrambling and the macabre sound of huge wings flapping together. Then the creature flew off into the night. Elena stood transfixed, listening to the sound. Ryan took advantage of the moment and made a lunge for the rifle. Angrily he pushed her to the floor. Ryan was close to the edge of hysteria. He still recalled only too clearly the sight of his wife pointing the rifle at his chest.

"Oh, God," Elena sobbed, "What is going to become of me?"

Ryan glared at her, his body trembling. Then he strode away from her, not answering. He grabbed a blanket from the bed and stalked out of the house. The cramped quarters of a car would be a bed of roses compared to a bed shared with a murderer. Ryan hunched up in the car, reviewing the shambles of his marriage. What had happened to Elena? Had she been living in an imaginary world of the sinister side of the occult and become trapped by it?

He thought back to his proposal of marriage and pondered anew her cryptic acceptance. Had Elena been playing dramatic games, selling herself a line about "bad karma" and filling her head with exotic baleful predictions? Had she ever really loved him, or had she made him a character in her bizarre secret world?

It seemed in retrospect that the demon had first come to her when she was pregnant with Robert. Had she realized her error then, or become resentful of him for cluttering up her imaginary world with a very real baby and its inherent responsibilities? But Ryan, too, had seen the demon, and he had heard the flapping noise as something huge and with wings had taken off from the roof. Could it be that a demon was truly trying to possess her? Had Elena's ignorant dabbling in the occult attracted some fiend to her, eager for a fleshly portal into the physical world? That vile thing! He thought again of its hideous visage and shuddered.

No, he could not accept simple insanity as the answer. He had to admit to himself that some ghastly denizen from another realm of reality had brutally plunged itself between them, and would not leave them until either the demon won—or Elena died.

A sound outside the car distracted Ryan from his thoughts. It was Elena, shivering with cold. Her face was streaked with tears.

"Leave me alone," Ryan told her. "I need to think."

Elena began to cry softly. Finally Ryan opened the car door and she gratefully crawled in with him. Still weeping, she curled into his arms. Ryan did not close his eyes until he was sure that she was sleeping. When he was certain that she was asleep, Ryan slipped into the farmhouse and made a telephone call.

The next morning the Harrises hastily packed all their belongings and shoved them roughly in the car. Elena seemed to guess what was on Ryan's mind. She cuddled against his side and kept her gaze away from his. When they stopped for a snack, she clutched his hand and would not relinquish it until they were back in the car.

When they arrived at the Sanchez home, Ryan jumped out of the vehicle and quickly unloaded all of Elena's personal belongings. Without saying another word, Ryan slid behind the driver's seat once more, leaving his wife standing on the porch, her personal effects stacked around her. As he drove off the tears fell freely down his cheeks. A glance through the rear view window showed Elena standing on the porch, waving good-bye. Her face held a look of desolation and despair impossible to describe.

Two and a half months later Ryan received a letter from his mother-in-law. Elena had been legally declared insane and placed under a doctor's supervision at a state mental hospital. Ryan called Mrs. Sanchez immediately, and the two shared their mutual grief over the telephone.

"That creature from another world stole my wife," Ryan said, concluding his story. "Was I a coward for not remaining with her to fight the monster? I ask myself that question again and again. But I had no knowledge of such things from the darkness, and I had no means of combating the demon. I visit Elena as often as I can, and sometimes I take the children to see her. I pray that one day she will be free of whatever it is that seeks to possess her—whether it is a monster created by her mental obsession with the occult or a demon from another world that has chosen her as its victim—and be able to return to her family."

Haunted by the Dybbuk

In the January/February 2007 issue of *Biblical Archaeology Review*, Hershel Shanks wrote of the more than 2,000 magic incantation bowls that have survived from the third to the seventh century C.E. in Jewish communities in Babylonia. The incantation bowls were inscribed in Jewish Aramaic, thus complementary and representative of life reflected within the Talmud, and were created to be used in rituals designed to combat demons.

Recently, according to Dan Levene (*Biblical Archaeology Review*, March/April 2009), the collector Shlomo Moussaieff acquired a rare inscribed skull that bears an incantation which invokes a magic formula for warding off demonic influence. The Moussaieff incantation skull joins only four other such inscribed skulls known to be in existence. Two of the skulls—one at the University of Pennsylvania, the other at the Berlin Museum—make reference to Lilith and the "other Liliths," her son and grandsons and offer mystical formulae designed to keep her away or at bay. On one of the incantation bowls there is a de-feminized image of Lilith allied with a serpent possessing a victim.

A good part of the mystery of the inscribed skulls is the baffling contradiction of Jewish law that forbids contacting the dead and, indeed, even touching a human corpse. Obviously, the inscription on human skulls indicate that necromancy was, at least on occasion, practiced and that some individuals may not only have sought access to the supernatural realms but certainly believed that demons needed to be thwarted for a variety of reasons.

In Jewish folklore, the spirit who possesses a human being is called a "dybbuk." The word itself is Hebrew for "cleaving" or "clinging." Rabbi Gershon Winkler told Jeff Belanger (*Ghost Village*, November 29, 2003) that while most contemporary Jews don't believe in demonic possession, they do accept the possibility that on rare occasions there can be the possession of a living person by the soul of a deceased human whose spirit has left the body, but not the world. In most cases, the discarnate spirit is seeking

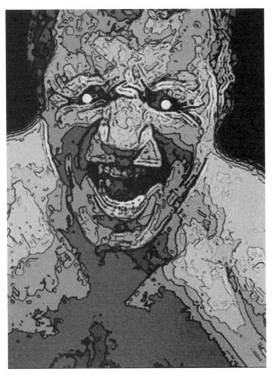

In Jewish folklore, the Dybbuk is a spirit who possesses a human in order to complete some task or purpose that it feels it must finish before leaving physical reality (illustration by Ricardo Pustanio).

to complete some task or purpose that it feels it must finish before leaving the physical reality.

Jewish traditions are full of ghost stories, but their concept of demons (*sheydim*) is that they were created in the final hours after the human being was fashioned and that they are neither of this world nor of the other, but a little bit of both. Thus, not all demons are evil. Some, such as the master demon Ashmedai, taught the mighty King Solomon a great deal about the mysteries of the unknown and of sorcery.

If a rabbi deems that someone has been truly possessed by a dybbuk, an exorcism is performed by a rabbi who has mastered practical Kabbalah. After the invading spirit has been exorcised, the rabbi and the others who participated in the ceremony can determine what its problem might be and pray for it to continue its journey to the afterlife.

Possessed for 30 Years by a Dybbuk that Claimed to Be Her Uncle

Young Teri Vruche lay in bed, restless and unable to sleep. She was 22 years old and soon to be married. Her thoughts were of her husband-to-be and the years of married life stretching before them. At the same time, though, she could not dismiss from her mind thoughts of her Uncle Sandor, recently and quite suddenly deceased. Uncle Sandor had been a pleasure-loving man, unmindful of his prayers and synagogue duties. Teri was troubled for her Uncle Sandor's soul.

As the girl lay in bed reviewing these things, she suddenly became aware of a strange creeping sensation covering her entire body. Teri lay still, her eyes widening with growing fear, while her ankles swelled beyond recognition. With horror she noticed that her body was ballooning out of shape.

Hungarian-born Teri was at a loss as to what was happening to her, and she was badly frightened. She struggled mentally with her fear, realizing that she had to do something about her condition. Then the voice spoke to her.

"Teri, it is I, Uncle Sandor. Teri, listen, you've got to help me. You were always my favorite and now you must help me."

In a desperate tone the voice continued to explain to the girl that his hedonism while in the flesh had robbed him of eternal rest. Sandor had discovered, though, that Teri's strict adherence to her faith and its many laws had put her in good stead with those "above."

"You must share your good deeds with me," the spirit pleaded, "so that I can gain forgiveness and enter the Eternal Rest."

Teri Vruche closed her eyes in a state of shocked paralysis. She could not scream. She could not even begin to scream. She could only realize slowly that she was being possessed by a dybbuk, a demon of the kind she had often heard about in the old country. This was the Bronx, though, and Teri shuddered to think that the whole bizarre sequence that had just passed could be possible.

That initial contact was in 1931. For 30 years thereafter, until February 18, 1961, Teri Vruche Goldenberg was plagued with a demon claiming to be her own Uncle Sandor. The dybbuk was present in Mrs. Goldenberg throughout her married life and the rearing of her children. She was a widowed grandmother before the exorcism rites were pronounced that banished forever the obsessive spirit from her presence.

According to Eastern European beliefs, a dybbuk is a demon—the soul of a restless and sinful person, which, after the death of its own body, seeks refuge in the body of a still-living, God-fearing person. According to ancient folk beliefs, the dybbuk resides in its human host, hoping that the good deeds practiced by the possessed person will atone for the grave sins committed by the contrite sinner.

The presence of a dybbuk is intolerable to the unfortunate host, for he or she is in the impossible position of supporting two souls with his or her actions. It is believed that only a great rabbi, who is also one of the Hasid and who has mastered the Kabbalah, can exorcise the unwanted spirit.

Mrs. Goldenberg suffered for three decades before she was able to find a Hasid (literally, "devout") of the Kabbalistic school to rid her of her demon. In that time the dybbuk never ceased petitioning the harassed woman for sanctuary. It implored her to desist from asking for the rites of exorcism, for only through her, it stated, could it hope to find peace.

Every night for 30 years Mrs. Goldenberg's inner ear rang with the demon's incessant pleas. It employed a number of tactics. Some evenings it would try to coax or to persuade. Other evenings it would curse Mrs. Goldenberg, speak cruelly to her and hint darkly at the fate awaiting her if she did not help it.

If Mrs. Goldenberg were particularly stubborn, the demon would retaliate by causing her eyes to smart to such a degree that she suffered temporary blindness. Other times, the entity would cause intense stomach pains. Then, while Mrs. Goldenberg lay doubled up in an agony of pain the dybbuk would whisper insidiously that she would never find a moment's peace if she did not allow it to stay within her, "or if you do not agree to share with me all your spiritual rewards."

Mrs. Goldenberg staunchly refused to give in to the demon, but she was not rewarded for her steadfastness until after her fiftieth birthday. It was in this later period that the by now extremely religious lady came under the spiritual guidance of Rabbi Salomon Friedlander.

Rabbi Friedlander was a remarkable man, revered throughout the Jewish Diaspora as a miracle rabbi, or *admore*. The word *admore* is a contraction of the Hebrew for "our master, our teacher, our rabbi," and it confers upon anyone so titled the honor of

He claimed to be her uncle, but she knew he was really a creature from the Darkside.

being the highest religious authority in all of Hasidism. According to the Kabbalah, the name given to the mystical literature of centuries of Judaism, the powers of the *admore* descend in a pure line from Moses, who was first given this title by God Himself. Only a rabbi of this stature is deemed capable of ridding a possessed person from a dybbuk. Therefore, it was to Rabbi Friedlander that Mrs. Goldenberg finally brought her story of 30 years of torment.

Rabbi Friedlander studied all the astrological data, as is given within the Kabbalah. At length, his research revealed that the morning of February 18, 1961, at precisely 6:30 A.M. would be the most propitious hour to begin the long rites of exorcism.

Mrs. Goldenberg, tense and visibly nervous, arrived punctually at the Lisker Congregation Synagogue. She quietly took her place before the Holy Ark which contains the sacred Torah. Attendance of the exorcism was strictly limited to Mrs. Goldenberg, Rabbi Friedlander, and a group of 10 elders of the synagogue, called a *minyan*.

Prior to the actual exorcism rites, the rabbi had followed a carefully delineated plan of preparation and consecration of himself to the task. This preparation had included a nine-day fast from "all unworthy and sensual things," and a three-day fast from all food. The actual ceremony began when Rabbi Friedlander solemnly donned a special long white robe, and in a low, mellifluous voice, began to chant an esoteric prayer. The minyan joined their rabbi in prayer while Mrs. Goldenberg shuddered under a white shawl especially designed for the ritual. All light in the synagogue came from the muted glow of 36 black candles.

After the introductory prayer, Rabbi Friedlander reverentially approached the Ark. After giving thanks for the privilege of touching the sacred scroll containing the Torah, the Rabbi removed the holy writings from the Ark. Then, speaking in Hebrew and holding aloft these Books of the Law, Rabbi Friedlander began his exorcism of the dybbuk.

"Hear me, O thou stubborn and unlawful spirit," he called forth loudly. "I order you to depart from this woman's body, and go in peace from whence you came. Go, now, and peace be with you!"

As the rabbi closed his mouth, the cantor stepped forward with the *shofar*, which is a ram's horn blown to symbolize the last trumpet which the Old Testament states is the herald of resurrection. The cantor held the horn in his left hand, then raised it to his lips and blew nine times into it. After each blast the rabbi and the 10 elders chanted in unison, "The Lord shall fight for you, and ye shall hold your peace."

The rabbi's voice roared above those of the others gathered. "I command thee to leave, thou sinful and unclean soul. Depart at once from this tormented body. Hearken unto me or I shall have to excommunicate you, to your utter disgrace. Go now in peace."

The minyan answered, "Amen," and the cantor blew upon the shofar 10 more times. This entire process outlined so far was repeated nine times, and each time the emotional intensity crescendoed. Throughout this display, the dybbuk remained unimpressed. The rabbi chanted, the minyan prayed, the cantor blew the shofar, but the dybbuk was silent.

Rabbi Friedlander was undaunted. Putting yet more power into his voice he called upon mightier powers than he against the resisting spirit. Even so, there was no response. "I curse thee by the name of God, and by my sacred work. I hereby order thee to render to me the submission that must be given to thy Maker!" the Rabbi said with great authority.

Still the dybbuk was silent.

With a sudden, dramatic move, Rabbi Friedlander moved three steps back from the Holy Ark. The tendons in his arm stretched violently as he held the Torah as high above his head as his reach would allow. In a voice of supernatural strength he called forth once more: "May every curse and every ban in the Chapter of Curses fall on thee if thou dost not immediately forsake the body and soul of our beloved sister, Teri Vruche Goldenberg!"

> *Rabbi Friedlander was undaunted. Putting yet more power into his voice he called upon mightier powers than he against the resisting spirit.*

"Amen!" cried the elders, as the rabbi swept into a recitation of the Psalm 91. Again the synagogue echoed with nine blasts from the shofar, followed by seven more. The voices and trumpet blasts had been swirling round the synagogue, but now, for the first time, the room was drenched in ghastly silence. As if coming out of a trance, Mrs. Goldenberg slowly opened her eyes and shook her head gently. A great sigh of release escaped her lips.

"The Lord be praised!" she cried. "I am free!"

In an overwhelming surge of emotion, Mrs. Goldenberg rushed to Rabbi Friedlander and prostrated herself at his feet. With tears streaming down his face, Rabbi Friedlander lovingly kissed the Torah and returned it to its sacred resting place. Then he removed himself to his own private sanctum to pray and to regain his spent energy.

Renewed study of the Kabbalah by Rabbi Friedlander revealed to him that the dybbuk of Uncle Sandor had "repented of his sins and the Holy One had granted him shelter in the Eternal Rest." Upon this announcement, the *Zidduk Ha-Din* was recited, which is the prayer for acknowledgment of divine justice and usually intoned only at burials.

Mrs. Goldenberg, for the first time in 30 years, slept peacefully that night, uninterrupted by the dybbuk's entreaties.

The Secondhand Sofa
Came with the Spirit of a Vampire

From time to time, I receive accounts from readers of my books wherein they have kept meticulous records—almost a daily diary—of the paranormal events that they have experienced. Such was the case with Brooke Robinson, who told of an eerie series of encounters with the spirit of a vampire, a grotesque and loathsome entity who had focused his attacks on young boys. Here is Brooke's record of the encounter.

When Brooke and Ethan Robinson saw the refinished couch and easy chair in the secondhand furniture store, they jumped at the opportunity to replace the dilapidated old sofa that they had inherited from Ethan's grandmother when they were first married nine years ago. It never occurred to either of them that they were acquiring anything more than second-hand furniture—and surely not the spirit of a vampire.

The Robinsons loaded the two pieces into the back of their SUV and took them home with them immediately. Brooke was so delighted to get rid of the old sofa that she insisted Ethan load it into the van and take it to the city dump. While Ethan was doing so, Brooke happily rearranged the furniture in the living room to accommodate their new acquisitions.

The next morning, Brooke arose at her customary early hour and did what little housework there was. She thought again how handsome the furniture looked in the living room. She was pleased with the purchase. The couch had been something they needed, and the price had been reasonable. Still feeling pleased, Brooke went into the kitchen to make breakfast.

Brooke dispatched Ethan to his office, then gathered up the children to drop six-year-old Hailey at school and little Nathan, four, at the day nursery on her way to her job as receptionist for Dr. Epstein at Lakeside Dentistry. It was early spring in northern California, and the weather was beautiful.

The Robinson family got much more than they bargained for from the secondhand sofa they bought. It was like something out of a Stephen King novel.

Later that night, Brooke sat alone, watching television. The rest of the family was asleep. The program had nearly concluded when Brooke noticed a dark shadow to the left of the new chair, positioned between the brightly-lit dining room and equally well-lit living room. When she focused her eyes directly on that spot, she could see nothing. Brooke decided that her eyes were undoubtedly tired. She resumed watching the television program.

A few minutes later, Brooke saw the shadow again. This time it seemed to cross in front of her, moving directly toward the couch. Again, Brooke could see the shadow out of the corner of her eye, but not when she focused directly upon it. Brooke shrugged and jovially addressed the shadow:

"Are you a ghost?" she inquired politely. "I don't happen to believe in ghosts, but if you are one, you appear harmless enough. Stick around if you want."

Chuckling at her declaration to an invisible being she knew wasn't there, Brooke turned off the set and went upstairs to her bedroom. By morning she had forgotten the entire episode.

The next day, Brooke put in a particularly difficult day at the dental office. After the supper dishes were cleaned and the children were in bed, it felt good to curl up in the big easy chair with a bit of escape fiction. Ethan watched television for a while, then confessed that he was quite tired and was going to bed. Brooke told him that she would be up to bed after she finished the chapter that she was reading.

Ethan nodded and flicked off the television. Brooke listened to the sound of his footsteps going up the stairs, then she settled back into her book. An innocuous house sound caused her to raise her head several moments later. She was surprised to see the shadow again. As with the previous evening, the shadow crossed in front of her and seemed to settle itself on the couch.

"Okay, ghost," Brooke addressed the shadow facetiously. "If you want the couch tonight, you just go ahead and take it. I am way too tired to play games tonight, so good night! I'm going to bed."

Brooke dropped a bookmark between the pages of her romance novel and lay the closed volume on the table. As she was going upstairs, she discovered herself inadvertently glancing back over her shoulder. Once again, she caught a shadowy image moving near the sofa. Brooke shrugged and wondered if it was time to have the prescription changed for her glasses.

> *As she was going upstairs, she discovered herself inadvertently glancing back over her shoulder. Once again, she caught a shadowy image moving near the sofa.*

Earlier that week, Ethan and Brooke had received a letter from Ethan's sister Patricia, reminding them that her planned vacation had arrived. She would be coming to the Robinson house for a nice, long visit. Patricia arrived early the next morning, just before Ethan left for work. Ethan and Brooke had a few moments to hug and kiss their most welcome visitor before leaving for their respective offices. The children were jumping up and down with enthusiasm for their favorite aunt.

"Oh, boy!" Nathan said. "Now I don't have to go to nursery school. I can stay home and play with Aunt Patricia."

Aunt Patricia gathered the little boy up in her arms. "That's right, Nathan. We'll have lots of fun together." Hailey was noticeably disappointed that she could not stay home and join the fun and games, but both Ethan and Brooke had prepped her by reminding her that she was a "big girl." Brooke smiled her thanks at Patricia, then kissed Nathan goodbye and took Hailey's hand as they walked to the car.

"I am a big girl," Hailey said aloud, convincing herself as much as seeking her mother's verification. "I go to school."

Brooke returned home and found a tempting meal prepared by Patricia. Later, the older woman helped Brooke change Hailey and Nathan into their pajamas, as well as read them a bedtime story.

"You're wonderful," Brooke told Patricia, as the two women went back downstairs to join Ethan. "Why don't you extend your vacation for several months." Brooke heated some coffee, and the three of them settled back for the enjoyable business of catching up on each others' lives. Patricia had all the news of the family, and was eager to relay any messages from the Robinsons.

"By the way," Patricia noted approvingly. "I see you've made a few new purchases since I was here last. This couch and chair are new, aren't they?"

"Sort of new," Ethan told her. "We bought them second-hand."

Talk of the couch reminded Brooke of the shadow she had seen the past two evenings. "Say, that reminds me," Brooke said. "Has anyone seen old Barnabas tonight?"

"Barnabas!" Ethan exclaimed. "Who's he?"

Brooke chuckled. "Barnabas is somewhat wispy in nature. Nevertheless he floats around here every evening and keeps me company when I'm up late."

Patricia chuckled at her sister-in-law's little joke. "Brooke, you're not saying this place is haunted, are you?"

Brooke leaned over and whispered to her. "Yes, honey, we have some kind of a ghostie or goblin. He seems harmless, but he just loves to float around the room."

Brooke stood up to demonstrate, but as she was wafting around the room in mock imitation of the shadowy figure that she had seen, she suddenly felt a chill of fear tingle her spine. It seemed as though her innocent joke was seriously offending someone or something—for all at once she felt surrounded by ugly hatred. On some nonverbal level of her mind Brooke knew that her joking had prompted very serious and dangerous hostility between her and "Barnabas." Brooke dropped her play-acting and sat down heavily.

"Anything the matter, Brooke?" Patricia asked.

Brooke managed a smile. "No, nothing. Tell me, how did you say Mom was doing to get Dad out of her hair now that he's retired?"

Having safely rerouted the conversation, Brooke nodded at the appropriate moments. Her mind, though, was occupied with the strange shift in the house's atmosphere that she had undeniably felt. As she was musing over this, Brooke became aware of something cold and invisible moving up the stairs. Brooke stiffened with fear, as she realized that whatever it was she had offended, it had decided to get even with her by going for her children.

Brooke was ready to jump and cry out that something terrible was going to happen, but Nathan's screams beat her to it. Brooke was several steps ahead of Ethan and Patricia, as everyone started running upstairs. Something in the boy's voice seemed to tell them all that this was no ordinary nightmare. Brooke reached Nathan's room first. She was almost afraid to go in, uncertain of what she would see. Her concern for Nathan overrode her fear, though, and she rushed to her son's side.

"What is it, Nathan?" she asked, holding him in her arms and trying her best to soothe him.

"There was an ugly old man with long teeth in my room!" he cried, gulping for air. "He was awful! He just stood there and sort of smiled at me with his big teeth, only I knew it wasn't really a smile." The little boy began to cry softly, still terrified of the ghostly visage he had seen. While Ethan went into Hailey's room to reassure her that Nathan had just had a bad dream, Patricia and Brooke comforted him. Aunt Patricia fetched another bedtime storybook and started to read it to Nathan. Finally, the boy was lulled back to sleep, and they went back downstairs.

Brooke was reluctant to turn out the lights that evening. She walked throughout the house, trying to catch sight of the elusive shadow. The shadow was nowhere to be seen, but everywhere Brooke turned she felt surrounded by burning hatred. With a growing sense of dread, Brooke decided to leave all the lights on that night. She was beginning to feel a vague premonition of evil. She slept in Nathan's room that night.

It was almost a pleasure to go to work the next morning and leave the oppressive atmosphere of the house. Brooke looked closely at Ethan and Patricia to see if they, too, felt the presence, but they were apparently unaffected. Hailey, too, seemed unaware of anything extraordinary about the house. Only Nathan seemed to sense something, but Brooke could not be certain. Just before Brooke's noon break, she received a call from Patricia.

"Brooke, I'm terribly sorry to bother you at work, but it's Nathan. He claims to have seen the old man with the big teeth again, and I can't quiet him down. He keeps screaming that the old man was waiting for him up in his room this morning. I don't know what to do."

Their son kept seeing the image of an old man with big teeth (illustration by Ricardo Pustanio).

Brooke felt a feeling of dread spread through her body. She went into Dr. Epstein's office and arranged for the rest of the day off. Patricia and Brooke made a concerted effort to keep the children occupied the rest of the afternoon. When Ethan came home the whole family went to a movie, then played in the park nearby. Hailey and Nathan were so exhausted by the time they reached home that they fell asleep almost immediately upon getting into bed.

All the lights were turned out early in the Robinson house that night. The three adults had only been asleep a few hours when Nathan's terrified screams again filled the house. Brooke and Ethan rushed to Nathan's room and Patricia headed for Hailey's bedroom. As Brooke stepped over the threshold, she was shocked by the chill in Nathan's room. The temperature was several degrees lower than the rest of the house. Brooke could see nothing, but she was sure the evil force had been frightening Nathan again.

"Oh, Mommy, Daddy, I had the terrible dream again! I can't stand it. I get so scared," the boy cried. It took nearly an hour to calm Nathan. When he was finally sleeping again, Ethan and Brooke were both exhausted.

"Ethan, I've got to talk to you," Brooke said quietly. "Ever since I was joking with you and Patricia about the 'ghost' in the house, I have felt an evil presence. I don't know what it is, but it's full of hatred, and for some reason it's concentrating on Nathan."

Brooke saw Ethan's scowl. It was clear he did not believe her. "Ethan, listen, there's more," she said hurriedly. "Just before Nathan woke up screaming last night, I felt some cold, invisible thing moving down the hall to his room. I was about to jump up and say something when Nathan started screaming."

Ethan sighed heavily. "I wish you hadn't said all this, Brooke. I don't think it helps Nathan any to have you going around saying these things."

"But I haven't said a word in front of Nathan! I just feel it, and I wanted you to know."

"Okay, honey, okay," Ethan nodded. "I know you wouldn't say anything to Nathan. I just don't think it helps any to have you thinking these things." He added, "Listen, why don't we take Nathan to a pediatrician tomorrow morning. Maybe there's some other reason he's having these dreams. Make an appointment first thing, all right?"

Her thoughts were on "Barnabas" ... and his malevolent intent. How could it be that only she and Nathan were aware of it?

Brooke nodded. Her thoughts were on "Barnabas," though, and his malevolent intent. How could it be that only she and Nathan were aware of it? Brooke decided wearily to let the matter rest and get what sleep she could.

Brooke was able to get an appointment for Nathan by mid-afternoon. Dr. Mason seemed unperturbed by her report that her son was having nightmares. "It's nothing to trouble yourself about, Mrs. Robinson. Many children experience nightmares and other frightening things at this age. He'll grow out of it."

In spite of the doctor's reassurances, Nathan woke up the household the next several nights with his screams of terror. Frequently he would claim to see the "ghost of the old man" in the daylight. All this time, Brooke continued to feel the hatred smothering the house.

For two weeks the night terrors continued, and though Brooke continued to feel the evil presence and Nathan continued to see it, Brooke was unable to see a thing. Only her instincts reassured her that she was right to worry as she did. One night Brooke was taking a restless walk through the house, and as she walked she felt certain that the presence was mocking her every step of the way.

"You may be frightened now," an inner voice seemed to tell her, "but this is nothing like the fear you will be experiencing shortly."

Brooke began feeling helpless. She still did not know what she was fighting, nor how to go about combating it. Brooke was shaken by these thoughts. She crept uneasily into Nathan's room, fearful again of what she would find there. All she saw was the tousled head of her little boy, sleeping peacefully. For some reason that night Brooke was reluctant to leave the room. She gathered the boy into her arms and kept watch the rest of the night. Sleep was impossible.

The sun began to rise and Brooke got up to prepare breakfast. She stopped in the bathroom and regarded her haggard reflection in the mirror. What was happening to her? Was she starting to go mad? Brooke determined to put an end to the intolerable situation.

"I refuse to live like this," she told herself firmly. "I won't let it get me down. Everything is all right." Brooke went to the dental office feeling better than she had in weeks, despite her sleepless night. The day went beautifully. By the time she was ready to go home, Brooke was convinced that nothing could crumble her newly acquired strength.

As her car pulled into the driveway Brooke could see Ethan outside playing with the children. Brooke turned off the ignition and got out of the car. Ethan came over to her and pecked her on the cheek. Hailey rushed excitedly to her mother and Brooke swung the girl into her arms. Brooke looked around for Nathan. The boy was standing sullenly in front of the house.

"How about you, Nathan, don't you have a big kiss for Mommy like Hailey?" Brooke walked toward Nathan. She knelt in the grass in front of him with outstretched arms.

"I don't want to kiss you," he said with venom precocious for his four years. "I can't stand you. I don't want to be near you."

Brooke was shocked and hurt. She glanced quickly at Ethan and saw the look of astonishment on his face. This was not their loving little boy speaking. Brooke strove to be calm.

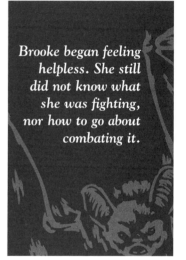

Brooke began feeling helpless. She still did not know what she was fighting, nor how to go about combating it.

"All right then, Nathan. I'm going in the house. If you change your mind, you can bring your kiss to me in there."

Brooke rose and walked into the house. Nathan did not follow. A few minutes later he entered the house for supper, but Nathan refused to let his mother touch him. His sister could hug him, Aunt Patricia could kiss and cuddle him, Daddy could wrestle with him and show his affection, bur Mommy could not get near Nathan. Brooke saw the confusion in Nathan's face, and she knew that there was a great part of him that longed to throw his arms around her. Something else was holding him back, though, and that something frightened Brooke.

Suddenly he broke into a run and hurled himself into Brooke's arms. "Mommy, sometimes I do love you," he cried. "I do." Brooke sat on the floor and pulled Nathan into her lap. All at once Nathan's smile was replaced by an evil sneer. As if repulsed, he slid out of Brooke's lap.

"Why can't you just leave me alone!" he shouted as he ran from the room. "Leave me alone. I don't love you anymore."

Brooke sat on the floor in despair. Hailey stood in the corner, uncertain what to do. She wanted to comfort her mother, but felt instinctively that she should remain quiet. The kitchen door swung open, and Brooke heard her husband's measured tread approach her. A strong, sympathetic arm was placed on her shoulder, and a hand came down to help Brooke rise.

"I heard the whole thing," Ethan said. "Let's not talk about it now, though. We'll eat dinner, put the kids to bed, then we'll talk."

Ethan's eyes lit on Hailey, standing uncertainly in the corner of the room. He motioned to her. "Hailey, can you help Mommy with dinner? She would really like that."

Later that evening, after the children were sleeping, Brooke and Ethan sat at the kitchen table to discuss the change in Nathan. They invited Patricia to join them.

"I heard that scene this afternoon, too," Patricia told Brooke. "I'm sure he didn't mean it."

"I'm afraid we're going to have to take Nathan to a psychiatrist," Ethan announced soberly. "He keeps insisting that he sees some old man in his room. Now he has had a complete personality change and refuses to let his own mother touch him—the mother he has always loved very much. A drastic change like that indicates a troubled mind."

"Ethan, there *is* something in this house, I know there is!" Brooke said. "There is something evil and awful in this house, and slowly but surely it's entering Nathan's mind and causing him to act as he does. Don't you see that this thing is trying to possess our son?"

Ethan replied swiftly and coldly. "Brooke, I don't see anything, Hailey doesn't see anything, and Patricia doesn't see anything. Don't you see that your persistence in this silly thing only aggravates Nathan's problem?"

Patricia had been listening quietly, reluctant to enter the family discussion. She began to speak hesitantly. "Brooke, Ethan, don't you think there's a possibility it might be something else altogether? I mean, Brooke, I don't intend this as a slight, but do you realize that you are the only mother in the neighborhood who works? Maybe Nathan resents not having his mother at home like all the other kids, and he doesn't like going to the nursery. He's been so glad to stay at home this past week with me here. Maybe by saying he doesn't like you, he's really saying that he doesn't like it when you leave him."

Ethan strongly disagreed. Patricia offered the suggestion that maybe Nathan was just acting out because he missed his mother because she was gone at work all day.

Ethan nodded at Patricia's analysis. He agreed that his sister may have discovered a possible source of the problem, but he urged that Nathan be taken to see a psychiatrist. Brooke agreed in order to maintain peace. She was determined to do whatever was right for her son.

Later that afternoon, Patricia's vacation time had come to an end, and she reluctantly began to pack her suitcase. "I wish that I could stay a few more days," she told Brooke. "I really wish that I could help you and Ethan reach some kind of resolution with Nathan. I am so sorry about whatever it is that is going on with him." Patricia left within a few minutes after Ethan had returned home from work. She declined their offer to take her to a restaurant for a farewell party, saying that she could get many miles "down the road" before she stopped to eat.

Late that night, after everyone else in the family had retired, Brooke mulled over the desperate situation with Nathan. As she was sitting on the couch she felt the temperature in the room drop inexplicably. A warning alarm went off in her head, and she feared to raise her eyes and look around the room.

A death-like chill permeated the room. The atmosphere of hatred seemed to strengthen and swirl around Brooke's head. She knew that something monstrous and evil was in the room with her. Cautiously, Brooke raised her head. There, in front of her, was the shadow image that she had first seen weeks ago and playfully named "Barnabas."

The hands and face of the shadow appeared lighter than the rest of the form, and Brooke was able to make out its features. Dark-rimmed, soulless red eyes stared hollowly at her. The being was grossly emaciated, and the yellowish-green skin clung tautly to its high cheekbones. Long hair flowed to its shoulders.

The face was truly horrifying to see, but what seized Brooke even more were the creature's fangs and skeletal hands. The thing's arms were outstretched, its fingers separated, its hands palms down. The crooked claws of the entity's bony hands stretched in front of it, as if grasping for her.

At last Brooke knew fully what the sepulchral being intended to do. All her fears and suppositions were confirmed as the hideous being materialized in front of her. It intended to take her son's life force, to steal his soul, and inhabit his body. Slowly, the form dematerialized before Brooke's frightened eyes. The chill lifted from the room and its natural temperature was restored. With a sudden jolt of fear, Brooke ran upstairs into Nathan's room. She sat on his bed and gathered his sleeping form into her arms.

The form materialized before her: Surrounded by a sepulchral haze with red eyes blazing hatred and its stained fangs dripping slime, the ghastly creature came toward her (illustration by Ricardo Pustanio).

She must find a way to thwart the creature's evil intent. Inadvertently she visualized his ghastly form. She saw the lips curl into the vile sneer, and her body shook when she realized that this was the sneer she had seen on Nathan's face earlier that evening. It was clear that the being was trying to possess Nathan, and that its plan was well underway.

Brooke tried to clear her mind of extraneous distractions. Naturally, she thought, the entity would attack Nathan, since he was the youngest and most vulnerable to such an approach. But how could she hope to fend off such a hideous being? Brooke thought of her husband and wondered how she could get him to believe her. How could she persuade anyone to believe such a bizarre circumstance?

She was alone, she realized despairingly. Completely alone. If anyone was to save Nathan, it would have to be she. Brooke lowered her head and allowed a few tears to well in her eyes. As she did so, a mocking, spiteful laugh filled the room. With a start, Brooke noted that the creature could both hear her thoughts and respond to them. Brooke held the body of her son all night while he slept. Brooke had no desire to sleep.

She knew she had to formulate a plan to thwart that of the evil creature inhabiting their home.

When Nathan awakened, he saw that his mother held him, and he sneered, just like the hideous entity that Brooke had faced. He struggled free of Brooke's arms and began walking with his arms outstretched, hands palms down, and fingers crooked in an exact imitation of the obsessing entity.

Ethan bent over to hoist Nathan up in his arms, but he jerked back when the boy snapped at him and tried to bite him.

"What's that, Nathan?" Ethan asked from the doorway of his son's room. He had been getting ready for work and had stopped by Nathan's room to check on him. "What are you doing?"

Nathan glanced at his father with a scowl of annoyance. "That's the way the old ghost looks at me," he said, as if he had expected his father be fully aware of the entity's appearance.

"Ghosts are just pretend, though, aren't they?" Ethan said. "They are just in movies and television shows. Right?"

"Yeah, I guess so," Nathan responded offhandedly. "Except for Barnabas. He lives with us now. He used to live by himself. He said that he really likes little boys, but I told him that I don't want him to drink my blood or to eat me like he did some of the other kids."

Ethan was momentarily speechless. His eyes darted from his son to his wife. "Where is he getting that stuff?" he wanted to know. "We don't let him watch those kinds of program on television."

All at once Brooke saw an opportunity to convince Ethan of the ghost's validity. She acted quickly. "Nathan, you go ask Hailey to help you get ready for nursery school."

Nathan scowled at his mother and refused to leave. "I know what you're up to," he said in a low, rasping voice. "You want to talk to him about Barnabas. Well, I am not leaving this room, bitch!"

Ethan was stunned for about three seconds, then he stormed across the room toward Nathan. "Don't you ever talk to your mother that way!" Ethan bent over to hoist Nathan up in his arms, but he jerked back when the boy snapped at him and tried to bite him.

"And don't you ever try to bite your father!" Ethan said, shaking his son before setting him down on the bed.

Nathan spat at his father and growled as if he were a vicious animal. "Someday I'll have long teeth just like Barnabas and I can bite anyone I want to, including you, you bastard!"

That did it for Ethan. He grabbed Nathan and turned him over his knee to administer a sound spanking—something Ethan had always said he would never do.

"Daddy, Daddy," Nathan cried, "what are you doing? What are you doing?"

Ethan froze, his hand poised over his son's bottom. He looked at Brooke, completely confused and perplexed.

Brooke nodded. "Nathan is back again," she said softly. "Our little boy is in trouble. Now will you listen to me? Now will you help me?"

Ethan removed Nathan from across his knees, straightened his Pooh Bear pajamas, and told him to go to his sister. "Tell me everything that's been going on around here," he said to Brooke.

Ethan called work to say that he would be in a bit later than usual, then he drove Hailey to school and returned home. Nathan had refused to attend nursery school, and under the circumstances, they thought it was best to allow him to play alone in his room. As soon as it seemed that their son was occupied with his toy trucks, Brooke told Ethan the entire story of the incredible events that she had experienced in their home late at night.

Brooke could tell from her husband's expressions and demeanor that he was skeptical of her account of the weird occurrences that had taken place around the secondhand sofa, but he retained a respectful silence while she told him every detail of the ghostly encounters that she had experienced. He agreed that he would sit up with her that night and see for himself if "Barnabas" would put in an appearance.

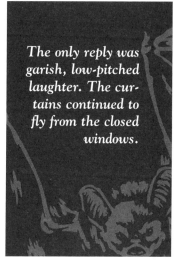

The only reply was garish, low-pitched laughter. The curtains continued to fly from the closed windows.

That evening Ethan was very quiet. Throughout supper he sat lost in thought, scarcely eating his food. Brooke, on the other hand, felt herself growing almost jubilant. She was convinced now that she had a most important ally with whom she could defeat the terrible entity that had disturbed the sanctity of their home.

Since Nathan had expressed his dislike of his mother throughout the evening, Brooke confined her attention to Hailey at bedtime, and Ethan had assumed the responsibility of putting Nathan to bed. Before that morning's episode, Nathan had never rejected affection from his father, yet this night he suddenly scowled at Ethan and refused to let himself be touched.

"You're getting as bad as she is," Nathan snarled, indicating his mother.

A stricken look crossed Ethan's features. Brooke hurriedly entered the room.

"Nathan's a big enough boy to put on his own pajamas," she said smoothly. "He can put himself to bed. Good night, dear."

Brooke reached for her husband's arm and led him out of the bedroom. The two entered the living room, determined to get involved in something on television. They finally become engrossed in a documentary program for several minutes when the windows began to make a fearsome noise. They were shaking violently, but there was no wind outside.

Ethan started to get up to investigate, but Brooke told him to try to ignore the manifestations. The drawn curtains began to flail wildly. Ethan got to his feet.

"Ignore it, Ethan. Please," Brooke pleaded.

No sooner had Brooke spoken than she heard a voice from inside her mind. The bodiless voice dripped with malice: *"You cannot ignore me. I am stronger than you."*

With a start Brooke realized that Barnabas was communicating with her telepathically. With all her concentrated attention Brooke returned a thought: *"We are stronger than you are. You cannot defeat us. Now get out of our house!"*

The only reply was garish, low-pitched laughter. The curtains continued to fly from the closed windows. Ethan began to pace nervously. "My God, Brooke, I can't take it. We've got to take the children and get out of here!"

"It's too late for that, Ethan," Brooke said. "We've got to stick it out and fight him now, otherwise we'll never be free. He knows the showdown is approaching, Ethan. Nathan wouldn't let you near him and he openly hates me. The horrible creature is already too strong within Nathan for us to run away."

"Do you mean this thing can hear what I say?" Ethan asked, stupefied.

"Not only can it hear what you say, it can read your thoughts," Brooke told him. "It can communicate with you. It's been talking to me. We've got to be strong, Ethan."

Eventually, the wind from nowhere died down, and the draperies once more settled quietly against the windows. After things had settled down for the time being, Brooke persuaded Ethan to lie down in their bedroom and get some rest. Then she stole noiselessly into Nathan's room. Brooke gathered her sleeping boy into her arms and tried to prepare herself for whatever was to come. Somehow she knew that this night would be the crucial one, and she feared she was not yet strong enough to combat such a powerful force of evil.

Brooke pondered the situation as calmly as she could, determined to conserve her energy. However, the combination of many sleepless nights was beginning to take its toll, and Brooke had to fight to remain alert. Sometime after 2:00 A.M., her eyelids wearily closed.

All at once Brooke was wide awake, suffused with a terror beyond anything she had ever experienced. Her throat was dry, her skin tingling with dread. She feared intensely for her own life and the life of her son. In desperation Brooke closed her eyes tightly and prayed for strength and protection. Her eyes flew open as she felt the chilling approach of the detestable being.

The entity knew that this night was his last chance, for Brooke and Ethan were getting stronger. Tonight the thing would have to make its final effort to possess the living body of four-year-old Nathan—and destroy anyone who would try to stop it.

Brooke eased herself away from Nathan and glanced wildly around the room. She wanted some kind of weapon, something that she could place between the being and her own vulnerable self. She was shaking with fear, uncertain as to her plan of action.

Brooke walked slowly out of Nathan's room and down the hall. The death-like chill seemed concentrated most heavily at the end of the hallway. That would have to be where the entity was waiting. Brooke had only gone halfway down the hall when the form materialized before her. Surrounded by a sepulchral haze and with red eyes blazing hatred, the ghastly visage came slowly toward her. Its bony hands were outstretched, palms down, and an almost irresistible force seemed to flow from the yellow-green claws. Brooke thought that if those hands should once touch her, her soul would be ripped to agonizing shreds.

The being stepped closer, and for one moment Brooke faltered. Her mind started to swirl, and she knew she was yielding against her will to the being's demoniacal power. From faraway, she heard its soulless laughter.

The sound of that laughter was all Brooke needed to pull herself together. "I will not let you defeat me!" she shouted. Somewhere inside of her Brooke seemed to have tapped a primeval energy source. Centuries of culture and sophistication slipped away, and Brooke was an enraged animal protecting her young. She boldly stepped toward the evil creature.

"You thought you could possess my son, but I am stronger than you are. You are beaten! Leave my son, leave my house. You can no longer harm us!" As Brooke moved forward she saw the creature step hesitantly back. Feeling a tremendous surge of power, Brooke continued to move in on him, no longer afraid. "Leave us!" she commanded. "Go back to wherever you belong."

The entity continued to retreat from Brooke, growing smaller as it went. Brooke was dimly aware that they were now in the living room. "Barnabas" was heading toward the couch. Brooke advanced on the couch, where the being seemed to be centered. As she approached, the thing became increasingly dimmer. The vaguely luminescent quality departed, and Brooke was staring at the formless shadow she had first seen weeks before. Finally that, too, evaporated into nothingness.

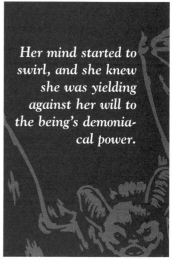

Her mind started to swirl, and she knew she was yielding against her will to the being's demoniacal power.

Without moving or taking her gaze from the couch, Brooke called to Ethan. When her husband arrived at her side, Brooke gave terse orders. She refused to move her eyes from the couch.

Brooke insisted that the sofa be taken from their house that night. She told Ethan to load the piece of furniture into the back end of the SUV. She would accompany him and they would unload it at the city dump. They bundled their two drowsy kids into the backseat, and as they made their desperate trip to the dump, Brooke explained to Ethan what had happened. She was convinced that she had cornered Barnabas in the couch, and that he was going on his last ride. She had ceased to sense his presence.

With only the pale light of a crescent moon to guide them, Ethan and Brooke lifted the couch from the car and placed it in a cleared area apart from the city's debris. As if for a ritual cleansing, Ethan held a lighter against the cloth and ignited the piece of furniture.

"It's over," Brooke whispered, clutching her husband's arm and watching the blazing couch. "It's finally over."

When the last flames had died down, Brooke and Ethan drove back home. Together, they climbed the stairs, Ethan carrying Hailey and Brooke cradling Nathan. They walked down the hallway to the children's rooms. Nathan remained sleeping serenely. Brooke laid him in his bed, tucked the covers beneath his chin, and placed her hand on his forehead.

"Mommy?" a sleepy voice asked. "Oh, Mommy, I love you."

Ethan came forward and smiled down at his son.

Brooke sighed deeply. "Thank God," she said. "We won."

Vampires from UFOs

The Ultimate Struggle for the Human Soul

In the view of military and aviation historian Trevor James Constable, the UFO beings are etheric, rather than physical, beings. As he sees it, the abduction of humans is symptomatic of the struggle for the soul of humans, rather than for the planet on which humans reside.

"Entities riding etherically propelled vehicles and obviously in mastery of psychic control in all its forms devise contact encounters with ingenuous human beings who can be used in various ways to serve certain ends," Constable said. "Investigators are led to believe that material craft are involved, if they are convinced at all that the experience was real. And if not convinced, then the contactee is just another 'flying saucer nut.'"

As for the true identity of the UFO occupants, Constable names the *Ahrimanes*, the fallen angels, who inhabit the space between Earth and the fixed stars. Constable reminds us that the Ahrimanic powers have for centuries held as their goal the total enslavement of humankind. If they are unopposed, the Ahrimanic entities will overwhelm humankind and make evolution wholly a matter of their control. Humans will win or lose the battle for Earth itself, for they are at once the goal of the battle and the battleground. The stakes in this battle are not the territory, commercial advantages, or political leverage of ordinary wars, but the mind and destiny of man.

In Constable's view, the objective of the Ahrimanic powers is to pull down all humanity. To this end, whatever political systems and philosophies exist among men are simply manipulated. Mundane party politics, political systems, and differences are therefore excluded from what is now being pointed out, because nothing definitive concerning the spiritual destiny of humanity can arise out of political studies or bickering. It is Constable's contention that humans are constantly being seduced into

Is there some other explanation for UFOs than aliens from other planets?

doing the work of the nether forces, because they simply do not recognize that such forces exist, let alone how they work *into* and *upon* Earth life.

"Ignorance of this kind persists in the face of an obvious motion of the human race toward a climactic period," Constable says. "Avarice is the main agency by which humans are seduced away from life, from positive work and positive thought. Incomprehension of spiritual forces and the institutionalized denigration of the spirit in formal education make humanity pitifully vulnerable."

"The battle for the Earth is a spiritual struggle but involves mighty temporal events," Constable writes in his book *The Cosmic Pulse of Life*. "In this battle we are called to redeem the Earth through the creation of a new humanity ... based on true brotherly love."

***

Charles is haunted by the memory of lying on a table in a small, metal-like room in some kind of vehicle. The light in the room is radiant, soft. He feels calm and trusting. Shadowy figures are moving around him, and he senses that they are deciding on the best procedure to follow with him. They take samples of his blood and remove tiny bits of his skin.

Charles is convinced that during that experience, which he believes was far more than a vision or a dream, something was implanted in his brain. Ever since that strange episode, Charles feels heat, pain, and hears a crackling, popping sound in his head. He believes that some integration process is trying to happen. His perceptions have changed dramatically. Charles's wife is very open to a discussion of his experience, and he is able to talk freely about the blackouts, the amnesia, and the urgent aching feeling that he experiences inside.

"I know what's happening," Charles says. "I'm being prepared for something. I feel so impatient. I just want to get on with it."

Charles isn't certain when his initial abduction occurred. It may have been one night when he was driving home late from work. It may have been another evening when he stopped by the side of the road because he felt sleepy after he had seen friends. But he recalls seeing not more than 10 feet above him a circular vehicle with a square bottom and a distended portion covered with white lights.

He remembers feeling groggy and hazy as he gazed at it. Then an invisible beam of energy shot through him, and his entire body, especially his chest, vibrated and got very warm.

"Something exploded in my heart," Charles said. "The sensation, like a kind of electrocution, lasted quite a while, then stopped, and I went into a deep sleep."

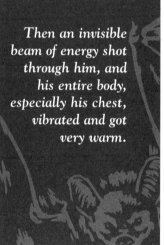

Then an invisible beam of energy shot through him, and his entire body, especially his chest, vibrated and got very warm.

But in spite of the deep sleep, certain impressions come back to haunt him. He has begun to recall images of strange reptilian-like entities working around him in that circular craft. Charles is convinced now that seeing UFOs or aliens is not necessary for the complete evolution of his thoughts and his awareness. He sees the physical experience as a crude level of blending and communicating. He feels that the actual process of communion is on a much subtler level. "I know them deep inside," he said. "I feel them. I sense them."

***

In order to focus, to relax, to escape from the pressures of work, Gretchen found great release in camping. Her father had been an avid camper and had taken her along on trips ever since she was a child of five or six. Gretchen took great delight in exploring the beautiful forest and lake country of Oregon on weekends. She remembers clearly that the incident occurred on a very lovely fall evening when she lay in her sleeping bag beside an idyllic forest stream.

She was letting the sound of the waters moving over the rocks lull her into a restful sleep when her half-opened eyes saw in the night sky a streak of light slash across the darkness and appear to come down in the forest. Her first response was that she was observing a meteor, but she knew that the light was too bright for any but the largest meteors—and that these were so rare as to not even be worth considering. She put all thoughts out of her mind, thinking that it had been merely a trick of the eye, perhaps due to her own fatigue.

She drifted into a light sleep when, about 3:00 A.M., she looked up from her sleeping bag and saw lights bobbing in the forest. She was astonished when she saw figures with unusually large heads emerge. In the shadows created by their source of illumination, they had grotesque, gargoyle-like appearances. They looked to her as if

What did the streak of light in the night sky really bring? (illustration by Bill Oliver).

they were snakes, or amphibians, two-legged toad-like beings. Their eyes were unusually large, and they appeared to have no lips, just a straight line for a mouth, again reminding her of a reptile or an amphibian. She could see no discernible nose.

One of the individuals was carrying a boxlike object in his hands. It was emitting strange, crackling sounds, and rays of light were shooting out from it. Suddenly the entity carrying the box stopped and began to let out high-pitched squeaking noises, which Gretchen assumed were sounds of excitement. The other entities gathered around the one carrying the box, and they began to look around them into the darkness of the forest.

A shiver moved through Gretchen when she received the clear impression that somehow the technology of that particular box had detected her presence, and now the toad people were looking for her. She lay there in utter silence, afraid to breathe, feeling sweat trickle down the back of her neck. A dry feeling entered her throat, and she was just at the point of leaping up from her sleeping bag and running into the woods. She decided that she would do her best to escape the strange entities that were emerging from the forest. She could count as many as six or seven of them, and her conclusion was that it was better to try to make a break for it and try to outrun them. After all, she had been a medalist in her high school track days. She should be able to outrun the short-legged, amphibious creatures.

Just as she was about to bound from her sleeping bag and head for the woods, she felt a strange peace come over her. As if in a dream, she remembers being lifted out of her blankets and carried a short distance.

When she awakened at sunrise, snug in her sleeping bag, the grotesque entities were no longer present, but they had left her with numerous small pock-like marks which indicated that they had taken several samples of her skin and flesh.

The Vampires Are Out Tonight

Deb, who has a great deal of psychic ability and is very much aware of her angelic guidance, has written to me many times since she heard me on a radio program discussing "spirit mimics," or "fallen angels appearing as Extraterrestrial beings." Somehow, she writes, trying to explain how she has been able to view such entities, "they seem drawn to my 'inner light.'" "Often," Deb says, slightly bemused, "the beings get irritated that I notice them, and they want to let me know it. By the way, I don't smoke or drink, and during all the experiences that I have had, I was very aware." Deb has generously taken the time to share a number of experiences in which she was able to detect the "ETs" or whoever or whatever they are, but an encounter in Croatia stands out for many significant reasons. Deb related the following story.

I was in Hvar, Croatia with my husband, my daughter, and my husband's parents walking through the city. I love to look around and study people. On this particular evening at around 7:00, I was scanning the crowds at restaurants when I saw five females with heavy make-up on sitting at a table. Their ages ranged from perhaps 27 to 35.

I locked eyes with one of them. I turned away and made a comment to my husband, "Whew, the vampires are out tonight!" I said it just to be funny. On the surface, I just thought they were a group of women friends enjoying a social night out.

Later when we returned home, I was taking a nap with my daughter and received this message from my Angels … my Higher self?

I realized:

1. All the women looked alike except for different hair-styles—short, long, fuzzy, curly, etc. They all had very, very platinum blond hair— almost white. One wore her hair long, straight down the back. Another had a bob, curly-frizzy shoulder length hair. They all had kind of out-dated hairstyles.

2. All had odd clothing, all black or dark-colored, long sleeved, long skirts, boots. None of them had the proper end of summer clothing for a tropical island resort.

3. They all had wide eyes, thin noses, small lips. They had very white skin, and they had applied theatrical dark kohl eye-makeup so black and ringed around their eyes that it looked clownish. Later, when I thought about it more, I realized that the one with whom I had locked eyes didn't necessarily have dark make-up on eyes. It seemed, rather that her eye sockets were deeply embedded in her skull and only appeared shadowy? Maybe they sent a "screen memory" that they were wearing make-up.

4. All five women sat up, straight, rigid, in their high backed chairs. They appeared to be observing the crowd, looking in all different directions, when I walked by. The two facing me looked in my direction at the same time, oddly cocking their heads to the side, like a dog does when it is confused. I locked eyes with the one to the right. I was carrying my daughter in my arms; her body was facing outward. I believe my daughter also has high energy. I think they may have been curious and drawn to our energy.

5. I felt their insecurity on how they should act. They held their menus oddly, as if wondering, "What do we do now?" They seemed to project an overall feeling of contempt and disgust toward the people around them.

6. They were very, very tall, all the same height—six feet maybe or a little more. They were graceful, yet heavy looking.

I got the feeling that the one with her back to me sensed that I saw them, and it was alarming to her. She did not expect that.

When I locked eyes with this being, I cannot describe in words the intensity of her essence. This was a very pure being. When you look into the eyes of someone you know is a kind and warm person, you can see it in the eyes. But her eyes were almost liquid pools—blackish, no light. Her energy was ancient, intense, wise. It almost looked as if she had layered eyelids—a lid on top of another. There was a clear one, and it closed and opened with regular eyelids, as if looking through the lens of a camera. Perhaps the best way to describe the feeling that I received is that she was intelligent in the mind, but emotionally challenged and awkward in social settings.

It was hard to keep staring, and I did look away and state out loud, "Whew, the vampires are out tonight," in a joking way to my husband. My husband looked at the women and immediately mentioned that their odd energy was too much for him.

I've seen some of these beings before. This time I was better prepared to not look away, but I didn't want to be around them anymore. And I got the feeling they were not good news. They had no emotion or warmth, no tenderness, empathy, or compassion. They were not evil, but they had no "aliveness." They seemed emotionally "flat-lined."

A Secret Group of Alien Trackers

I was astonished by the synchronicity of receiving Deb's communication just a few days before I was contacted by a group of scientists who had previously been connected with a major university and who now said that they had left the edu-

cational establishment to track and to study the very type of alien, extraterrestrial, or multidimensional beings that she had encountered so often in her life. One of the scientists, who seemed to be the leader of the group, told me that some of the entities that Deb had encountered were alien-human hybrids. For obvious reasons, I am using pseudonyms for the members of this group of scientists. According to my correspondent within the group, whom we will call Benjamin, they had recently encountered a family of aliens living in a Midwestern state:

Last summer, we were [in the upper Midwest], connecting with a young man of unusual capacities, and we ran across a couple of [aliens] (male-female with a child) at a soup place off the highway. My companions were two others from the scientific investigative group.

[The aliens] were already in this restaurant when we entered. My colleague Brian elbowed me lightly and motioned my attention toward them. They too took notice of us, so we proceeded to get our food (it was a self-serve type of place) and found a table almost across from them.

All the while, we are being "checked out," because none of us were experiencing fear or friction toward them. We noticed, though, that they were not making any sort of contact with anyone else in the restaurant.

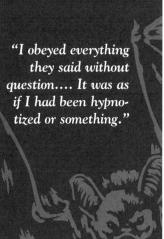

"I obeyed everything they said without question.... It was as if I had been hypnotized or something."

All of us were more curious than anything, and they knew it. So I tried mind-on-mind with the male and, lo and behold, I get an answer. This surprised them to no end, and they immediately began to make preparations to leave. By then we were seated, and I smiled at him, telling him inwardly that they had nothing to fear from us. So he calmed down, she calmed down, and the little girl with them (couldn't have been more than five years old, by appearance) began to quiz me about how is it that I (we) knew they were not from here. All of this, mind you, is taking place telepathically in the midst of the usual decibel of noise in a busy restaurant.

I answered all of her questions, and then turned the tables on her. I asked her if I could ask her questions. The male, whom I took to be the biological father, said it was OK, and I proceeded to engage in a most disconcerting conversation: Yes, they were not from here. Yes, they've been here for a while. Yes, she was born here. Yes, they come from another place. She didn't have a clear notion of what to call where they were from, until the father stepped in and informed me they were from a planet in what we know as the Lyra system.

I asked them about a certain "project" we knew to be ongoing in that part as more or less of a test. Much to my surprise, the woman begins to tell me about it, chapter and verse, as if it was already public knowledge (maybe to them). This to us established their clear bona fides.

By then, they were getting ready to leave. I asked them a couple of final questions, one of the female and one of the male. I asked her where they lived. She said it was south of there, near a lake. I asked him what they were doing there, and he replied that he worked as an engineer making carriages (which on image I understood it to be recreational vehicles), but that he was preparing to go work on the north end of the west coast. I asked if it was California, Oregon, or Washington state. He replied it was Washington, but wouldn't clarify location. I didn't press, and then he told me that now that they knew "us" (i.e., the three of us), that they would remain "in touch" with us from time to time. They have!

Oh, he also told us that there were many more of "them" here in the region. So, tell Deb she did not have an unusual experience at all!

An Interrupted Journey from Denver to Phoenix

On a November night in 1978, something that defies any easy explanation happened to Lois and her friend Gina while they were driving from Denver to Phoenix. While they were negotiating a lonely stretch of highway, they saw a hitchhiker standing at the side of the road. Although Lois had never before picked up a hitchhiker under any circumstances, she found herself slowing her automobile and stopping.

Even at a distance, there seemed to be something decidedly different about this hitchhiker. He was dressed casually in a plaid flannel shirt and jeans. He was extremely clean-shaven. His hair was long and blond, and his eyes were a brilliant sky-blue.

With a peculiarly warm smile of welcome, he leaned forward toward the window that Gina had opened. "I'm so glad you've come," he said in a soft, almost musical voice. "We've been waiting for you."

Lois remembers that there was something strangely familiar about the hitchhiker. "As crazy as it might sound," she said, "it was as if I had known him all my life. Gina is usually kind of shy around strangers—especially males—but she was smiling from ear to ear, as though she were greeting an old friend."

Lois's memory becomes very sketchy after the hitchhiker's statement that "they" had been waiting for them. She doesn't remember driving her car off the highway. It was more as though something had picked up her car and "floated" it toward a large craft that was hovering over the desert.

"Gina and I were separated," Lois stated, "and I didn't see her again for quite a while. All of a sudden, I was surrounded by strange entities with large, staring eyes." Lois's clothing was removed, and she was told that she must lie on a table so that she might be examined.

"I obeyed everything they said without question," Lois said. "It was as if I had been hypnotized or something. I just did whatever they told me. Nothing they did hurt that much. They took some blood, some samples of hair and skin here and there. I was not married at that time and had no children. I had a sense that a lot of the tests had to do with my fertility … or lack of it."

Lois was given a gown to wear. "They still seemed to be examining my clothing, my purse, everything that I had with me. I had been really nervous when they brought us aboard the space vehicle, but a voice kept saying over and over that Gina and I had nothing to fear, that they would not hurt us."

Lois had no concept of how long she might have been in that room, staring spellbound at what seemed to be colors and lights swirling past the window. "The next thing I remember is when an elderly bearded man in a robe came into the room," Lois said. "He looked like a regular, normal earthman. He was a bit above medium height and well proportioned."

She remembers only snatches of their conversation: "They said that I had been taken on board because I was one of them," Lois said. "They wanted to examine me to see if I were well. They cared about me because I had a 'key.' When I asked what key that was, they said that I would remember when the time was right."

The next clear memory that Lois has is of waking in her car along a lonely desert road, far from the main highway. Gina was once again beside her. They were both hungry and thirsty. They looked at each other but said nothing. After the two confused women drove to the nearest town, they discovered to their amazement that *five days* had passed. They hurriedly made reassuring calls to the anxious friends and relatives who had been expecting them nearly a week ago in Phoenix.

The next clear memory that Lois has is of waking in her car along a lonely desert road, far from the main highway.

In the years that have passed since their UFO abduction, Lois and Gina have seldom exchanged memories of the incredible experience. "Actually," Lois explained, "Gina refuses to discuss it at all. She regards the whole thing as some kind of high spiritual encounter that should not be denigrated by analyzing it. She thinks that we were blessed and that we should let it go at that."

Lois, on the other hand, remains disturbed by the abduction. Then, too, shortly after her marriage, she began to experience poltergeist phenomena in her home. "Doors would open and close of their own volition," she stated. "Telephones would ring at weird times of the night, and there would never be anyone there. Lights would blink on and off. My husband went nuts with all this happening. He thought he had married a witch."

Lois would have periodic dreams of the hitchhiker at the side of the road. He would smile and remind her that she had the "key."

One night when her first child was about five years old, the child awoke screaming, calling in terror for her mother. When Lois ran into the child's bedroom and took her in her arms, the girl sobbed: "Mommy, Mommy, they're in the house, and they want to see you. They say that they've come for the key."

Lois swore that she had never told her young daughter about the hitchhiker, the UFO, the abduction experience—anything. "I had never even told my husband about the experience," she stated firmly. "And yet here was my daughter repeating the same phrase to me that I had been told directly. I had the 'key.' Somehow the beings had contacted my daughter in her dreams and managed to get her to pass on a message to me."

After this nightmarish contact, the physical manifestations in the home became so violent that the family was forced to move. As an additional tragic side effect, Lois's marriage ended. Lois had told no one of her experience until she visited my wife, Sherry, and me.

"I have kept all this weirdness to myself. I have virtually suffered in complete silence for all these years," she said. "I have really undergone a hell because of that experience. I still have no idea what they meant when they said that I had the 'key.' The whole thing is really driving me crazy."

Although we have lost touch with Lois through the years, the last we heard from her, her second daughter, who was then four years old, had one day looked up from her toys to remark: "Mommy, it won't be long now before the hitchhiker comes back to see you."

Close Encounters of the Terrifying Kind

Some UFO contactees/abductees see handsome Nordic men and women approaching them from alleged alien spacecraft. Others see small gray figures with unusually large heads and bug-like eyes. (illustration by Ricardo Pustanio).

From 1967 to 1989, I conducted hypnotic regressions of dozens of men and women who claimed to have been abducted for brief periods of time by crew members from UFOs. Many of these contactees/abductees claimed to have been given some kind of medical examination. In some instances, they were left with peculiar punctures and markings in their flesh.

During some encounters, the abductees saw entities that were human-like in appearance. However, in the greatest number of such encounters, the UFO occupants were described as standing about five-feet tall and dressed in one-piece, tight-fitting jumpsuits.

Their skin was gray, or grayish green, and hairless; their faces were dominated by large eyes, very often with snakelike, slit pupils; they had no discernible lips, just straight lines for mouths; they seldom were described as having noses, just little snubs, if at all; but usually the witnesses saw only nostrils nearly flush against the smooth face. Sometimes a percipient mentioned pointed ears, but on most occasions the abductee/contactee commented on the absence of noticeable ears on a large, round head.

It has seemed to me for many years now that the UFO occupants may be reptilian or amphibian humanoids, and I believe that they have been interacting with Earth for millions of years.

Assessing the experiences of certain abductees, I conclude that the citizens of Earth are encountering at least two representatives of extraterrestrial or multidimensional worlds. There appear to be those intelligences associated with the UFO phenomenon who are genuinely concerned about our welfare and our spiritual and physical evolution, and there are those who seem largely indifferent to our personal needs and our species' longevity. If the Forces of Light and Darkness are about to square off on our turf, humankind could find itself the unwilling pawn in the ultimate battle—the final struggle between Good and Evil.

Black-Eyed Beings

It was probably in the autumn of 2003 that people began to write to me describing their encounters with a strange group of boys, ranging from pre-teen to teenaged, who had coal black eyes and very strange and menacing ways. The first report that I received proved almost to be a prototype of the accounts that would follow.

Carter and his girlfriend Suzanne, were double-dating with their good friends Greg and Karen on a pleasant fall evening in Seattle when they encountered the strange lost boys. Carter remembered that they first saw them as they were leaving a seafood restaurant. "There were four of them," he said. "They looked like a bunch of teenagers just lounging around the park near the restaurant on a Saturday night. No school the next day. No dates. Nothing to do. Just hanging out."

Carter opened the car door for Suzanne and walked around to the driver's side. As he was getting behind the wheel, Suzanne asked if he knew the boys in the park.

"No," he said, and wondered why she had asked.

"Because one of them is waving and I thought he called your name," she said.

Puzzled, Carter looked toward the park and saw that the group appeared to be coming toward the car. "Don't know any of them," he shrugged.

Greg suggested that they leave. "They might be a bunch of hoods trying to make trouble," he said. Suzanne laughed and said that they were just kids and that one of them had called Carter's name.

Greg was insistent that they leave immediately. "Kids like those very often carry guns and rob people," he said. "Let's get out of here." Carter thought that Greg's assessment of the situation made sense. The teens must have heard Carter's name when the couples left the restaurant and one of them called his name to gain proximity for a robbery. He had heard that it was a common ploy for criminals, whatever their ages, to attempt to deceive their victims with a sense of familiarity.

Although most of the strange, black-eyed boys appear to be in their early to mid teens, some are much younger and seek to appeal to homeowners taken in by their apparent helplessness and need for shelter (illustration by Ricardo Pustanio).

"As I backed out of our parking space," Carter said, "I made eye contact with the boy who appeared to be the leader. I wish that I had not done so. His eyes were like black marbles. When I glanced at the other boys, they, too, seemed to have no ordinary pupils. Just black marbles. I felt a shiver run through me and I burned rubber leaving the lot."

Greg asked if Carter had spotted any guns or other weapons on the kids. "No, weapons," Carter answered, "but did any of you see their eyes? They were solid black."

Suzanne laughed and said that the kids were all trying to be cool and wearing sunglasses at twilight. "They all want to be hip-hop or rock stars," she said.

Karen agreed. Her kid brother was always wearing "shades," trying to appear cool. Their mother was always on him, warning him that he would ruin his eyes.

The two couples went to a recently released film that they had all wanted to see. Carter said that the four of them were cheerily engaged in a mock intellectual debate over the quality of the film when he spotted the same four teenaged boys leaning against the wall of a Chinese restaurant across the street. When he directed his friends' attention to the group, they voiced the same question almost in unison: How did they get here? How did they know what movie they were going to see?

The four boys waved at them in an exaggerated gesture of friendliness. They all wore broad smiles. One of them asked them how they enjoyed the film. Greg wanted to know how the kids had been able to tail them. Did anyone notice that they had a car when they first spotted them as they came out of the restaurant? Did anyone notice that they were being followed? Even Suzanne's cheerfulness had diminished, and she expressed her opinion that they should get out of there ... fast.

"As I looked at the four teenagers leaning against the wall, I couldn't help thinking of Kiefer Sutherland and his vampire gang in the old movie *The Lost Boys*," Carter said. "We got into the car as soon as possible, and I drove to one of our favorite watering holes on the edge of the city. I was determined to get as far away from the teenaged terrors as possible. Greg kept lookout in the backseat all the way to the bar to see that we weren't being followed."

Although Carter said that it may seem beyond all belief, when they left the bar at one in the morning, the four teenagers were lounging on the curb across the street. "To say that we were all unnerved is to make the understatement of the year," Carter said. "Greg wanted to call the cops. Suzanne wanted to go straight home. Karen accused Greg or me of arranging a hoax to frighten the girls. She insisted that one of us had the most stupid sense of humor in the world and that we had set up the whole thing. One of us had given the teenagers our itinerary for the evening. It was all just a stupid joke. The worst one that anyone had ever thought up since the fall of Rome."

After 20 minutes of Carter and Greg vowing that the "Lost Boys" had not been their idea of a joke and that they had no explanation for the bizarre events of the evening, Carter dropped Greg and Karen off at their respective apartments and he and Suzanne headed home.

Suzanne knew that the appearance of the boys and their subsequent stalking of the group of friends had been no joke. She was frightened and said very little on the drive back to their apartment. "We had not been home for more than a few minutes," Carter said, "when someone rang the doorbell. We live on the first floor and the steps lead from the street right up to our door. I looked out the peephole, knowing exactly who I was going to see. It was the Lost Boys, their black eyes reflecting the lights from the street. The one I determined to be their leader was leaning on the door. The other three sprawled on the steps."

Carter grabbed a baseball bat and asked through the door what they wanted. Suzanne clutched his sleeve, insisting that he not open the door.

Carter grabbed a baseball bat and asked through the door what they wanted. Suzanne clutched his sleeve, insisting that he not open the door. The leader asked Carter to open the door. Carter replied that that wasn't going to happen and told them to leave before they called the cops.

"I need to make a telephone call," the leader said. "Can I use your phone? I'll be quick. Just one call? We need to have someone come and pick us up."

No.

"We need to use your bathroom. Please let us come in to use your bathroom. We really have to go bad. Please open the door. We won't make a mess. Just in and out. Okay?"

No.

"Can you give us something to eat? We haven't eaten all day. We are starving. Can't you spare us a little food?"

No.

"C'mon, we are really hungry. Let us in. Give us just a little snack. Please!"

The leader's voice was becoming louder more insistent. Then the other three joined in, almost chanting their demands that they be allowed to come in and get something to eat. Carter was unaware that Suzanne had called the police shortly after the black-eyed lost boys had begun asking to be allowed inside.

"As the squad came around the block, the boys simply disappeared," Carter said. "They vanished in the blink of an eye. All we could tell the police officers is that a gang of rowdy teenagers had been pounding on our door, but they ran away when they heard the squad car coming. When the officers asked for descriptions, we gave accurate descriptions—except for the solid black eyes."

Who are the mysterious black-eyed boys who appear and disappear from nowhere, but who plead to come inside people's homes? (illustration by Dan Allen).

Since I received Carter's remarkable account in 2003, men and women have been reporting similar encounters with the Lost Boys with the black eyes all over the world. On a number of occasions, witnesses have also reported encounters with black-eyed adults. At this point, no one knows for certain who these beings are, but I will once again champion their place of origin in some multidimensional corner of the universe. The modus operandi of the entities is basically the same whenever they manifest.

1. They knock on the door and appear as boys in their early teens. There are two, sometimes four, beings who are dressed as typical teenagers. The leader, usually the taller of the boys, asks to use the telephone or the restroom.

2. The homeowner senses that these are not ordinary children, and the sight of the black eyes fills him or her with fear.

3. When the homeowner refuses to allow them admittance, they continue to speak politely, but they plead that it is too cold or too hot or some other matter of great urgency.

4. When the homeowner continues to refuse their requests, the boys begin to plead that they must come in, they need to come in.

5. The homeowner is increasingly overwhelmed by feelings of fear. After absolutely refusing to let them enter the home, the black-eyed boys walk away—and disappear.

In his article "Are Black-Eyed Beings Walking Among Us?" on www.rense.com, May 5, 2008, Ted Twietmeyer listed some common characteristics of black-eyed beings that he had discovered.

1. The black-eyed beings sometimes dress in inconspicuous clothing that will fit in with the general population, but they are often reported wearing clothing that appears out of sync with contemporary times. Sometimes they seem to favor odd color combinations.

2. Black-eyed children approach adults quite forcefully, and they do not act with the shyness expected of most normal children. While they may be verbally forceful in demanding entry into a home or an automobile, they seldom become physical.

3. Evil is the most common characteristic that eyewitnesses report feeling after encounters with both black-eyed children and adults.

4. The fact that the black-eyed adults and children alike ask permission to enter a home or a vehicle suggests the ancient spiritual law that forbids evil to enter a person's domain without that individual granting it permission to do so.

5. The black-eyed entities appear to be solid beings. They are not ghosts or other disembodied creatures.

6. The great majority of encounters with the black-eyed ones occur after dark. Some researchers have suggested that these beings may not be able to tolerate direct sunlight.

There is some evidence that at least some of the black-eyed boys may be paraphysical beings and that they find other ways of gaining entrance to someone's home.

Tommy Wants to Stay in Our House

One night in January 2007, Maya and Michael Rodriquez were relaxing with a glass of wine and the newspaper when a book suddenly became airborne from a coffee table and crashed to the floor. The two went to investigate and found that, though it had been closed on the coffee table, the book had fallen face down on the carpet at the exact page that Maya had paused in her reading earlier that evening.

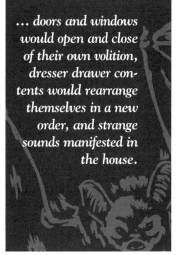

... doors and windows would open and close of their own volition, dresser drawer contents would rearrange themselves in a new order, and strange sounds manifested in the house.

The airborne book was only the beginning of the phenomena. Thereafter, doors and windows would open and close of their own volition, dresser drawer contents would rearrange themselves in a new order, and strange sounds manifested in the house. The Rodriquezes were confused about the phenomena, but not greatly concerned. They were open-minded about such matters. If their house was suddenly hosting a ghost, as yet the pranks had been completely harmless.

Then, one night, Maya heard their seven-year-old daughter, Maria, talking to someone in her bedroom. Curious, Maya climbed the stairs to see to whom Maria was speaking. Maria did not have permission to have a friend over to play after dark. The child fell silent as Maya entered the room. There was no one else there.

"To whom were you talking, Maria?"

Maria looked annoyed. "No one," she said sullenly. "I was just playing." Maya shrugged her shoulders and left the room.

The next night the Rodriquezes lost their complacency regarding the strange phenomena visiting their home. They were sitting in the living room, watching television, when low moans seemed to be coming from Maria's room. Maya jumped to her feet and turned down the volume control on the set, then she inclined her ear toward Maria's room. The moans were most certainly coming from Maria. Maya and Michael went upstairs to investigate, each unmistakably worried. Michael strode forward and switched on the light. Maya screamed.

Somehow, Maria had been stuffed inside her pillow case. Her pitiful cries were muffled by the cotton fabric. Maya extricated her daughter and brought the girl downstairs with them. Together Michael and Maya comforted her until the little girl seemed to have recovered from her frightening experience. Then Maya picked Maria up and swung her into her arms.

"Time for little girls to go back to bed," she said as she headed for the staircase. Maya stepped into the room and gasped with surprise. She and Michael and Maria were the only people in the house, and they had all been downstairs. Yet, somehow, someone had taken the pillowcase in which Maria had been imprisoned and placed it back on the pillow. The bed had been completely remade, as though Maria had not yet retired for the evening.

Maya tried to hide her uneasiness from Maria as she turned down the covers once more and tucked the girl into bed. She gave Maria a distracted kiss good night and went back downstairs.

"Michael, are all the doors and windows locked?"

Michael looked mildly surprised. "Of course, Maya. Everything is locked up."

Maya explained to her husband what had happened.

"No one could have been in that room, yet somehow the bed was completely remade. It scared me."

Maya remained lost in thought for a few minutes. Then she tentatively raised her head and spoke hesitantly to her husband. "Michael, you don't suppose that my mother—God rest her—is trying to communicate with us, do you? Trying to tell us she's all right? She's been gone now for five months. What if her soul is not at peace?"

Michael smiled at Maya. "You know that your dear mother is at peace. There's got to be a logical explanation for all these things. We'll find out what it is. You wait and see." Maya was not quite so confident that a "logical" explanation could be found. Two nights later Michael was nearly ready to agree with her.

It was almost midnight when the talking and singing began. Michael and Maya's bedroom was on the ground floor of the house, directly below Maria's. The Rodriquezes were just beginning to doze off when they heard Maria talking to someone in her room. At the same time, another voice could be heard singing. The voice of the singer was that of an older *male* child. As Michael and Maya climbed the stairs, they could hear the voices more clearly. When they opened the bedroom door, however, both voices stopped. Maria looked at them with her wide, child's eyes.

"Maria, who were you talking to just now?" Maya asked.

"That's my friend, Tommy. He comes and plays with me lots now."

The Rodriquezes looked around the room. There was no one else there but the three of them.

"Where is your friend, Honey?" Michael asked. Maria pointed directly in front of her. "There."

The Rodriquezes looked at each other, puzzled. They could see no one else. Michael asked where Tommy lived and why he was in their house and not at home with his mommy and daddy. Maria told them that one day when she got home from school and Mommy and Daddy were in the kitchen, Tommy knocked on the door and asked if he could come in. Maria had minded her manners and invited him into the house. Then they went up to her room to play. Tommy didn't really have a Mommy and a Daddy or a home, so she asked him to stay.

Later, Maya and Michael discussed the incident. They knew that it was not uncommon for children to have invisible friends, but invisible friends that could sing in a voice that others could hear? From then on, Maria talked frequently with her invisible friend.

Late one evening the Rodriquezes were all seated in the living room when the temperature suddenly dropped dramatically. Icy eddies swirled around their feet.

"Tommy, stop that!" Maria cried. "You're making me cold." Immediately the eddies left, and the room temperature returned to normal. Other phenomena continued to plague the Rodriquez home. Lights would turn on and off of their own will, and cold spots became common in various parts of the house.

Tommy wasn't your child's average imaginary playmate.

One morning Maria came downstairs for breakfast with a number of small red spots on her right arm. One of the punctures was bleeding slightly. When Michael asked to see the "owie" on his daughter's arm, Maria explained that Tommy had bitten her during the night while she was sleeping. Puzzled, Maya took Maria's arm in her hand and looked closely at the wound. "Maria," she asked quietly, "did you bite yourself?" Maria threw her toast angrily down on the floor. "I told you that Tommy did it."

The Rodriquezes decided to purchase a puppy for Maria, to try to divert her attention from her "friend." The first night "Bowser" was in the house it began to growl at something neither Michael nor Maya could see. Its hair stood on end, and it ran to the kitchen table, cowering beneath it. Whatever invisible entity was in their house, it was clear that the dog could see it.

Later that night, Maya heard Maria in her room saying over and over again that something was too bad, but that's the way things had to be. When she went to investigate, she found Maria kneeling beside the puppy's little bed. The dog was dead.

"Tommy said that we didn't need any damned dog," Maria said with only a tinge of sadness in her voice. "We have each other."

Maya was shocked by the words that had come from her seven-year-old daughter. Maria did not curse. Or at least she never had done so. The puppy appeared to have been strangled or smothered. Its mouth was open as if gasping for breath, and its little body was twisted grotesquely. Maria could not have done such a thing.

"What happened to your sweet little Bowser, Honey? Please tell me how just an awful thing could have happened to the puppy."

Maria shrugged. "Tommy said that he needed the puppy's breath so he could get stronger. If he had Bowser's breath, then he wouldn't need to bite me as much. It hurts when he bites me."

The atmosphere in the room suddenly became harsh and malevolent. A chill came upon the room. Maria began to whimper.

"Oh, he's coming toward me, Mommy!" Maria suddenly cried. "Tommy is mad that I told on him."

"No, no!" she cried to herself, staring at the hideous thing in the closet that now seemed to be floating toward Maria.

The girl slumped in her mother's arms. Maya cried out and shook her. "Maria! Maria! Answer me!" The little bundle in her arms did not move. At the sound of laughter in Maria's closet, Maya looked into the shadows and was startled to see the image of a young boy of about 10 or 11. The image wavered, then became stronger. Maya gasped when she saw that the boy had coal black eyes.

Maya was frantic, confused. She did not know what to do. Then Maria stirred. The little tousled head turned upward and stared sardonically at Maya. A low chuckle escaped her lips. Maya stared in horror as a glint of evil shone in Maria's eyes. The little girl threw back her head and started to laugh coarsely. Maya jumped up and let go of her daughter, as though she were something diseased.

"No, no!" she cried to herself, staring at the hideous thing in the closet that now seemed to be floating toward Maria. Maria welcomed the presence of the entity with obscene chortles of laughter. Maya ran from the room and almost collided with Michael on the landing.

"What in heaven's name is going on?" he demanded.

Maya could only shake her head mutely. Michael tore past Maya and entered Maria's room. He was aghast at the sight awaiting him. Maria sat with her back to the door, almost doubled up with the hideous laughter. Michael made the sickening realization that the vile sound was coming from his seven-year-old daughter.

Maria started to turn toward the door, her face contorted into an expression of centuries-old evil. Michael was shaken by her look. The instant that Maria's eyes fell upon Michael, however, the expression vanished. The horrifying laughter died on her lips. She sat on the floor as if dazed.

"Maria?" Michael asked, uncertainly.

"Is she all right?" Maya asked from behind him. "And what about the *thing* in the closet?"

"Hi, Daddy," the little voice greeted. It was once again the sound and expression of their daughter.

"Maria, are you all right?" Maya asked, looking cautiously toward the closet and checking to see if "Tommy" was present.

"Sure, I'm all right," the girl replied. "Why are you here?"

Michael walked quickly toward the girl, picked her up and carried her to her bed. "Because little girls should not be out of bed at this hour, that's why," he declared.

"But tonight," Maya interrupted, "Maria gets a treat. She gets to sleep downstairs with Mommy and Daddy."

Michael caught the look in his wife's eyes, and cheerily agreed. He carried Maria downstairs, placed her in bed, and pulled the covers around her. Then he softly withdrew from the room, closing the door behind him. He put his arm around Maya, and together the two walked into the living room. "Now, then, tell me exactly what happened."

Maya sat down in a large easy chair and told Michael about the short life of Bowser and what Maria had said about Tommy. Then she summoned her courage and told Michael what she had seen in Maria's closet, the specter of a little boy with coal black eyes. Michael listened carefully, without comment.

Maya winced as the maniacal laughter echoed down the stairs and filled the hallway.

When Maya had finished her narrative, the two reconstructed the past several days in their house, starting with the floating book from the coffee table. They carefully listed the various kinds of phenomena they had experienced, including the icy spots in the house and the reaction of the poor little puppy to their home's atmosphere. They realized that they had been lulled to complacency by the relative harmlessness of the psychic activity around them. By harboring the manifestations in their home, they feared that they had attracted less kindly disposed beings. These negative aspects were now attacking Maria, who, as the youngest, was the most psychically attuned of the three and the most vulnerable to a negative purpose.

Both Michael and Maya were lapsed Roman Catholics or they would have called a priest. Instead, they remembered meeting a medium at a New Age Psychic Exposition who went to people's houses and exorcised ghosts. From all reports, the woman, Alexandra, was very good.

"I think we should call her," Maya said.

"But that woman exorcises ghosts who are haunting houses," Michael said. "We've got some kind of weird entity haunting a person—our Maria. Can a medium cast that thing out before it possesses Maria altogether?"

"Well," Maya replied grimly. "Let's put it this way. We had better try." Michael agreed that they should call Alexandra.

Before he went to bed that night, he sadly ascended the stairs and removed the body of Bowser from Maria's room. Gently, he wrapped the puppy in an old blanket that he had once had in the trunk of their car and carried the little body to the backyard where he buried it under the soft light of a quarter moon.

The next day Alexandra responded to Maya's emergency call for help. She made arrangements to visit the Rodriquez home later that same day, after the dinner hour. When the medium arrived, Maria was playing quietly upstairs. The instant the front door was opened to admit the medium, however, Maria experienced another seizure, such as the one she had undergone the night before and they all heard a young boy's voice screaming curses.

Maya winced as the maniacal laughter echoed down the stairs and filled the hallway. Michael offered his hand distractedly to the medium; his face was ashen.

"Let us go up there at once," Alexandra announced in a brisk, yet sympathetic, tone. "There is no need to prolong this."

The medium reached into her purse and drew out what appeared to be a kind of wand with a crystal embedded in its tip. With the crystal wand in her right hand and a medium-sized wooden crucifix in her left, Alexandra began climbing the stairs. Maya and Michael followed closely behind her. As the medium entered Maria's room, the laughter abruptly ceased. With an utterly evil expression on her face, Maria looked up and snarled at the medium.

"Your attempts will be futile, you fool," the little girl hissed, with a vocabulary far beyond her seven years. "I am here in this house now, and I intend to stay here. Recite your silly lines, wave that puny cross. And you know where you can put that wand. Your methods are useless with me."

Maya gasped and clung to her husband's arm. They could see clearly the image of Tommy standing directly behind Maria. It was the black-eyed little boy who was speaking through their daughter. Alexandra remained unperturbed. "Leave that body at once, and return from whence you came. You are no longer welcome in this house."

So saying, the medium advanced slowly upon the child, holding the cross and the crystal wand in front of her. Maria began to squirm, yet the demon's voice within her remained firm. "I was invited into this home," Tommy said. "Once I am invited in, you cannot make me leave."

Alexandra once again commanded him to leave.

"You stupid hulk of flesh," Tommy taunted. "Put down that absurd cross and primitive crystal and leave me be."

Still the medium slowly advanced. She began to pray softly in a monotone. Her voice started to rise, still preserving the chant-like quality of her praying. The image of the black-eyed boy started to curse, using vile terms. When the medium was within two feet of the demon, she suddenly thrust the cross and the crystal wand before her until they were inches away from the now-cowering form of Tommy, whatever he truly was.

"In the name of the Great Spirit, the Blessed Harmony that governs the universe, the Oneness of Love, and the Power of Light, I command you to leave this child," the medium thundered. "Depart now. Feel the power of the Light envelop your darkness and nevermore show thy face or thy characteristics on Earth. Depart now, relinquish the unholy hold you have over this body!"

There was a lot more that Alexandra said, step by spiritual step, driving the essence of the black-eyed boy back into the vortex from which he came, back into the dimension that had spawned him.

With a loud cry Maria fell over on her face. The medium raised her hands toward the ceiling and spoke rapidly in what sounded to Maya and Michael like some

Native American language. When she brought her arms down to her side, little Maria looked up at her parents and began to cry.

Maya and Michael did not hold back their own tears of gratitude that their blessed little girl had been returned to them as she was, free of the taint of a tormented spirit that had desperately sought refuge in her body and in their home.

The Shadow People

The concept of "Shadow People" began to be popularized on the late-night talk shows in about 2003. There seemed scarcely a night when someone didn't call in to report an encounter with a shadowy figure that he or she had caught moving quickly about the room. It seemed that in most instances, the percipient viewed the figure with his or her peripheral vision, but nonetheless, was convinced that "something" had been there.

Stories of strange skirmishes with Shadow People continue to be popular with radio audiences. Lively debates over whether these beings are spirits of the dead, aliens from another world, or energy-seeking vampires from other dimensions continue to keep listeners up until the wee hours of morning.

Entities of the Shadow have been with humankind for centuries. As beings from another level of our multidimensional universe, they are often summoned by human emotions, especially fear, self-doubt, and greed. Very often, they are invited into a human's space by someone dabbling in the occult. Curious and previously innocent minds can offer a wide-open portal to this world when some individuals begin "playing" with such devices as the Ouija board.

"Playing" with the Ouija Board Invited Shadow People to Cross the Portal between Worlds

As Erica tells her story.…

A few years back my sister and I were "playing" with a Ouija board. We thought it was just a game, but we soon found out that it really wasn't when weird occurrences

Some researchers have theorized that the Shadow People are energy vampires that enter from some other dimension of reality to steal the spiritual essence of their victims (illustration by Dan Allen).

began to happen. At first, it was like footsteps in the hall and on the ceiling. Then there would be loud thuds, like someone wearing boots or heavy shoes. Sometimes we would hear wind chimes inside the house when we knew it was impossible, because we had no wind chimes in or outside.

Then things started to get more strange. One night while I was in bed I started to stare into a dark corner of my room. I was about to close my eyes when I noticed that the shadow began to get darker and darker. I couldn't quite understand what was happening so I just continued to stare.

Then the shadow took up almost the entire corner, and I could see a silhouette of a person. Fear sunk in at this point, and I could feel him staring right through me. I then saw this "shadow" man step out into the light and everything was visible except for the features of his face. From what I could tell about his clothing (from later research) was that he was an officer from Revolutionary War times. I could see everything right down to the golden buttons.

Then he walked right past my bed and out into the hallway. He seemed like an intelligent sort of shadow person or spirit. I was extremely scared, and I didn't tell anyone about it for a while. I'm not sure whether it's the same "shadow" person or not, but since then I've seen it quite often. Sometimes in the living room, and once it even ran across what is now my room while the room light was on. My sister was the one who was now in the back bedroom, and she yelled for me just as it happened.

I see him or it mainly in the daytime or while the lights are on. To be honest I can't explain it as hard as I try to debunk it all. I have also seen a figure of a woman in a white gown float down my hallway. My sister has seen her once. We have also seen the images of a little boy and girl—the boy mostly. They both seem harmless, and I do not resent that they are in the house. I just live with it.

I have seen the boy in my niece's room. He was kneeling beside a dollhouse that she had at the time, almost as though he were playing with it. The boy has also been seen outside of the house by my sister's boyfriend. He was standing by her boyfriend's car as if he wanted to take a ride. I've also heard both the boy and girl laughing together from the hallway. My sister's boyfriend has heard the girl giggle while he was in the bathroom. I think that made him uncomfortable about the house. I've had my hair lifted up while I was in the shower. It caught me off guard, but by that time I was used to such manifestations and had accepted that I lived alongside these spirits.

But there are things that are harder to accept. The darker things began only a couple years ago and things seemed to spike after a horrible, and extremely vivid, nightmare that I had. I didn't know what fear was until the end of that "dream."

I dreamt that I was in a desert, and when I woke up I could still feel the sand on my face. After I had experienced the same dream for about five or six days straight, I would see shadow creatures from the dream following me in the house.

When I would be out in public places, I would see people with no whites in their eyes. Their eyes would be totally black. I tried to ignore all these things, and I decided that my imagination had gotten the better of me. One night when I was in the shower, I thought that enough was enough and I declared that demons did not exist.

All of a sudden, I began choking. I became extremely afraid. It felt as though I was being choked from the inside out. Whatever it was, I sensed that it would not stop until I said that "demons did exist." After I thought that I had made peace with the entities by conceding their existence, I was sitting down in the house by myself when, just out of nowhere it felt like something reached into my chest and began to squeeze my heart. I thought I was having a heart attack. It felt like something was trying to pull my heart out of my chest.

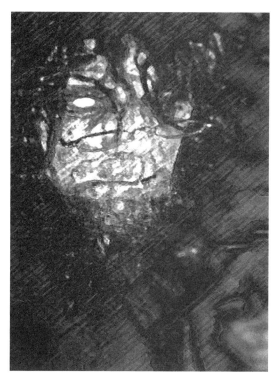

Many people have reported humanoid shadows moving from room to room in their homes (illustration by Ricardo Pustanio).

I honestly thought that this was it, and I asked for God/the Great Spirit to spare me. I begged him—and as soon as I asked for spiritual help the pain started to subside.

Since that time, I have been awakened by a loud, hissing growl coming from the middle of my room. I heard scratching on the wall at the head of my bed. Another night I was about to go to sleep when, as I closed my eyes, I could hear two people screaming, and two people in the foreground arguing.

Connecting with the Light
to Protect Ourselves from the Darkside

Erica was nearly at the end of her wits with the Shadow People after she and her sister had inadvertently allowed the beings to enter our dimension through their innocent "playing" with a Ouija board. I emailed her some very effective techniques that Sherry and I have developed over the years for banishing negative entities and they seemed to be effective. I also discussed the case of Erica with Lee, a friend who has had a number of years experience in dealing with Shadow People and other entities from the Darkside. Lee made these comments, which are worthy of sharing.

A person who has opened the door to other dimensions by ignorant action must learn to shut the door by a deep trust in the Light. When we pray—seriously—we make the connection with the Light. The words aren't important, just the act of trust and the seeking of protection from Evil. Ten thousand Crosses, 100 Bibles, 600 Mandalas, 500 Dream-Catchers, and 1,000,000 Candles will never have any effect if the soul seeking protection has no relationship with the Light. We live in a Quantum Multiverse where one particle/wave must be "bonded" … "harmonized" … with the other in order to have any effect on the other. This is true with the soul and the Light just as much as with the soul and Evil.

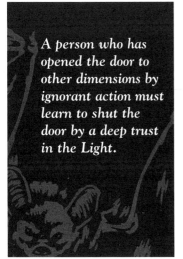

A person who has opened the door to other dimensions by ignorant action must learn to shut the door by a deep trust in the Light.

The soul which formed a bond with Evil must now form a bond with the Light. We need not break that link with Evil. We can't. We aren't that strong. The Light, by the act of joining with us in relationship, breaks that bond. It displaces the old bond and replaces it with a new one. The Light makes us "new born" … a "new man/woman." We, like a simple quantum particle, have our orbit, our orientation, shifted to another.

When we are confronted by negative entities, we must simply let the Light speak through us. How do we protect ourselves from Darkness? We turn on the Light. This process works in a simple room at night, and it works in the Soul in life. Standing in the Light you are not in Darkness.

The process is simple, but no one can mutter words, burn incense, light candles, or read from a sacred text, you must put the Light inside your soul. You are the one who must let the Light ignite you. No one can convince another of this. We can witness to our own knowledge. We can report. But it is for each soul to choose. This is our Free Will. This is the one choice.

Encountering the Gray Men

Kari wrote inquiring about manifestations of the "Gray Men," a kind of variation of the Shadow People. Endowed with a high degree of spiritual and psychic sensitivity, Kari was much better equipped to deal with shadow entities than many who suddenly find themselves faced with the unknown. Kari related the following.

At a young age, I watched humanoid shadows cross the hallway in my home, moving from one room to another. Often I could catch the movement out of my peripheral vision and would be staring directly at them when they moved across open space. My brother and mother also witnessed them.

There was no sense of fear, alarm, or dread accompanying the sightings. (Note that I had ruled out natural causes that may create a movement of shadows in many of these instances. The shadows moved independently of any backdrop and passed across open space without any distortion of distance or angle.)

A note: The house was the first built in that location and anything present in the house was there probably because we, the inhabitants, attracted the presences. My family has a history of members with psychic sensitivity.

Around age 10 or 11, I became fascinated with auras, which naturally led to a study of the relationship between energy and organic bodies. The generation and channeling of energy led to a practice of meditation and "energy manipulation" (a term my brother and I shared for the basic affecting of energy through will and concentration, often with the aid of visualization techniques). Around this time, I took to warding my room so that: "None with ill intent may enter."

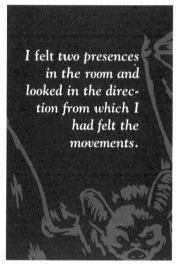

I felt two presences in the room and looked in the direction from which I had felt the movements.

About a year later, my parents transformed the backmost room of the house into a sort of guestroom (it had previously been a porch, transformed into an aviary, and then a guestroom). I decided one night to spend the night in the backroom. I was awakened in the middle of the night by two shadows passing over the bed. I *felt* two presences in the room and looked in the direction from which I had felt the movements. I saw two, solid looking, dark, human-shaped shadows standing at the end of the bed.

The moment I saw them, I became paralyzed and felt a weight pressing down on my chest. Note that there was no sense of suffocation, just a weight that would not allow me to get up. When I realized I couldn't move, I became frightened and began to pray. I couldn't speak, so I prayed loudly in my head. The figures seemed unaffected by my prayer for protection and lingered a few moments before moving toward the back door of the house and disappearing.

The pressure and paralysis had left the moment they turned away, but I remained still until they were gone. It then dawned on me that the room I was in was not shielded. I took the time to establish a simple ward before returning to sleep. I remained undisturbed for the rest of the night and slept untroubled. The next day, I told my brother what happened and he said that he had not experienced anything like that in the room, and didn't know why the shadows would be in there. However, afterward, we agreed to extend our own personal wards, which were for our bedrooms, to encompass the whole of the house.

Looking back on the event, I sensed no maliciousness or evil from the shadow men, or shadow walkers as I began to call them. The experience was terrifying only while I was experiencing paralysis, a sense of inability to act.

My first reaction upon waking was curiosity, and I actually wanted to *ask* questions of the visitors, but when I discovered I was unable to move, I became fearful of

They appear even blacker than the darkness against which they manifest (illustration by Bill Oliver).

their intentions. Now, I consider it an instructional experience, made forceful because a point was being made, a lesson given that I would not forget: Remain aware of the potential dangers of wandering spirits/entities, and not to leave myself unguarded. Since then, I have taken personal steps toward spiritual protection (primarily deep faith in a higher power, and in my own force of will).

It was soon after the experience that while sitting on my bed meditating, I noticed a new presence in my room. It was a man-like figure dressed all in white with pale hair, oval face, a fair complexion, and eyes shadowed but full of light. He was just watching me, observing me, and he followed me around long enough that I ceased to pay him any mind. I got the feeling that he inhabited that same, overlapping realm that the shadows were from, but possibly a different level. I know that he was separate and apart from them, but still from the same place.

Not long after, I began to sense other presences, though all I saw were vague, man-shaped gray images. They began to come into my room soon after the white-man appeared and would wander around the house, almost inspecting it. I actually felt *safer* with them around, and their presence, though neither positive nor negative, was slightly warm and nice. The best way to describe it would be to feel the warmth of sunlight while standing under a night sky.

Over time I became sensitive to their presence. I learned that thinking about or concentrating on them could attract their attention, and likewise, their presence. I invoked this often when I fell into the habit of taking late night walks around the edge of the college campus. When at least one was with me, I felt strangely safe. If I was attacked or accosted, I didn't know what would happen, but I had the uncanny feeling that my "escort" was not powerless to interfere, even if that interference was to make themselves visible to others in order to scare them away or make me appear not to be a lone target.

A nice side benefit of many being present together, is that they radiate a sense of warmth. If I was cold while walking, I would visualize one moving close to me and I would immediately warm up.

The last significant encounter that I've had was with *the* gray-man, as I think of him. I first noticed him when, late one evening, I was with the man who is now my husband, and we were visiting an old covered bridge in the local area. Something in the woods seriously spooked him , and he insisted that we get into the car and leave. I noticed a gray-man that I had never seen before, standing and watching us leave. I saw him in amazing detail, more than ever before. He made random appearances for the next two weeks, just observing me. I got the feeling that I was being *evaluated*. He wouldn't even give me a name to call him by.

At the end of those two weeks, I was napping in my dorm room at the college and I woke up to find him standing at the end of the bed, watching me. For the second time in my life, I couldn't move, but I had no fear this time. If anything, I was annoyed with the knowledge that if I closed my eyes and gave myself back the ability to move, when I opened them, he would be gone. So I waited for an undetermined amount of time before he seemed satisfied and left. I freed myself from the paralysis and sat up.

My experiences with other entities are not limited to those detailed in this summary of my life up until now (I am 23 yrs old). I have had a variety of encounters with other entities.

Multidimensional Mimics

In my book *Shadow World* (Signet 2000, Anomalist Books, 2007), I introduced the concept of spirit mimics, other-dimensional beings that often pose as ordinary men and women in order to accomplish goals that seem beyond our present human perspective to comprehend. In appearance, these beings seem to be about 97 percent just like us, but there is always that three percent or so that betrays them. Perhaps it is something in their manner of speaking or their choice of wearing apparel that just doesn't seem quite right.

In his *Adventures with Phantoms* (Quality Press, 1946), it seems as though British author Thurston Hopkins might also have been onto the spirit mimics. He said that he had come to recognize a kind of spirit that appears to occupy a spiritual "no-man's land," and he described them in this way: "They are creatures who have strayed from some unknown region.... They dress like us, pretend they belong to mankind, and profess to keep our laws and code of morals. But in their presence we are always aware that they are phantoms and that all their ideas and actions are out of key with the general pitch and tone of normal life."

I have said many times that I am puzzled by the spirit mimics' true agenda. Perhaps they are among the entities—the real vampires of ancient times—who seek to enslave the souls of humankind. If this is true, their numbers and their ventures into our world are happening more often and becoming more common. Indeed, it often seems of late that their program of dominating, controlling, and enslaving humankind might have been accelerated according to some larger cosmic plan to which our species is not privy.

A Perfume Salesperson Out of Time Sync

Whitney wrote that she had an experience a few years ago that still makes her hair stand on end. Such a fright should not have occurred to Whitney. She is a ghost researcher and has worked in the paranormal field for many years.

I was home, alone, in the garage, cleaning, when I see this girl about 16 to 18 years old standing at the end of my driveway. She had this blank look on her face and was staring not at me but past me. So I asked her if she needed anything, and she began to speak in old American slang: "Golly, gee, Miss, it sure is hot out side. I am selling perfume, and leapin' lizards it sure smells good. Would you like to mosey on over here and take a whiff?"

At the time I was living in L.A., and I do not know anyone who speaks like that. She had a feel of plastic that had come alive, because when she was looking at me she was actually looking past me. I got the feeling that you get when you are a kid and a stranger asks if you want some candy. Something just wasn't right. I just knew that if I walked down the driveway and looked in the perfume box something bad was going to happen.

I asked her what type of perfume she had, and she gave me weird answers and said such things as the perfume smelled like a new car. When she left, there were only two ways to go: to the right or to the left. And whichever way a person went, they would be visible for quite a distance. She just disappeared.

Dining Out Next to a Very Strange Couple

One of my correspondents, who has pronounced psychic abilities and is usually able to "read" people with remarkable accuracy, wrote recently to share this encounter with spirit mimics, or beings from another world.

I was eating at a restaurant with my husband and daughter. I noticed a weird vibration emanating from this couple right next to us. When my husband left to get our drinks, I looked over at the couple and made direct eye contact with each of them. They were both:

1. Very tall and thin and perfect looking. My rational mind thought they must be professional models.

2. They had high-cheekbones, very elongated. Very blue eyes. No flaws on their faces.

3. They were very well-dressed. His hair was perfect in that modern, short, blunt cut; hers, that short stylish bob. She had red hair, blue eyes. He had reddish-

brown hair, blue eyes. He wore very stylish jeans and a nice crisp shirt/jacket. She had a stylish sweater, slacks, and boots. (Usually these beings are not well-dressed).

4. They exuded a sense of eerie specialness, separateness, entitlement. No warm fuzzy feelings toward us or our daughter.

What really struck me when I made eye contact was that I could not read them. They blocked me. I think they knew that I sensed they were very human-looking ETs. I love to people-watch and often people watch my daughter. She is very cute, so I make a lot of eye contact and sense people's goodness and humanity. These beings looked human, but I did not sense "human," but "other." They did eat, very small amounts of soup, yogurt, maybe some tea.

After we made initial eye contact, I think I spooked them. They rose up at the same time and walked off in opposite directions. I saw he had no keys in his hands; she had no purse. They didn't even say good-bye to one another or hug or do the "chit-chat" good-bye that normal people might do.

I have seen these beings—or some like them—so many times over the years, but this was the first time I was not really afraid … but very curious.

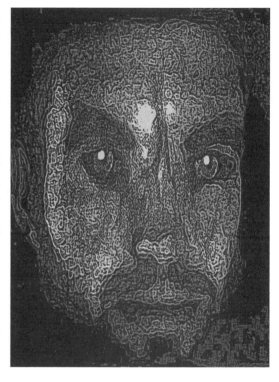

A number of those who have encountered spirit mimics have seen their eyes turn black. Are they somehow related to the black-eyed boys, who knock on doors asking to be allowed inside a human's dwelling place? (illustration by Ricardo Pustanio).

A Gas Station between Dimensions

Gary, 67, said that in the spring of 2003 he was driving through Oregon and stopped for gas at a small station off the regularly traveled highway in the area. He was drawn to the station because it reminded him of some of the old gas stations that were popular when he was a kid back in the late 1940s in the Midwest.

"When I walked inside, I had the strangest feeling that I had walked into a movie set depicting American life a few decades ago," Gary said. "The man who was the obvious owner of the station wore coveralls with the emblem of the gas company prominently placed on the chest of the uniform. A white-haired lady behind a small lunch counter gave me a warm, motherly smile. Two men in plaid shirts and jeans who seemed to be typical bearded lumberjacks, nodded in my direction and then went back to examining a display of fish hooks. A boy, maybe 10-years-old, sat at a table reading comic books that he had removed from a rack of magazines. As I passed the magazine spindle, I thought that they must all be collector's issues for sale, because I saw the covers of *The Saturday Evening Post, Colliers, Look, Argosy,* and *True: The Man's Magazine.*

Some witness to spirit mimics have been attracted to their eyes, which sometimes appear unusually bright (illustration by Ricardo Pustanio).

When I saw that the kid was flipping through a *Captain Marvel* comic, I couldn't resist telling him to treat it gently. It was worth a lot of money."

As Gary walked across the cozy interior to pay for his gas, the man in the coveralls seemed uncertain what to do with the hundred dollar bill that he handed him. "I'm sorry," Gary said. "That's the smallest that I have. I've been on vacation and I always try to save the large bills for emergency. Now I'm out of money and needed gas, so it's kind of an emergency."

The man held the bill, smiled, and looked toward the woman behind the counter. "Look, I have credit cards, if that works better for you," Gary said. The woman, the All-American Mom, had crossed to the cash register and taken the bill from the man's hand. "Oh, Paw never was good at numbers," she said, laughing at the awkwardness of the situation. "I'll make change for you."

While she was counting out the bills, one of the lumberjacks spoke to Gary. "Where you heading, Pardner?" Gary said that he almost laughed and asked if he were in a bar in Texas cowboy country. Although he had been to a lot of bars in Texas and no one had ever called him "Pardner." Gary said that he was driving back to Redlands, California. Both of the lumberjacks nodded in unison. The one who had not yet spoken said, "That's nice. That's a nice drive. You will enjoy it."

Gary could not shake the feeling that he had walked into an automated display at Disneyland or some other amusement park. "None of the people in the place looked quite real," he said. "If I would have really thought about it at the time, it probably would have freaked me out." The All-American Mom asked him what he liked to eat. Gary said that he had not stopped to eat, just to get some gas, thank you.

"But what kind of foods do you like to eat?" she persisted. Gary chuckled and was about to ask if she was doing a survey, but he indulged her and named a few of his favorite foods. One of the lumberjacks expressed his opinion. "That's nice."

"Do you live in a house or an apartment?" the other woodsman asked. Gary was increasingly becoming uneasy.

"Really, I've got to get going," he said, "I'm running a bit behind on my schedule."

"Who gives you a schedule?" the station owner asked. "Does the government, the ruling class, give you a schedule?"

That did it for Gary. He was becoming really uncomfortable with the entire set-up. Everyone in the station seemed to be automatons made of plastic or some other life-like covering. Their voices seemed pre-record-ed. The kid looking at the comic books never moved from his seat, but his arm kept flipping back and forth, back and forth over what seemed to be the same pages. Gary found himself staring at the boy's arm, and for a few seconds he felt as though he were losing consciousness, as if he were going to faint or go into trance.

Gary bolted for the door and ran for his car. "I was completely creeped out. I didn't really feel phys-ically threatened, like I had stopped at some place where I was going to be the victim of another ver-sion of *The Chainsaw Massacre*, but there was defi-nitely something not right about that gas station."

And then, Gary said, this was the truly weird part, the part that he doesn't really expect anyone to believe: "When I drove by the place about a month later, there was no gas station there. Noth-ing. And it looked as though there never had been. I knew exactly where I had been. I had taken note of all the highway and road markers. I drove to a number of small towns in the area and asked about the old gas station at such-and-such a spot, and everyone consistently denied that there had ever been a gas station at that location."

At the time that I asked Gary what he thought the meaning of his eerie experience might be, he had had a few months to think it over. "I believe that I had stopped at some kind of extrater-

Perhaps the spirit mimics, the multidimensional beings, the fallen angels, the Ahrimanes, the Jinn walk always among us, striving to seduce into their cause of earthly domination and control. (illustra-tion by Ricardo Pustanio).

restrial or multidimensional testing or examination decoy," he said. "You know, just like a duck hunter will set up a blind and put out a bunch of decoys on the pond to lure in the real ducks. I think that I was a specimen, one of the human species, who entered the little replica of a gas station that they had created in order for them to study human responses, reactions, emotions, and so forth. Their replica of a gas station was a bit dated, however. If I hadn't been a man in my sixties who was drawn by nos-talgia to stop at the place, they might have sat there quite a while before any speci-men stopped for analysis. On the other hand, I have to consider an alternate to the above statement and consider that they drew their replica from my memories. I am not an egotist by any means, but as I think back on the encounter, it was obvious that the charade was all about me—or at least my kind."

Do the spirit mimics, the multidimensional beings, the extraterrestrials, the fallen angels, the Ahrimanes, the Jinn walk among us? Do they strive to enlist humans into their cause? Are the real vampires, the night stalkers, the creatures from the Darkside exercising their powers by blending with us and accelerating their plan to enslave us?

Choose to Serve the Light

The real vampires and creatures from the Darkside have always sought to activate human disciples to help preach their lies and to perform their perverse and cruel creeds. The daughters and sons of Lilith have whispered into the ears of thousands of men and women over the centuries and convinced them to join blood cults and to sacrifice the lives of their fellow humans. Since the beginning of time, the fallen angels and the Cacodaemons of Ahrimanes have possessed the vulnerable and the weak and deceived them with the promise of becoming like unto gods. These multidimensional shape-shifters have always been devoted to their goal of enslaving the human race and capturing our soul energy.

The only effective protection against such creatures of darkness is—and has always been—to choose to serve the Light. Since humankind has been blessed with free will, each individual has the gift of choice. There comes that moment in nearly everyone's life when he or she must make the choice between creeping stealthily in the shadows or walking openly in the Light. When we choose to walk in the Light as free spirits, we are able to see clearly the path that lies ahead and discern any pitfalls that may loom before us. To choose to walk in Darkness is to crawl as slaves to the feet of cruel masters who only desire to bind us to their will, to exploit us as chattel, and to steal our life force.

Vampires: A Chronology

The following chronology was originally published in *The Vampire Book: The Complete Encyclopedia of the Undead* by J. Gordon Melton. It has been updated here by Brad Steiger.

Prehistory:	Vampire beliefs and myths emerge in cultures around the world.
c. 4000 B.C.E.	Lilitu becomes known as a demonic presence of the night that drains the blood of sleeping victims. In Hebrew folklore, Lilitu (now Lilith) was Adam's first wife before the creation of Eve, the true chosen mother of humankind. The children of Adam and Lilith are the terrible night creatures known as the incubi, who prey on women, and succubi, who thirst for male blood.
731 C.E.	Venerable Bede's *Ecclesiastical History of England* describes an array of demonic and vampiric monsters that haunt the night.
774 C.E.	*The Chronicles of Denys of Tell-Mahre* describes night creatures that terrorized the region known today as Iraq.
1047	First appearance in written form of the word *upir* (an early form of the word later to become "vampire") in a document referring to a Russian prince as "Upir Lichy," or wicked vampire.
1190	Walter Map's *De Nagis Curialium* includes accounts of vampire-like beings in England.
1196	William of Newburgh's *Chronicles* records several stories of vampire-like revenants in England.
1233	Pope Gregory IX founds the Inquisition to eradicate the practice of witchcraft, shape shifting, vampirism, cannibalism, animal familiars, and the invocation of demons.
1278	A woman in Toulouse, France, is found guilty of having sexual intercourse with an incubus and of giving birth to a child who is half snake.
1305	The wealthy and powerful Knights Templar are accused of heretical acts, such as having sexual intercourse with succubi and worshipping demons.

1312 In spite of hundreds of witnesses for their defense, the Templars are tortured and burned at the stake. Their order is officially disbanded by Pope Clement V.

1313 The Grand Master of the Knights Templar, Jacques de Molay, is burned to death on a scaffold erected for the occasion in front of Notre Dame. He condemns the pope and the king, who both die soon after his execution.

1428/29 Vlad Tepes, the son of Vlad Dracul, is born.

1440 Gilles de Rais is tried and burned for child murders and for worshipping Satan in both human and animal form.

1447 Vlad Dracul is beheaded.

1458 *The Book of Sacred Magic of Abramelin* is translated from the Hebrew. The manuscript deals with the summoning of tutelary spirits.

1462 Following the battle at Dracula's castle, Vlad flees to Transylvania. Vlad begins 13 years of imprisonment.

1475 Vlad resumes throne of Wallachia.

1476/77 Vlad is assassinated.

1486 *Malleus Malificarum,* the infamous "Hammer of the Witches," is authored by Heinrich Institoris and Jakob Sprenger. The book quickly became the "bible" of the witch hunters and focuses on seeking out those under the spell of the fallen angels who are intent on destroying the human race.

1560 Elizabeth Bathóry is born.

1610 Bathóry is arrested for killing several hundred people and bathing in their blood. Tried and convicted, she is sentenced to life imprisonment.

1614 Elizabeth Bathóry dies.

1645 Leo Allatius finishes writing the first modern treatment of vampires, *De Graecorum hodie quirundam opinationabus.*

1657 Father Françoise Richard's *Relation de ce qui s'est passe a Sant-Erini Isle de l'Archipel* links vampirism and witchcraft.

1672 Wave of vampire hysteria sweeps through Istra in Russia.

1679 A German vampire text, *De Masticatione Mortuorum,* by Philip Rohr is written.

1680 Catherine Montvoisin goes to the stake in Paris after claiming she performed satanic blood sacrifice with over 2,500 infants.

1710 Vampire hysteria sweeps through East Prussia.

1725 Vampire hysteria returns to East Prussia.

1725–30 Vampire hysteria lingers in Hungary.

1734 The word "vampyre" enters the English language in translations of German accounts of the European waves of vampire hysteria.

1744 Cardinal Giuseppe Davanzati publishes his treatise, *Dissertazione sopre I Vampiri.*

1746   Dom Augustin Calmet publishes his treatise on vampires, *Dissertations sur les Apparitions des Anges, des Demons, et des Espits, et sur les revenants, et Vampires de Hundrie, de Boheme, de Moravie, et de Silesie.*

1748   The first modern vampire poem, "Der Vampir," is published by Heinrich August Ossenfelder.

1750   Another wave of vampire hysteria occurs in East Prussia.

1756   Vampire hysteria peaks in Wallachia.

1772   Vampire hysteria occurs in Russia.

1797   Goethe's "Bride of Corinth" (a poem concerning a vampire) is published.

1798–1800   Samuel Taylor Coleridge writes "Christabel," now conceded to be the first vampire poem in English.

1800   *I Vampiri,* an opera by Silvestro de Palma, opens in Milan, Italy.

1801   "Thalaba" by Robert Southey is the first poem to mention the vampire in English.

1810   Reports of sheep being killed by having their jugular veins cut and their blood drained circulate through northern England.

       "The Vampyre" by John Stagg, an early vampire poem, is published.

1813   Lord Byron's poem "The Giaour" includes the hero's encounter with a vampire.

1819   John Polidori's *The Vampyre,* the first vampire story in English, is published in the April issue of *New Monthly Magazine.*

       John Keats composes "The Lamia," a poem built on ancient Greek legends.

1820   *Lord Ruthwen; ou, Les Vampires* by Cyprien Berard is published anonymously in Paris.

       June 13: *Le Vampire,* a play by Charles Nodier, opens at the Theatre de la Porte Saint-Martin in Paris.

       August: *The Vampire; or, The Bride of the Isles,* a translation of Nodier's play by James R. Planche, opens in London.

1829   March: Heinrich Marschner's opera *Der Vampyr,* based on Nodier's story, opens in Leipzig, Germany.

1841   Alexey Tolstoy publishes his short story "Upyr" while living in Paris. It is the first modern vampire story by a Russian.

1847   Bram Stoker is born.

       Varney the Vampyre begins lengthy serialization.

1851   Alexandre Dumas's last dramatic work, *Le Vampire,* opens in Paris.

1872   "Carmilla" is written by Sheridan Le Fanu.

       In Italy, Vincenzo Verzeni is convicted of murdering two people and drinking their blood.

1874   Reports from Ceven, Ireland, tell of sheep having their throats cut and their blood drained.

1887 The Order of the Golden Dawn is founded. Largely based on the *Sacred Magic* of Abramalin, the order restores a fascination with vampires, werewolves, and spirits of darkness. Among its members are the notorious Aleister Crowley and Nobel Prize winner W.B. Yeats.

1888 Emily Gerard's *Land Beyond the Forest* is published. It will become a major source of information about Transylvania for Bram Stoker's *Dracula*.

Jack the Ripper terrorizes London with his vampiric blood letting and mutilations of prostitutes.

1894 H.G. Wells's short story "The Flowering of the Strange Orchid" is a precursor to science fiction vampire stories.

1897 *Dracula* by Bram Stoker is published in England.

"The Vampire" by Rudyard Kipling becomes the inspiration for the creation of the vampire as a stereotypical character on stage and screen.

Vacher the Ripper mutilates and kills as many as twenty victims before he is apprehended in France.

1912 *The Secrets of House No. 5*, possibly the first vampire movie, is produced in Great Britain.

1913 *Dracula's Guest* by Bram Stoker is published.

1920 *Dracula*, the first film based on the novel, is made in Russia. No copy has survived.

1921 Hungarian filmmakers produce a version of *Dracula*.

1922 *Nosferatu*, a German-made silent film produced by Prana Films, is the third attempt to film *Dracula*.

1924 Hamilton Deane's stage version of *Dracula* opens in Derby, Ireland.

Fritz Harmaann of Hanover, Germany, is arrested, tried, and convicted of killing more than 50 people in a vampiric crime spree.

Sherlock Holmes has his only encounter with a vampire in "The Case of the Sussex Vampire" by Sir Arthur Conan Doyle.

1927 February 14: A stage version of *Dracula* debuts at the Little Theatre in London.

October: An American version of *Dracula*, starring Bela Lugosi, opens at Fulton Theatre in New York City.

Tod Browning directs Lon Chaney in *London after Midnight*, the first full-length vampire feature film.

1928 The first edition of Montague Summers's influential work *The Vampire: His Kith and Kin* appears in England.

1929 Montague Summers's second vampire book, *The Vampire in Europe*, is published.

1931 January: Spanish film version of *Dracula* is previewed.

February: American film version of *Dracula* with Bela Lugosi premieres at the Roxy Theatre in New York City.

Peter Kürten of Düsseldorf, Germany, is executed after being found guilty of murdering a number of people in a vampiric killing spree.

1932   The highly acclaimed movie *Vampyr,* directed by Carl Theodor Dreyer, is released.

1936   *Dracula's Daughter* is released by Universal Pictures.

1942   A.E. Van Vogt's "Asylum" is the first story about an alien vampire.

Gordon Cummins, London's "Wartime Jack the Ripper," is apprehended.

1943   *Son of Dracula* (Universal Pictures) stars Lon Chaney, Jr. as Dracula.

1944   John Carradine plays Dracula for the first time in *Horror of Frankenstein.*

1953   *Drakula Istanbula,* a Turkish film adaptation of *Dracula* is released.

Eerie No. 8 includes the first comic book adaptation of *Dracula.*

1953–1955   Elisfasi Msomi takes the flesh and blood of at least 15 men, women, and children to make his magic as a witchdoctor in Natal more powerful.

1954   The Comics Code banishes vampires from comic books.

I Am Legend by Richard Matheson presents vampirism as a disease that alters the body.

1956   John Carradine plays Dracula in the first television adaptation of the play for "Matinee Theater."

Kyuketsuki Ga, the first Japanese vampire film, is released.

1957   The first Italian vampire movie, *I Vampiri,* is released.

American producer Roger Corman makes the first science fiction vampire movie, *Not of This Earth.*

El Vampiro, with German Robles, is the first of a new wave of Mexican vampire films.

Ed Gein, the Wisconsin vampire/ghoul/cannibal, is arrested.

1958   Hammer Films in Great Britain initiates a new wave of interest in vampires with the first of its *Dracula* films, released in the United States as *The Horror of Dracula.*

First issue of *Famous Monsters of Filmland* signals a new interest in horror films in the United States.

1959   *Plan 9 from Outer Space* is Bela Lugosi's last film.

1961   *The Bad Flower* is the first Korean adaptation of *Dracula.*

1962   The Count Dracula Society is founded in Los Angeles by Donald Reed.

1963   The police in Ciudad Victoria, Mexico, disband a cult that had sacrificed 12 victims to ancient gods and drank blood passed from member to member in a ceremonial goblet.

1964   *Parque de Juelos* (*Park of Games*) is the first vampire movie made in Spain.

1964   *The Munsters* and *The Addams Family,* two horror comedies with vampire characters, open in the fall television season.

1965   Jeanne Youngson founds The Count Dracula Fan Club.

The Munsters, based on the television show of the same name, is the first comic book series featuring a vampire character.

1966   *Dark Shadows* debuts on ABC afternoon television.

Richard Speck brutally slashes eight student nurses to death in Chicago.

1967   April: In episode 210 of *Dark Shadows*, vampire Barnabas Collins makes his first appearance.

1969   First issue of *Vampirella*, the longest running vampire comic book to date, is released.

Denholm Elliott plays the title role in a BBC television production of *Dracula*.

Does Dracula Really Suck? (a.k.a. *Dracula and the Boys*) is released as the first gay vampire movie.

The Charles Manson "family" commits a satanic mass murder in Beverly Hills with suggestions of blood drinking and cannibalism.

1970   Christopher Lee stars in *El Conde Dracula*, the Spanish film adaptation of *Dracula*.

Sean Manchester founds The Vampire Research Society.

Stanley Dean Baker brings his unique problem to Monterey County, California, police offers: he was trying to be the new Jesus by eating human flesh and drinking mugs of their blood.

1971   Marvel Comics releases the first copy of a post-Comics Code vampire comic book, *The Tomb of Dracula*.

Morbius, the Living Vampire, is the first new vampire character introduced after the revision of the Comics Code allowed vampires to reappear in comic books.

1972   *The Night Stalker* with Darrin McGavin becomes the most watched television movie to that point in time.

Vampire Kung-Fu is released in Hong King as the first of a string of vampire martial arts films.

In Search of Dracula by Raymond T. McNally and Radu Florescu introduces Vlad the Impaler, the historical Dracula, to the world of contemporary vampire fans.

A Dream of Dracula by Leonard Wolf complements McNally's and Florescu's effort in calling attention to vampire lore.

True Vampires of History by Donald Glut is the first attempt to assemble the stories of all of the historical vampire figures.

Stephen Kaplan founds The Vampire Research Center.

1973   Dan Curtis Productions' version of *Dracula* stars Jack Palance in a made-for-television movie.

Nancy Garden's *Vampires* launches a wave of juvenile literature for children and youth.

1975   Fred Saberhagen proposes viewing Dracula as a hero rather than a villain in *The Dracula Tape*.

The World of Dark Shadows is founded as the first *Dark Shadows* fanzine.

1976   *Interview with the Vampire* by Anne Rice is published.

Stephen King is nominated for the World Fantasy Award for his vampire novel, *Salem's Lot*.

Shadowcon, the first national *Dark Shadows* convention, is organized by *Dark Shadows* fans.

1977   A new, dramatic version of *Dracula* opens on Broadway starring Frank Langella.

Louis Jourdan stars in the title role in *Count Dracula*, a three-hour version of Bram Stoker's book, on BBC television.

Martin V. Riccardo founds the Vampire Studies Society.

1978   Chelsea Quinn Yarbro's *Hotel Transylvania* joins the volumes by Fred Saberhagen and Anne Rice as a third major effort to begin a reappraisal of the vampire myth during the decade.

Eric Held and Dorothy Nixon found the Vampire Information Exchange.

1979   Based on the success of the new Broadway production, Universal Pictures remakes *Dracula*, starring Frank Langella.

The band Bauhaus's recording of "Bela Lugosi's Dead" becomes the first hit of the new gothic rock music movement.

Shadowgram is founded as a *Dark Shadows* fanzine.

On January 2, Richard Trenton Chase, the Vampire of Sacramento, is charged with six counts of murder and sentenced to die in the gas chamber at San Quentin.

1980   The Bram Stoker Society is founded in Dublin, Ireland.

Richard Chase, the so-called Dracula killer of Sacramento, California, commits suicide in prison.

The World Federation of Dark Shadows Clubs (now the Dark Shadows Official Fan Club) is founded.

1981   James P. Riva II listens to the voices who declared him a vampire. After developing a taste for blood from several small animals, he murders his grandmother and drinks her blood from the bullet holes in her body.

1982   The notorious Chicago Rippers, a savage gang of rapists, murderers, and blood drinkers, is apprehended.

1983   In the December issue of *Dr. Strange*, Marvel Comics' ace occultist kills all the vampires in the world, thus banishing them from Marvel Comics for the next six years.

The Dark Shadows Festival is founded in order to host an annual *Dark Shadows* convention.

1985   *The Vampire Lestat* by Anne Rice is published and reaches the best seller lists.

Richard Ramirez, the "Night Stalker," receives 19 death sentences in Los Angeles.

1986   Sean Sellers, a self-proclaimed "Devil Child," becomes, at age 15, the youngest prisoner on Oklahoma's death row. According to his testimony, he allowed the demon Ezurate to possess him before he committed several murders.

1988   Teenagers Terry Belcher, Robert McIntyre, and Malisa Earnest are apprehended after they have traveled around the country performing their blood-drinking rituals and acts of human sacrifice.

1989   Overthrow of Romanian dictator Nikolai Ceaucescu opens Transylvania to Dracula enthusiasts.

Nancy Collins wins a Bram Stoker Award for her vampire novel, *Sunglasses after Dark*.

A satanic/cannibal/blood drinking cult headquartered in Matamoros, Mexico, is disbanded.

Daniel Rakowitz attempts to found a new religion by drinking human blood. On September 18, Rakowitz is arrested after police make the disgusting discovery that he made a soup out of his girlfriend and was ladling out samples to the homeless.

1991   *Vampire: The Masquerade*, the most successful of the vampire role-playing games, is released by White Wolf.

Annette Hill stalks and kills Charles Reilly so that her lesbian lover, Susi Hampton, can feed on his blood.

1992   *Bram Stoker's Dracula*, directed by Francis Ford Coppola, opens.

Andrei Chikatilo of Rostov, Russia, is sentenced to death after killing and vampirizing some 55 people.

Jeffrey Dahmer is convicted on 16 charges of murder, mutilation, and cannibalism.

Joss Whedon's movie *Buffy, the Vampire Slayer*, starring Kristy Swanson, is released.

1994   The film version of Anne Rice's *Interview with the Vampire* opens with Tom Cruise as the vampire Lestat and Brad Pitt as Louis.

CBS releases the series *Forever Knight*, featuring a homicide detective named Nick Knight, who is a vampire from the thirteenth century trying to do penance for his misdeeds as a member of the undead.

1995   In May, the International Transylvanian Society of Dracula sponsors the World Dracula Conference in Romania.

A very bizarre vampiric monster first rears its ugly head in Puerto Rico in the summer of 1995. The creature still continues its bloody forays and bears the name "Chupacabras."

1996   Members of a vampire "cult" led by Rod Ferrell are arrested for the murders of two people in Florida. They are subsequently tried and convicted.

Jon C. Bush is convicted of 30 sexual crimes against eight underage girls whom he molested during an initiation rite into his family of vampires.

1997　The centennial of the publication of Bram Stoker's *Dracula* occasions a flurry of activity through 1997 and into 1998, including the publication of a number of commemorative books, many television programs, and the issuance of postage stamps (Canada, Ireland, United Kingdom, and the United States).

June 13-15: "Dracula the Centenary" is held in Whitby, England. It is sponsored by the Whitby Dracula Society.

August 13: Serial killer Ali Reza Khoshruy Kuran Kordiyeh, known as the Tehran vampire, is publicly executed in Iran.

August 14-17: Dracula '97: A Centennial Celebration is held in Los Angeles and is the largest of several events commemorating the hundredth anniversary of the publication of *Dracula*. The event is sponsored by the American and Canadian chapters of the Transylvanian Society of Dracula and the Count Dracula Fan Club.

The Hunger is released. The film is based on a novel by Whitley Strieber, directed by Tony Scott, and stars Catherine Deneuve.

Buffy, the Vampire Slayer, the television series based on the movie, airs in March 1997 on the WB network, with Sarah Michelle Geller as the "slayer." The popular series will run for 144 episodes, ending in May 2003.

1996　Wesley Snipes stars as the title character in *Blade*, in which he is a half-human/half-vampire protector of humans. Kirk Jones assumes the role of Blade in a short-lived 2006 television series.

1999　David Boreanaz appears as the title character in *Angel*, a spin-off from *Buffy, the Vampire Slayer*. Portrayed as Buffy's vampire lover in the original series, Angel is a private detective attempting to expiate his prior sins as a vampire.

2001　Charlaine Harris publishes his *Dead until Dark*, the first of her "Sookie Stackhouse" novels about a waitress in a small Louisiana town. Harris writes of a time when most vampires and mortals coexist peacefully, and the vampires imbibe an alternative to human blood.

Seventeen-year-old Matthew Hardman stabs 90-year-old Mabel Leyshon to death at her home in Llanfairpwill, Anglesey, Wales, then drinks her blood from a saucepan. He was convinced that this heinous act would serve as his initiation into life as a vampire.

2003　The motion picture *Underworld* creates an alternate reality in which vampires and werewolves (lycans) have been at each other's throats for centuries—a true war of the monsters.

2004　Twenty-year-old Micah White kills his mother and aunt with sharpened stakes, then burns their bodies, believing that they were vampires.

2005　Six members from a Romanian village are sentenced to six months in jail for the unlawful exhumation of a body. The vampire killers had unearthed a body and impaled its heart in order to stop the corpse from rising at night and drinking blood from its victims in the community.

Mohammed Bijeh, the Tehran Desert Vampire, is publicly executed in Pakdasht, Iran, for the deaths of at least 17 children and three adults.

The "Twilight Saga" is launched by Stephenie Meyer with *Twilight*, the first of what would become a series of four novels, concluding with *Breaking Dawn*.

2006 Voices of the Vampire Community (VVC), the leadership network for the modern vampire community, begins an exhaustive survey and study of the contemporary vampire—sanguinary (blood-drinking) or psychic. This massive undertaking is later updated in 2009.

The sequel to the movie *Underworld*, *Underworld Evolution* continues the saga with a Romeo Lycan and a Juliet Vampire seeking to bring their tribes together.

A 30-year-old woman in the Ukrainian city of Odessa is arrested for drinking the blood of teenaged boys while conducting magic rituals.

2007 CBS, the network that had a fairly successful series in *Forever Knight*, tries its luck again with vampires in *Moonlight*. Mick St. John (Alex O'Laughlin) is a vampire who was transformed by his wife 60 years ago. Like some other well-intentioned vampire, the character is a private detective working to save humankind.

Tiffany Sutton, 23, of Phoenix, Arizona, is sentenced to 10 years in prison for aggravated assault. After telling her boyfriend that she liked to drink blood, she bound him, then slashed his leg, arm, shoulder, and back. Prison records bore out Sutton's claim that she believed herself to be a vampire.

2008 Charlaine Harris's *Dead until Dark* is turned into the HBO series *True Blood*.

Twilight is released as a motion picture that gains a huge fan base made up primarily of teenaged girls.

2009 Santiago Meza Lopez of Mexico City, Mexico, is arrested by police for turning as many as 300 victims into "stew" in vats of acid for a Mexican drug lord.

Jonathan Albert Sharkey, who ran for Minnesota governor as "The Impaler" under the Vampyres, Witches, and Pagans ticket, is sentenced to 90 days in prison on two counts of harassment of a 15-year-old girl. Charges of coercion to inflict bodily harm and coercion to expose a secret are dismissed.

Underworld 3: The Rise of the Lycans, a prequel to *Underworld*, delineates how vampires first became the rulers of the lycan slave class.

THE HOTEL ROOSEVELT, HOLLYWOOD'S MOST HAUNTED

Check into the Hollywood Roosevelt Hotel, and you just might encounter the ghosts of Marilyn Monroe, Montgomery Clift, or Carole Lombard.

Lombard shared her fabulous top-floor suite with Clark Gable, and the elegant decor is basically the way the ill-fated actress left it. The essence of romantic Hollywood is nowhere more powerful than this glamorous star's favorite hideaway. Numerous guests who have shared the romance of this suite have also experienced an encounter with the gorgeous ghost of Carole Lombard.

Marilyn Monroe posed for her first print advertisement on the diving board of the Roosevelt's pool, and she stayed often at the hotel over the years, preferring a second-floor Cabana Room overlooking the pool. Her favorite mirror is on display in the lower elevator foyer, and numerous individuals have claimed to have seen Marilyn's sensuous image near—or superimposed over—their own when they stop to look in the reflecting glass.

In December of 1990, while my wife, Sherry Hansen Steiger, and I were in the lower elevator foyer taping a "Ghosts of Hollywood" segment for a Japanese television program, a hotel guest, curious as to what we were filming, stopped to watch the proceedings. Suddenly, he stepped briskly aside as if to avoid a collision with some unseen person and stifled a cry of surprise, which interrupted the scene that we were filming.

When the director asked the man what was wrong, he replied, somewhat shaken, "Didn't you see that blonde woman who just brushed by me? If I didn't know Marilyn Monroe was dead, I would have sworn it was her!"

As we quizzed him about his experience, he appeared only mildly interested when we explained that the full-length mirror in the foyer had once been a personal favorite of Marilyn Monroe. "But the woman who brushed by me was solid flesh and blood, " he insisted. "She was no ghost!"

The man stalked off a bit indignant, fixing us with an incredulous glare, when we, together with the director and the camera crew, tried to make him understand that there had been no woman visible to the rest of us in the foyer.

Montgomery Clift lived at the hotel for three months during the final stages of filming *From Here to Eternity*. He would often pace the hall outside of his ninth floor apartment, rehearsing his lines, and sometimes practicing bugle calls—much to the consternation of nearby guests, who were trying to get some sleep.

Kelly Green, one of the personable staff members of the Roosevelt, told us of the dozens of guests who had heard Clift's bugle blowing long after his death in 1966. In November of 1990, a witness to the ghostly bugle blasts had been interviewed for inclusion on our segment on Hollywood ghosts for *Entertainment Tonight*. In October of 1992, Sherry and I wanted to return to the hotel and try to catch the ghost of Clift in the act for ourselves for the new "Haunted Hollywood" segments that we were filming for the 1992 Halloween edition of HBO's *World Entertainment Report*.

The night before filming, Kelly Green made arrangements to place us in the room next to Clift's haunted room on the ninth floor. It was our intention to film in the room early the next morning, so Sherry and I were disappointed to hear a variety of sounds coming from Clift's room, as if it may have been occupied by a family with children.

We couldn't imagine that the thoughtful Ms. Green would book guests—especially a family—in a room that we wished to utilize the next morning for filming, but we really didn't feel that we could complain. It was really quite enough that she was making the room available for us to film the segment the next day.

Sherry and I went to bed, sincerely hoping that the next-door guests would check out very early in the morning—a hope that we increasingly felt was in vain, since our neighbors stayed up most of the night, moving noisily about their room. Perhaps it wasn't a family with children next door, for it certainly sounded like a party was in progress with little consideration for the neighbors.

Neither of us seasoned ghost hunters could suppress a small shiver that next morning, when we learned that Ms. Green had indeed left orders at the desk for the Clift room to remain unoccupied for the convenience of our filming. The thumps and bumps that we had heard all night had been the ghost of Montgomery Clift and his circle of spooks welcoming us to his portion of Haunted Hollywood.

Later that day, Sherry recalled that she had been awakened sometime during the night by what she had thought at the time was one of the rambunctious kids next door blowing on a horn, but she had been too tired from the seminar that we had just completed at a Los Angeles area college for the eerie significance of the bugle blasts to register fully in her sleep-numbed consciousness.

INDEX

Note: (ill.) indicates photos and illustrations.